W9-AAW-417

# MIndful Education
# for ADHD Students

# MIndful Education for ADHD Students

*Differentiating Curriculum and Instruction Using Multiple Intelligences*

**Victoria Proulx-Schirduan**
**C. Branton Shearer**
**Karen I. Case**

*Foreword by Bruce Campbell*

Teachers College
Columbia University
New York and London

continuum

Published simultaneously by Teachers College Press, 1234 Amsterdam Avenue, New York, NY 10027, and Continuum International Publishing Group, The Tower Building, 11 York Road, London, SE1 7NX.

The authors express their gratitude for the use of the following, used by permission:

Figure 3.3, "Human Intelligence Hunt," from T. Armstrong, *Multiple Intelligences in the Classroom*. Alexandria, VA: ASCD. © 1994 by the Association for Supervision and Curriculum Development. To learn more about ASCD visit www.ascd.org.

Figure 3.5, "Whole Word Reading Introduction" and Figure 3.6, "Visual-Spatial Reading Techniques," from L. K. Silverman, *Upside Down Brilliance: The Visual-Spatial Learner*. Denver, CO: DeLeon Publishing. © 2002 by Elizabeth Maxwell.

Appendix A, "A Diagnostic Criteria for ADHD," from the *Diagnostic and Statistical Manual of Mental Disorders, Fourth Edition, Text Revision*. Washington, DC: APA © 2000 by American Psychiatric Association.

*British Library Cataloguing-in-Publication Data*
A catalogue record for this book is available from the British Library.

*Library of Congress Cataloging-in-Publication Data*
Proulx-Schirduan, Victoria.
   MIndful education for ADHD students : differentiating curriculum and instruction using multiple intelligences / Victoria Proulx-Schirduan, C. Branton Shearer, Karen I. Case.
      p. cm.
   Includes bibliographical references and index.
   ISBN 978-0-8077-4926-5 (pbk. : alk. paper) — ISBN 978-0-8077-4927-2 (hardcover : alk. paper)  1. Attention-deficit-disordered children—Education.  2. Learning disabled children—Education—United States.  3. Multiple intelligences.  I. Shearer, C. Branton.  II. Case, Karen I.  III. Title.
   LC4713.4 .P76
   371.94—dc22

                                                                        2008039680

Continuum ISBN: 978-1-4411-7993-7 (paperback)
Teachers College Press ISBN: 978-0-8077-4926-5 (paperback)
Teachers College Press ISBN: 978-0-8077-4927-2 (hard cover)

Printed on acid-free paper
Manufactured in the United States of America

16   15   14   13   12   11   10   09      8   7   6   5   4   3   2   1

*For my husband Jim, my rock, and Ryan and Mimi. For my mother, Pat, and for Ana.—VP*

*For my son, Dylan, who lives and breathes ADHD and daily grows beyond all expectations.—CBS*

*For Amanda, Mike, and Christopher, my 19-year-old superheroes of intelligence.—KC*

# Contents

# Foreword

FIFTEEN YEARS AGO I HAD a student named TJ. He was inattentive, impulsive, and at times disruptive. In my classroom, students work in small groups much of the time. Early in the year TJ seldom contributed to his group; spending much of his time wandering around the room and watching other groups. Curiously, whenever TJ's group rotated to a new work station, he knew exactly what to do even if the rest of the group didn't, because he had been watching the previous groups at each station. It didn't take long before others in the class realized that TJ was a valuable person to have in their group: He always knew what to do after each rotation. He came to take pride in this skill and was soon considered one of the best people to have in your learning group.

TJ was diagnosed with ADHD and learning disabilities, which were nothing more than his inability to focus on "the task at hand." He was actually a bright student and a very capable one, but his strength—awareness of the big picture of "seeing the forest but not the trees"—interfered with his academic work. By midyear, though, everyone wanted TJ in their group. Most students saw the trees but not the forest, and his strength complemented their deficit. More importantly, TJ's academic work improved immensely over the remainder of the year.

I have been both an elementary and a high school teacher for over 30 years, and I have seen many students like TJ, whose strengths are not acknowledged in most classrooms. Some, like TJ, are diagnosed with ADHD, some with learning disabilities, and some are simply considered behavioral problems. The problem is generally not the student; the problem is the system. With today's emphasis on state standards and high-stakes testing, we have become a deficit-based system: We focus on what kids can't do instead of what they can do.

Tickle Tune Typhoon, the children's performing group, has a song called *Everyone Is Differently Abled*. One line in the song is, "I will not be defined by my limitations but rather by my possibilities." Too often we tend to focus on what kids can't do instead of what they can do. The three highly qualified authors of *MIndful Education for ADHD Students* realize this and present a powerful antidote. Victoria Proulx-Schirduan, C. Branton Shearer, and Karen I. Case bring a wealth of personal and professional experience to the reader and present a rich and relevant approach to solving the dilemma of dealing with ADHD students in the regular classroom by focusing on what they can do.

The book is filled with examples of how students with so-called "deficits," or what the authors wisely refer to as "promises," can bridge from their areas of strength to their areas of challenge. Just like TJ, who by midyear was one of the most successful and productive students in my classroom, many of the students described in this book have also used their strengths to not only compensate for their challenges but even to excel in their work.

How is it done? The answer lays in the development of a systemic instructional model based on Multiple Intelligences Theory, a model that provides multiple entry points into any content area, at any grade level, and in any subject area. *MIndful Education* is full of effective interventions and teaching strategies that can help all students succeed. I can personally attest to the relevance and success of this approach. Since I began working with multiple intelligences in an intentional way over 20 years ago, I have seen countless students use an area of strength to bridge to an area of challenge. There was Roger who learned to read with music, Maria who learned her times tables through use of visual arts, Tareene who finally understood differential equations after three weeks of constant text messaging between the two of us, Cruz who learned the fundamental principles of physical science (force, energy, mass, speed, acceleration, causality) by applying these ideas to the dirt bikes he raced, and Myron who learned about state history through interviews of elders. Each of these students was diagnosed with Attention Deficit Disorder (ADD) or Attention Deficit/Hyperactivity Disorder (ADHD).

These examples testify to the efficacy of this multimodal approach to learning, of using strengths as bridges to weaknesses. They pale, however, before the host of illustrations provided in *MIndful Education*. Drawing on their wealth of experience, the authors present a comprehensive and inclusive methodology for working with ADHD students, and in my estimation, for all students. The instructional strategies in Chapter 3 are a treasure chest for classroom teachers, particularly those of reading, writing, and math. The advice for setting up a *MIndful school* is inspiring for educational leaders. The advice for parents is both practical and proven. The implications for ADHD students in school and the world beyond school are profound. No parent or educator could read this book and not come away with renewed inspiration and useful tools for meeting the needs of this oft-neglected segment of our population, one with far more promise than the system often recognizes. I'm keeping a copy on my desk this school year.

Bruce Campbell

# Preface

AS TEACHERS WHO HAVE TAUGHT students with attention deficit hyper-activity disorder (ADHD) at the elementary and secondary school level, as researchers who have examined the synergy of ADHD and Multiple Intelligences (MI) for over a decade, and as parents who have lived with a child with ADHD, we are pleased to present promising ways to rethink ADHD.

The employment of an MI lens enlarges our view of students with ADHD, providing avenues to investigate the ways these students learn best. Our goal is to aid teachers to recognize, employ, and develop Multiple Intelligences in their students with ADHD as well as ensure "best practices" in their classrooms. To that end, we've included two codes to access a free, valid, and reliable MI assessment: the Multiple Intelligences Developmental Assessment Scale (MIDAS™) for the ADHD student and his or her teacher. To our knowledge, this is the first book and series of research studies investigating students with ADHD in light of MI theory. (If codes to the MIDAS™ have been accessed by a former reader of this book, you can purchase additional codes at www.miresearch.org)

ADHD is one of the most common and most studied disorders among students, and yet we believe that students with ADHD comprise a population that is typically underserved in the traditional classroom. Our book provides a way to view students with ADHD as at-promise versus at-risk. A second goal of this book is to present a variety of tactics that teachers have used successfully while instructing students with ADHD. These instructional remedies are in the areas of reading, writing, and math skills. The included research, collected case studies, and vignettes represent powerful testimony regarding the application of MI theory. These examples speak to the need for change in instructional methods for students with ADHD. We invite you to apply the strategies offered throughout the book to bring about positive change in the learning of those students with ADHD within your classroom.

This text encapsulates new knowledge connecting ADHD to Multiple Intelligences (MI) theory. Harvard psychologist Howard Gardner developed MI theory. Unlike a traditional view of intelligence, which stresses verbal and numerical aptitude, Gardner situates intelligence in "real-world" application and problem solving to encompass not only linguistic and logical-mathematical intelligences, but also bodily-kinesthetic, musical, spatial, naturalist, intrapersonal and interpersonal intelligences. As witnessed through the lens of an MI curriculum, ADHD is not a disadvantage; it is rather an integral component of how the student processes information, makes sense of the world, self-regulates, and ultimately acts. Rather than a challenge or weakness, ADHD may be a useful starting point when used to the student's advantage.

Students with ADD/ADHD are unique, with their own combination of strengths and weaknesses. The inattentiveness, impulsivity, and hyperactivity evidenced by students with ADHD can be seen to occur on a continuum. We use the acronym ADHD throughout the book; however, ADHD may reflect a student with or without the "H," which stands for "hyperactivity." We will refer to our "at-promise students" as "ADHD students," or "students with ADHD" (though we believe that such labels pathologize students with ADHD). From a more practical and pragmatic standpoint as teachers ourselves, we realize that these labels may supply additional educational services to students. Finally, the data represented on students with ADHD from MI and "non-MI" or traditional schools comprise regular education, learning disabled (LD), and gifted students; those students taking medicine for their disorder and those who are not; and students primarily in elementary or middle school.

*MIndful Education for ADHD Students: Differentiating Curriculum and Instruction Using Multiple Intelligences* contributes to a *multimodal*, team approach when working with students with ADHD. This book has been derived from our collective experiences. The text is based on national and international data. It reflects teachers we've encountered, our collaboration with parents, and the administrators we've interviewed. We have learned from the private practice clients we've counseled and the many workshops we've conducted, as well as from our research. Most importantly, we've learned from the students we have taught and the ADHD children we've raised.

## BOOK OVERVIEW

Chapter 1 discusses ADHD (e.g., etiology, primary and secondary characteristics, traditional approaches, and so forth) and MI (e.g., definitions and descriptions) to present an initial framework. ADHD and MI theory are conceptually linked. ADHD is viewed from an at-promise lens. Anecdotes from students, teachers, and parents are introduced and continue throughout ensuing chapters.

In Chapter 2, the assessment of students with ADHD is explained, as are instructions for using the Multiple Intelligences Developmental Assessment Scale (MIDAS™). Procedures of reflection, observation, and discussion are explored as another avenue for uncovering the predominant intelligences of students with ADHD. The impact of MI profiles on teaching and learning is articulated, as are the interpersonal relationship and self-concept needs of students with ADHD. This chapter concludes with a comprehensive examination of how the ADHD student with "nonacademic" intelligences, such as naturalist and spatial intelligences, can best be educated inside and outside of the classroom setting.

In Chapter 3, traditional and innovative solutions to managing primary (e.g., inattentiveness) and secondary (e.g., poor academic skills, disorganization) characteristics of ADHD are presented and mindful curriculum planning is discussed. This chapter presents general and specific mindful instructional strategies for students with ADHD to ensure improvements in reading, writing, and arithmetic.

In Chapter 4, mindful leaders are cognizant of student intelligences. Professional development on topics ranging from training in ADHD, managing ADHD behavior, and raising test scores are examined. A look at MI schools in the United States and abroad concludes the chapter.

In Chapter 5, the partnering of schools and parents provides numerous bene-fits for teachers, parents, and students with ADHD. Conventional and unconventional methods for school–home partnerships and increased academic productivity are presented. This chapter ends with a Partnership Promise, a pledge to identify and support areas of difficulty for the student with ADHD.

Finally, in Chapter 6, the progression leading to college for students with ADHD and a focus on ability versus a disability outlook are discussed. This chapter concludes the book with recommended life choices for students with ADHD. Research findings are provided, correlating intelligences with careers and job placement.

## CONCLUSION

Students may experience a keen sense of failure as early as elementary school, and consequently may withdraw intellectually, emotionally, and physically from formal academic experiences. Although research has indicated that teachers, school staff, and parents respond helpfully when students with ADHD are entrenched in school failure, they may be seeking answers to ADHD in a host of traditional ways that may have little to do with how students with ADHD learn best.

*MIndful Education for ADHD Students* is based on the authors' combined years of extensive research on MI theory and direct experience working with students, teachers, and administrators. The authors' overarching goal is to offer practical, tested, at-promise strategies for teachers (and parents) who manage one of today's most prevalent and challenging school populations.

Educators—specifically, elementary and middle school teachers—and administrators make up the intended audience for this book. However, this work may also be helpful to high school teachers, parents, and individuals with ADHD. Additionally, *MIndful Education for ADHD Students* can serve as a college textbook or resource textbook in the areas of teacher education, special and gifted education, curriculum, and observation and assessment.

# Acknowledgments

A HEARTFELT THANKS TO ALL the teachers, ADHD students, parents, school staff, and administrators around the country and abroad. Second, thanks goes to Brian Ellerbeck, the executive acquisitions editor at Teachers College Press, for allowing us to write on an area that holds fundamental promise for students with ADHD. Thanks also to Aureliano Vázquez, Jr., for his diligent edits, and to Adee Braun, the assistant acquisitions editor, for promptly and kindly answering our questions and providing support.

Special thanks go to Steven Plogg of www.resultsproject.net, who willingly shared his stories with us and whose powerful anecdotes have made this book a better read. Thanks to Paula McClellan, for her dedication to those with ADHD and for her assistance in gathering anecdotes. Special thanks go to school administrators, especially Penny Jojin and Lisa Eells, who opened their school doors, and gave us their time and access to talented MI teachers. Our thanks to Bruce Campbell, a teacher who has developed a nationally acclaimed classroom model based on MI, for his inspired work with students that sets a great example for us all. Teachers can and do make a difference. Thanks to Dr. Linda Silverman and Betty Maxwell, APA, and ASCD, who allowed us to reprint material. Sharing work ultimately benefits the students we serve.

Thanks also go to the following people, who have assisted us in one way or another to make our book better: to Dr. John Ryan, for his expertise in ADHD; to Greg Palmerino and Dr. Judith Faryniarz, who read and edited early drafts of this work; to photographers Frank Bradley and Michael Teitler; and to Betty Proulx, Dr. Nancy Levine, and Dr. Linda Perry. We humbly thank you and our families for the support of our efforts to improve the lives of children.

# At-Promise Versus At-Risk

S TUDENTS WITH ADHD are often academically and socially marginalized in the classroom due to their unique cognitive and social differences. These differences may result in their being labeled "at-risk" for academic failure. Gardner's MI theory provides educators with curricular avenues to reach students without alienating them from the formal educational system. By philosophically recognizing students' strengths as opposed to weaknesses, students may view themselves as academically successful in spite of the MI cognitive profiles of many ADHD students—a weak language–logic intelligence profile, which is necessary to succeed in reading and math.

However, the MI cognitive profile reveals alternate intelligences, from which more traditional intelligences can be bridged. It is our contention that MI is the curricular response needed that will enable students with ADHD to live up to their fullest intellectual and emotional potential. Providing classroom experiences that offer successful task completion for the ADHD student avoids damaging student self-efficacy and esteem. It has been shown that students with ADHD face common challenges at school and at home. Traditionally taught subjects, interpersonal relationships, and "living up to" family and teacher expectations may be met by ADHD students with apprehension and eventual frustration. Regrettably, many educators continue to view students with ADHD as "at-risk," a label that may have a self-fulfilling academic prophecy. According to Winborne (as cited in Swadener & Lubeck, 1995), the problem may have more to do with the pathology of the phrase. "At-risk" terminology "appears frequently in education and social science literature, [and] comes from the medical field and alludes to the threat of disease or injury" (p. 22). When bandied about by educators, such terms have negative, even alarming connotations for parents and educators, often implying necessary remediation to make the student "normal" or "better," and thus, further pathologizing students.

Traditional classroom settings exacerbate the problem by failing to acknowledge nonacademic intelligences (Black, 1994), thereby disenfranchising students with unique learning abilities, and dooming them to educational failure. A Multiple Intelligences (MI) perspective provides the avenue whereby a positive and comprehensive understanding of the ways these students learn differently can be achieved. It also identifies what students do well by presenting intelligences and student performance as affirmation of ability. Students' unique skills and attributes can be witnessed as "at-promise" (Sleeter, as cited in Swadener & Lubeck, 1995, p. x). For example, Armstrong (1994) viewed MI theory as a means for understanding students because it "provide[s] a language for talking about inner gifts of children, especially those students who have accumulated labels such as 'LD' and 'ADD' during their school career" (pp. ix–x).

Sending students with ADHD the academic message that they are not teachable is not acceptable. Instead of molding students to fit the design of schools, schools must adapt to fit the needs of students. This process can only succeed through the actions and determination of caring, knowledgeable teachers and administrators. Parents and educators must advocate this change, urging those in charge of the curriculum to use methods to seek out the strengths and intellectual profiles of ADHD students. Gathered and assessed information should serve to personalize education. Schools need to assess intelligences and nurture interests and abilities to enable student passion. In turn, students become academically engaged and embrace learning in positive, constructive ways (Brown, 1998). Educators broadly and classroom teachers in particular have profound influence over how students with ADHD grow and develop academically. MI offers an important conceptual frame for understanding what students with ADHD can learn (curriculum), how they learn (instructional methods), and for the evaluation of that learning (assessment). This work introduces Howard Gardner's MI theory and illustrates how, as a diagnostic tool, the MI cognitive profile can identify a student's strengths.

## ATTENTION DEFICIT HYPERACTIVITY DISORDER (ADHD)

ADHD is one of the most commonly diagnosed (National Institute of Mental Health [NIMH], 2003), misdiagnosed, and overdiagnosed disorders of the 20th century.

### Etiology and Nomenclature

"There is disagreement among researchers as to the etiology of ADHD" (D'Alonzo, 1996, p. 89). Although few question the existence of ADHD (Stagg-Elliot, 2000; NIMH, 2003), parents often blatantly denounce the disorder. Cheryl, a mother of a boy who was labeled ADHD, explains, "I don't believe in ADHD or ADD, I believe in a style of thought." Physicians, psychologists, and educators do not know what causes ADHD (Bishop & Beyer, 1995). However, chief among the many causes that have been postulated is genetics (NIMH, 2006). Scientists have begun to identify genes that are associated with ADHD. Thus, the potential exists as to future genetic testing for the disorder (Fine, 2001).

As with etiology, nomenclature of the disorder has changed over the past 100 years. Today, however, ADD or ADHD are the names (acronyms) most of us associate with this profile. *ADHD* is the medically correct term for all individuals with the disorder, though a student may or may not have the "H," which stands for "hyperactivity." Dr. Russell Barkley (as cited in Moore, 2000), a leading authority on ADHD, delineates the two subtypes: hyperactive and inattentive. The inattentive subtype, whose symptoms include spaciness, underactivity, and dreaminess, is the group for which attention is a deficit.

This is best illustrated through Charlie's case. Diagnosed with ADHD in middle school, Charlie spent much of his time daydreaming, looking out the window or through the classroom door and into the classroom across the hall. Often distracted, when called upon, he would become confused due to inattention, much to the teacher's chagrin. Charlie's advocate, a relative with an extensive background in education, explained his lack of classroom focusing, stating that it occurred "not because Charlie wasn't smart. In fact, he was quite smart. He is a person who thinks a lot."

> I remember once he said "you know sometimes I just think too much and sometimes I think too deeply." This made *me* think that an ADHD person gets lost in their own thoughts. You know maybe that daydreaming in school is not "spacing out." I think when someone daydreams, they are reflecting on something and the person observing [teacher] may not see it as deep, reflective thought.

In other words, the inattentive subtype may be revealing a heightened tendency for focus and reflection.

The hyperactive subtype, according to Barkley (as cited in Moore, 2000), is a disorder of impulsivity and self-control (output), not attention (input). An "output" deficit affects executive functions in the brain and, thus, causes difficulty in controlling emotions and actions. Tommy's case illustrates this tendency. Heidi, Tommy's teacher, explained that Tommy was unable to follow classroom rules. She shared that there were the typical classroom rules: raise your hand, stay in your seat, respect others, and so on. "Day after day, he would break the rules. I had a heart to heart talk with him and Tommy said he was aware that he was breaking the rules in class, but simply could not control himself."

To read more about the symptoms associated with ADHD, see Appendix A, the Diagnostic Criteria for Attention Deficit Hyperactivity Disorder from the *Diagnostic and Statistical Manual of Mental Disorders*.

## Diagnosis and Characteristics of ADHD

Understanding why some children develop ADHD while others do not has been the subject of study. "While the diagnostic label of Attention Deficit Hyperactivity Disorder is relatively new, this particular combination of symptoms (inattention, impulsivity, and hyperactivity) in children has been recognized for over 100 years" (Braswell, Bloomquist, & Pederson, 1991, p. 6; NIMH, 2006). Peter, a hypersensitive and outspoken middle schooler, upon hearing his diagnosis 6 years ago, revealed that he was "officially diagnosed with having Attention Deficit Hyperactivity Disorder by a doctor in 1994. Now there's a negative diagnosis if I have ever heard one. Half the words in the name of my so-called problem are identifying me as a loser. I now have a 'Deficit,' I'm told!" Peter's words clearly pointed to the power of pathologizing language.

**Misdiagnosis, Underdiagnosis, and Overdiagnosis.** ADHD has been called one of the most misdiagnosed and overdiagnosed disorders (Jensen, 1998; Parmet, Cassio, & Glass, 2002). It is important, therefore, that the person who is evaluating the student gather information from a range of sources in order to determine the problem.

Generally, although only a physician is most qualified to diagnose a child with ADHD, teachers may assume a diagnostic role, as was the situation in Christine's case. Her mom stated, "When my daughter, Christine, was in second grade, the teachers decided she was ADHD. They gave me a form to fill out and they filled it out too. That is what the doctor used to diagnose her with ADHD. Yep, just that school form."

This practice, unfortunately, contributes to the widespread belief that ADHD is overdiagnosed. According to Kessler (as cited in Stagg-Elliot, 2000), doctors can be caught in the middle. Given the relatively short patient time in a doctor's office and the rather lengthy list of complaints, many physicians turn to their prescription pad as a quick fix. If medication improves attention or behavior, some assume that the ADHD diagnosis was correct. However, others would argue that medication will improve the attention and behavior of any student placed on medication.

Still, some believe that ADHD is underdiagnosed in our society. Barkley (as cited in Moore, 2000) believes that underdiagnosis may be attributed to media distortions and poor diagnostic criteria. Others contend that the prevalence of underdiagnosis of ADHD, specifically among poor minority populations, is related to economics and unequal access to proper medical care. In addition, experts assert that many girls are never diagnosed (U.S. Department of Education, 1994).

While diagnosis of the disorder is relegated to physicians in most states, teachers and school professionals do collaborate with physicians in the treatment of ADHD. To illustrate this, Benito, a kindergarten teacher, suspected that Mario had ADHD. In her classroom, he was displaying many of the characteristics of ADHD.

> I talked with the parents about options: more structure and discipline at home, and at school and possible outside assessments. They took him to the doctor and [after the doctor diagnosed him with ADHD] he began taking drugs. He was then able to control himself in class. The meds helped him achieve that control.

Teachers walk a fine line regarding their initial suspicions of a student who may be displaying the characteristics of ADHD. Often among the first to recognize ADHD, teachers are left with the task of informing the student's parents. For example, Martin, a 4-year-old came from a home of professional older parents and admittedly had had limited contact with young children. Martin's teacher was Mrs. Powers, a veteran with a lot of experience with children, who stated, "his parents were surprised when he started getting in trouble and not succeeding in school."

> He was bright and mature, and a good conversationalist. I asked his mom how he acted at home. She said, he plays with puzzles while he watches TV and plays with Teenage Mutant Ninja Turtles and then flips through the pages of a book. [This was done] all at the same time! His mom did not realize his behavior was different from other kids his age. He was an only child.

**Primary Characteristics.** The primary characteristics of the disorder are inattention, hyperactivity, and impulsivity. DSM diagnostic criteria include varied characteristics (e.g., student does not often follow through on instructions and fails to finish schoolwork; loses things necessary for completing tasks or activities such as school assignments, pencils, books, or tools; and is often forgetful in daily activities). Brett displayed primary characteristics and talked about his confusion, which resulted from living with the ADHD label.

> You know how frustrating it is when you lose your keys? Try dealing with that ten times a day. I would forget to write my homework down and then I wouldn't remember to do it. . . . I would forget my lunch, or forget a book

and my mom would constantly be driving back to school because I forgot a book or homework, sometimes I forget to take the medication.

Brett was in middle school and had experienced ADHD symptoms since second grade. He maintained, "I wasn't hitting anyone or falling out of my chair and I was very quiet, I never got into trouble [so I] wasn't diagnosed with ADHD until middle school."

Associated features of the disorder vary. However, predominant features—inattention, hyperactivity, or a combination of the two—define the disorder. Students commonly exhibit some clear symptoms of ADHD. As one teacher, Constantine, recalled:

Last year, I had a student Eddie, and Eddie, who was ADHD, was bright, interested, and quick to make connections. However, he found it very difficult to sit with us in a whole group without some exaggerated rolling on the floor, flopping down in the middle of things.

Brett and Eddie were enrolled in school when their teachers recognized their ADHD symptoms. Parents may notice symptoms of ADHD early on in their children. Common characteristics often occur before school's commencement. One parent revealed to us his early worries about Ken, a third grader with ADHD.

When he was a toddler he'd be going in 10 different directions, what to get into, not the next thing but [the next] 10 different things. He didn't stay with anything too long 15 minutes here, 15 minutes there. Bored with this bored with that. The longest thing that he's really been involved in is actually the Play Station.

His father describes his son as being "bigger than everyone in his class" and tells us that his son was a big baby and shares the same build as the father and Ken's grandfather. He adds that "If Ken could, he'd be outside all day either riding his bike or, we have a basketball hoop in the back, being outside doing activities constantly moving, ya know what I mean? He moves even when he's standing still" (Schirduan, 2000, pp. 168–169). Ken's profile indicates that he has some hyperactive, impulsive, or inattentive symptoms that have caused impairment prior to his age of 7 years. (ADHD characteristic: Is often "on the go," as if "driven by a motor.")

High distractibility may be the first symptom witnessed in the school setting. In the case of Sharon, a bright, amiable fifth grader, her teacher revealed, "Sharon was looking at the custodian changing the light bulb . . . and was saying 'excuse me that's distracting.' He was just looking at her . . . every little thing distracts her. She can't stay focused" (Schirduan, 2000, p. 187). (ADHD characteristic: Is often easily distracted by extraneous stimuli.)

The above anecdotes provide descriptions of how students with ADHD and their parents and teachers experience the characteristics associated with their labeling. Such experiences are in keeping with similar field research studies (Viadero, 2005).

**Secondary Characteristics.** During the elementary years, primary ADHD symptoms can lead to the development of secondary problems, such as academic difficulties, classroom conduct problems, peer rejection, and low self-esteem.

(Braswell, Bloomquist, & Pederson, 1991). Parson, a tall, lanky, brown-haired eighth-grade student, described how he "went to the principal's office twice a week like clockwork. . . . I had my own chair. . . . I was on a first name basis with the principal. . . ." Like many preadolescents with ADHD with conduct problems, Parson was affable one on one. However, in a group setting among his peers and under the supervision of authority, he experienced difficulty displaying appropriate conduct.

**Comorbidity.** Comorbidity, or having two or more diagnosable conditions simultaneously, is common for students with ADHD. "An estimated 40% to 60% of people who are affected by ADHD are also affected by a secondary disorder . . ." (Stanberry, 2003), such as depression, anxiety, oppositional defiant disorder (ODD), conduct disorder (CD), and learning disabilities (LD), as well as other disorders. In 2002, the Centers for Disease Control and Prevention (CDC) reported that approximately one-half of students with ADHD also have LD (Stanberry, 2003). This highlights the importance of deciphering whether an individual with ADHD has a coexisting condition or if the current condition is masquerading as ADHD. In other words, some conditions may look like ADHD but, in fact, may be something other than ADHD, such as anxiety (Watkins, 2002).

## Approaches to ADHD

Strategies to combat primary and secondary characteristics along with comorbidity issues include both medical and school-based approaches.

**Medical-Based Approach.** As diagnoses of ADHD have increased, so, too, has the demand for methylphenidate hydrochloride, also known as Ritalin. Stimulant medication (e.g., Ritalin, Concerta, Adderall, Dexedrine) may be the first step for teachers and parents in the treatment of ADHD (Miranda, Presentacion, & Soriano, 2002). Given this trend to medicate, a growing number of child advocates has become alarmed at the rate at which students with ADHD are being prescribed medication. There has been rising concern regarding the rate of stimulant medication, leading some to suggest that "Prescriptions are more the rule than the exception" for the treatment of children with ADHD (Hoagwood, Kellehert, Feil, & Comert, 2000, p. 206).

Given that some parents have a negative opinion of stimulant medications (Bailey, 2003), and the Food and Drug Administration (FDA) approval of a nonstimulant medication (e.g., Strattera), some parents are choosing to treat their child with ADHD with nonstimulants. Briana provides an illustration of how difficult it is to balance these prescription medications. A frail-looking 8-year-old girl with big brown eyes, Briana has a wide smile. Her parents and doctor have worked to balance her medications to treat her ADHD, choosing a stimulant and a nonstimulant medication.

> The doctor started her out on meds. The meds weren't working, so he changed her dose over and over again and tried different "brands" and everything. He then prescribed depression medicine. He said the side effects will not make her hungry. Since she was losing weight as a thin child. She was in the 10% of the weight charts. [As her mom,] I no longer was comfortable giving her drugs.

Briana's parents eventually gave up on prescription medications for ADHD.

Many parents chose to avoid medically treating ADHD due to the unknown long-term effects of these drugs. Even short-term effects have been known to worry parents. One mother noted that drowsiness and complacency in her daughter was a significant problem. Virginia, a sixth grader with ADHD, was entering the preadolescent stage where peers are considered paramount. Virginia's mother feared social rejection because of the characteristics associated with ADHD.

Virginia has always been a fun-loving, full of energy, loves life, goes down her own path, very unique individual. When she started school, she was diagnosed with ADHD. She was always in trouble when it came to classroom settings. She just couldn't control herself and pay attention and do what the rest of the class was doing. She was, and still is, easily distracted. When the doctor put her on medication for her ADHD, I observed her falling asleep in the car and it seemed as if the light inside of her was burned out.

Other side effects extend beyond the physical. When Camille, a third grader with ADHD, was placed on medication, her mother asked her how she felt taking them. "Her reply broke my heart. Camille said, 'If this is how everyone wants me to be, then it feels like I'm someone else.' I love my child, I didn't want to change her. I wanted to help her."

Parents and educators state that the primary reason for medicating students with ADHD is to improve the child's ability to focus in the classroom. Success stories related to safe and effective medical treatment in the past 50 years are believed by some to have been deemphasized (DeNoon, 2001). Approximately 70% to 80% of children with ADHD respond to stimulant medication (Parmet, Cassior, & Glass, 2002). In the following illustrations, medication was discovered to have helped Juan, Tess, and Bob to focus in school. One music teacher, Beverly, explained that she'd "known Juan for two years now. He is a third grader with ADHD in my music class. Last year, I didn't even get to know him because he wasn't able to settle down to do his work."

If he wasn't in time out, he was out coloring because he literally could not attend to anything. When he was in class, he would be making animal sounds, yelling, hopping, jumping, etc. I remember once he jumped over one of the xylophones in a performance! It was so sad to see him miss out in music class because I knew that he loved music and that he was gifted— especially in voice. Juan can sing anything! But he disrupted others learning. Juan went on meds. He is a different child. Sure, I have to talk to him once in a great while but after I give him a reminder, he takes care of it. He now sits still and is able to focus. It is a joy to see him now! He is a much happier student and learner.

Tess, a girl who often stood out in class in a mischievous way, was also placed on medication and, subsequently, was able to focus on academics. Her disposition improved. Her teacher described the scenario of having Tess in class.

Tess was a very likable fourth-grade student with ADHD in my music class and was on-task about only 30% of the time. The other times, if she was not in time out, which she got every day, she was crawling under tables, rolling across the floor, spinning, mooing, making sounds, etc. I am convinced she learned by osmosis! She was hearing *everything* that was going on even though she was off-task. When I could get her to focus I found that she was intensely musical and she'd be right there with us for the moment. She was put on medicine. It changed her life. She is still a great dancer and singer but also a model student. You can always count on her for everything. She is one of the brightest kids in the entire school. She's the kind of kid if you had a valedictorian in elementary school, she'd be it.

Bob was older than both Juan and Tess. He was in middle school and had a medium build, medium brown hair, and eyes with little affect. However, although this former client was sensitive, he was not outwardly expressive. Still, he cried with relief upon hearing his diagnosis of ADHD. He stated that his "doctor told him he was going to have to take medication every day to help him concentrate." As Bob explained further, "I took the medication the next day and I was finally able to think. I did my homework all by myself for the first time in 2 years." Many teachers readily maintain that they can identify the days when their students with ADHD have forgotten to take their medication. Jamie's teacher works diligently with students with ADHD and is very proactive when working with parents. She shared an incident about one student in particular.

> I can tell you when he's not on meds. I've called his father a couple times and said you didn't put him on meds this morning did you? Because, this kid has been all over the place. I [said] you have to give the meds. (Schirduan, 2000, p. 188)

Teachers aren't the only individuals who notice when youngsters fail to take their medication. Sasha, a whirlwind of an elementary school student, often appeared disheveled. She had tousled hair, skirt askew, and the contents of her backpack included torn and crumpled assignment pages. Her mother noticed a difference in her appearance and academic work after she started on medication.

> Oh yeah [I noticed a difference], I'll tell you when she first started [taking the medicine] her teacher had said "Oh my God!" right away [she] noticed the difference, [in Sasha]. [But before medication] it was a struggle for her to write in her journal. [She did] not even [write] a couple sentences. [Now] she went on to write a page and a half. I mean it was just so different. (Schirduan, 2000, pp. 188–189)

The research is inconclusive regarding the use of medications to control the characteristics of ADHD. It has been suggested that medication may improve behavior and academic performance (Zametkin & Monique, as cited in Schlozman & Schlozman, 2000). However, others maintain that "It has not been shown that academic performance improves at the same level [as improvements in behavior]" (Rapport, Denney, DuPaul, & Gardner, as cited in Miranda, Presentacion, & Soriano, 2002, p. 546).

Seymour was making the transition from middle to high school and, given the social and academic demands of high school, his parents were worried and wanted the transition to go smoothly. He was a reflective boy and expressed a desire to "fit in." His parents thought that medication may help overall with the transition and the problems he was having. Diagnosed with ADHD in middle school, Seymour was described as someone who "thinks too much and thinks too deeply." His guidance counselor shared his parents' confusion over the best possible course for their son. "It was at this time that the physician put him on Ritalin," his mother noted. "It didn't make a difference [in his academic performance or behavior]." It may be that prescribed medication fails to replace the mastery of skills and student responsibility for learning.

Medication need not be the sole educational intervention for students labeled as ADHD. "The limitations of pharmacotherapy for ADHD highlight a need for the augmentation of psychosocial and psychoeducational treatments" (Miranda, Presentacion, & Soriano, 2002, p. 546). A better understanding of the strengths and capacity of students with ADHD as learners via training may prove the more important intervention. At times, a student labeled with ADHD may present differently, depending on the subject and the teacher. A music teacher told the story of Lola, a typical 10-year-old, who had a select group of friends. She wore mostly pink, her favorite color, to school and loved to play the flute. Lola's strengths and interests were in music, which enabled her to mask her ADHD symptoms. In other classrooms, however, her behaviors were problematic. According to her music teacher, "I would not have known Lola, a student in my fourth-grade music class, had ADHD if it had not been for a note that was circulated to all of Lola's teachers."

> The note informed us that medication was being considered to treat Lola's ADHD. We were then asked to comment on her behavior. I have never had trouble with her in music because I think her interest in music overrode her distraction issues. She was not exceptional but I think the interest in music helped her stay focused and on-task in my class.

According to Swanson (as cited in DeNoon, 2001), parents are cautious about placing their children on medication. In fact, most parents resist having medications prescribed for their children. They often choose other approaches, such as behavioral therapy and or school-based approaches, before considering medication.

Although psycho-stimulants are the treatment of choice for most physicians (according to Greenhill, as cited in Hoagwood, Kelleher, Feil, & Comer, 2000), there is a "percent of the ADHD population whose symptoms don't respond to medication. . . ." (Kuo & Taylor, 2004, paragraph 13). Finally, given the limitations of behavioral therapies, the serious side effects of medicine (e.g., loss of appetite, sleep deprivation, and so on), and the uncertain long-term impact on academic and social skills, there is a strong need to introduce promising and alternative ways to meet the needs of students with ADHD.

**School-Based Approach.** Although public schools have spent billions on students with ADHD (National Institutes of Health [NIH], 1998), only some qualify for special services under IDEA (the Individuals with Disabilities Education Act). Students who meet the criteria receive an Individual Education Program (IEP). Whether the student with ADHD has an IEP or teacher-initiated plans, teachers, parents, and sometimes students themselves convene to identify specific problems (e.g., academic, social) and ways to address them.

Examples of school approaches that teachers have traditionally used with students labeled with ADHD include behavior modification, stimulus reduction, cognitive and behavior modification, and classroom management. As Barkley (as cited in Moore, 2000, paragraph 13) contends, a "carefully thought-out motivation and management program must be followed by both parent and teacher to ensure its success." In addition to designing an instructional plan, most teachers of students labeled with ADHD incorporate at least some accommodations in the instructional plan.

*Classroom Accommodations for Students with ADHD*
- Seating preference (e.g., front or near teacher)
- Minimizing distractible stimuli (e.g., avoid high-traffic areas, doorways, windows)
- Use of active participation and variety (e.g., interaction and rehearsing for critical information)
- Cueing for off-task behavior (e.g., hand lightly placed on shoulder, eye contact, or chosen word for off-task behavior)
- Timing of academics (e.g., morning versus afternoon and daily schedule structured to minimize transition problems)
- Extra time for written assignments as needed
- Organizational and study skills
- Case manager model (e.g., "academic coach")

When contemplating school approaches for students with ADHD, whether or not they receive special service, in order to be successful, the curriculum must (as the title IEP delineates) be individualized. It goes without saying that every child learns differently, and while one may find success with a particular technique, the same technique may fail when applied to another student. Perseverance is key to finding what works best.

The National Institute of Mental Health has called the lack of diagnosis and treatment of students with ADHD "a major public health concern" (Fine, 2001, p. 26). Such a statement serves to pathologize individuals who may or may not have behaviors that are deficit-based. Nonetheless, many experts contend that a variety of approaches may best serve the student labeled with ADHD (Hazelwood, Bovingdon, & Tiemens, 2002) in that the "core symptoms of inattention, hyperactivity and impulsivity can be reduced with medication, the social skills, work habits and motivation that have deteriorated along the course of the disorder require a multimodal treatment approach" (Brown, 1998, p. 37). Furthermore, "given the weaknesses inherent in any single treatment modality, the multimodal treatment approach is preferred here for treating most cases of ADHD. . . ." (Mash & Barkley, 2006, p. 83). Five to 8% of the general population has been diagnosed with ADHD, and of the population with an accurate diagnosis, few are receiving necessary multimodal treatment (Chapman-Booth, 1998). A holistic approach that addresses the concerns of the whole child—emotionally, physically, and intellectually—is the one espoused by the authors as having the most promise for students labeled as ADHD.

Chapter 3 weaves these and other approaches with MI theory to tackle learning problems for students with ADHD.

## MULTIPLE INTELLIGENCES (MI) THEORY

Multiple Intelligences (MI) theory represents a view of intelligence that is plural-istic and comprised of differing levels of strengths and weaknesses. According to Gardner's (1993a) MI theory, there are eight ways in which a person can display intelligence. These intelligences may vary from individual to individual. Intelligences can also be bridged from strongest to weakest. This conceptualization of intelligence lends a powerful instructional tool to teachers who may not only use it to identify students' strongest intelligence, but also can bridge their predominant intelligences to those that may be weaker. This curriculum method has significant potential for instructing students with ADHD and is diametrically opposed to traditional views of intelligence.

### Intelligence Theories

For many, intelligence is related to identity and achievement. The authors hold that a high Intelligence Quotient (IQ), which reflects strengths in math and reading, is only a small element in what makes up an individual's aptitude. While research indicates that IQ tests predict school performance (Neisser, Boodoo, Bouchard, Boykin, Brody, Ceci, et al., 1996) not all students achieve strictly in math and reading. Furthermore, IQ results have been found to be less predictive of college and career performance (Ackerman, 1996), both of which may comprise an overriding goal for educators of students with ADHD. MI theory has the potential to broaden current definitions of intelligence by drawing attention to talents not nurtured within the school and, thus, may serve to aid parents and teachers in their understanding of student capacities and talents. This is particularly true for students with ADHD, who may have experienced, due to constant classroom failure, a loss of self-esteem and efficacy.

### Howard Gardner's Contribution to Intelligence Theory

Thoughts on intelligence can be divided into two camps. One camp advocates the studies of Charles Spearman and supports a general factor of intellect (IQ). Others, such as Thurstone, challenged Spearman's findings believing instead in primary mental abilities (French, 1939). A broader view of intelligence has come to the fore. Howard Gardner (1993a), who espoused MI theory, is firmly entrenched in this second camp. His definition of intelligence is diametrically opposed to earlier views, which employ a standard psychometric approach (IQ test) to cognition or intelligence. Intelligence, as defined by Gardner (1993a), represents "an ability to solve a problem or fashion a product that is valued in one or more cultural settings" (p. x). Gardner identifies eight intelligences: linguistic, logical-mathematical, musical, spatial, bodily-kinesthetic, intrapersonal, interpersonal, and naturalist. Unlike his predecessors (those individuals who helped to create and advance IQ tests such as the Stanford-Binet and Wechsler Intelligence Scale for Children—Revised [WISC-R]) and many of his contemporaries, who endorse math and verbal skills as the standard of intelligence, Gardner's theory espouses that an individual possesses all eight intelligences, but with varying levels of skills. Gardner purposefully placed the aforementioned verbal and math intelligences alongside six other intelligences to give all eight intelligences parity.

"Just as we look different from one another and have different kinds of personalities, we also have different kinds of minds" says Gardner (as cited in Checkley, 1997, p. 9). Gardner did not choose to use the word *talent* or *strength* as is often done in the literature. Rather, he chose the word *intelligence*, because he wished to convey these intelligences equally. His theory advanced from an interdisciplinary base, borrowing from biology, anthropology, psychology, and psychometrics. He was less concerned with the nomenclature of intelligence, skill, strength, talent, or gifts than with the necessity of placing all eight intelligences on an equal footing.

A profile of intelligence, or intellectual disposition, can be detected early in life, and, given the development of these aptitudes, may prove to be enduring over the life cycle (Gardner, 1989, p. 151). Gardner recommends building on students' strengths and initiating formal learning from individualistic talents as opposed to a more traditionalist approach that concentrates on mathematical and verbal literacy. Such an approach has tremendous repercussions for how curriculum is developed and modified in schools.

Gardner's (1993a) MI theory identifies eight ways in which students are intelligent. Listed next are the intelligences, definitions, and descriptors for each of the ways students express their predominant intelligences.

### Multiple Intelligences

* *Musical: To think in sounds, rhythms, melodies, and rhymes*; to be sensitive to pitch, rhythm, timbre, and tone; to recognize, create, and reproduce music by using an instrument or voice; active listening and a strong connection between music and emotions
* *Bodily-kinesthetic: To think in movements and to use the body in proficient and complicated ways* for expressive and goal directed activities; a sense of timing, coordination for whole body movement, and the use of hands for manipulating objects
* *Logical-mathematical: To think of cause-and-effect connections and to understand relationships among actions, objects, or ideas*; to calculate, quantify, or consider propositions and perform complex mathematical or logical operations; it involves inductive and deductive reasoning skills as well as critical and creative problem solving
* *Spatial: To think in pictures and to perceive the visual world accurately*; to think in three dimensions and to transform perceptions and re-create aspects of visual experience via the imagination; to work with objects effectively
* *Linguistic: To think in words and to use language* to express and understand complex meanings; sensitivity to the meaning of words and the order among words, sounds, rhythms, inflections; to reflect on the use of language in everyday life
* *Interpersonal: To think about and understand another person*; to have empathy and recognize distinctions among people; and to appreciate their perspectives with sensitivity to their motives, moods, and intentions. It involves interacting effectively with one or more people in familiar, casual, or working circumstances
* *Intrapersonal: To think about and understand oneself*; to be aware of one's strengths and weaknesses and to plan effectively to achieve personal goals; reflecting on and monitoring one's thoughts and feelings and

regulating them effectively; the ability to monitor one's self in interpersonal relationships and to act with personal efficacy
- *Naturalist: To understand the natural world, including plants, animals, and scientific studies*; to recognize, name, and classify individuals, species, and ecological relationships; to interact effectively with living creatures and discern patterns of life and natural forces

Although it is true that individuals possess all of these intelligences, as well as the potential to improve in any of them at any time in life, they also display a natural proclivity at a young age toward one or two in particular (Fagella & Horowitz, 1990). These particular capacities are sustained throughout the adult life cycle. As persons mature and change over time, these predominant intelligences remain in the areas in which the adult finds it easiest to learn and grow. Gardner states that "My own belief is that one could assess an individual's intellectual potentials quite early in life. . . ." (Gardner, 1993a, p. 385).

There is a particular curricular logic to educating by complementing and building upon students' predominant intelligence. This is meaningful and poignant for students who may appear less successful than their peers. Whereas all children may experience rejection due to their lack of the more traditionalist intelligences, this may be devastating for the population of students with ADHD. Though students with ADHD are labeled at-risk academically and socially, one teacher commented, "I have found a lot of my students with ADHD to be very bright." The authors have heard this from parents as well as teachers throughout their interviews. Transferring this intellectual capacity to attaining traditional measures of intelligence, such as attaining "good" grades and standardized test scores, has remained out of grasp for many members of this population. The aiding of these students in meeting academic goals has also eluded many teachers.

It is our obligation as educators to seek alternatives to standard classroom practices for students with ADHD. One parent, Alicia, exasperated by her son's seemingly intermittent abilities shares, "Kurt can master *any* video game within 5 minutes. It interests him and he wants to do it. I have observed that my son is quite capable of attending to a task for a long period of time. What I don't understand is if he has the ability to focus and concentrate and do very well in this activity, why can't this be transferred to his schoolwork? Is it a matter of creativity? Why can't his teachers find a way to reach and teach him?"

## MI THEORY AND ADHD: AT-PROMISE VERSUS AT-RISK

A national study on ADHD and MI in Schools Using Multiple Intelligence Theory (SUMIT) and in non-MI sites was conducted by the authors (Schirduan, 2000; Schirduan, Case, & Faryniarz, 2002). SUMIT schools, defined by Harvard University's Project Zero, are "ideal" schools using MI theory. The study's purpose was to "identify, document, and promote effective implementations of MI" (Project Zero, 1999, paragraph 3). The studies conducted by the authors describe the multiple intelligences profile, self-concept, and achievement level of students with ADHD. Students labeled with ADHD had their profile of intelligences, or intellectual disposition determined. Teachers were queried from 1997 to 2007 regarding instructional and curricular rationale. The information that came forth offers additional insights and understandings regarding students labeled with ADHD and their intellectual promise.

As we begin our journey to discover the MI and ADHD connection in school-age students and move from at-risk to at-promise, we acknowledge that characteristics associated with ADHD impact the student's profile of intelligence, a profile that may be detected early in life. In fact, profiles of intelligence for students with ADHD who walk through classroom doors may turn out to be quite enduring, and as Gardner (1989) stated, "It is probably prudent to go with the grain, rather than wholly against it" (p. 151).

An example of this can be seen in the MI profile of Chris, a former client in our private practice. Chris, a middle school student, was short with his responses, and although he was polite, it was evident that he was present due to the urging of his parents. He scored highest in spatial intelligence. The parent interview revealed his early proclivity toward the spatial intelligence. "Chris was building with LEGO® Technic sets for age 12+ by the age of 5 and 6. He couldn't read but would follow the pictures [on the LEGO® boxes] to build." Past accomplishments such as artwork, drawing, and video games, and his success with school endeavors such as technical education, along with hobbies and interests (e.g., taking things apart and reassembling them, strategy games like Battleship, chess, computers, and drawing plans), indicated strengths in spatial intelligence. These skills should be utilized to bridge to other academic areas. Chris was referred by his parents on the advice of school personnel who maintained that he was having difficulty focusing and paying attention in class. This was negatively impacting his academic performance, especially in language arts and social studies.

Chris described a social studies project (a stated area of difficulty according to his teachers) as easy when photography (a primarily spatial activity) was incorporated into the project. Chris explains, "I took a picture of an empty theater to show loneliness. . . ." His ability to relay information and understand social studies concepts through his predominant intelligence illuminated Chris's capacity to excel in different academic arenas. It is the authors' contention that difficulty in one area may often be successfully overcome by rerouting a task through an individual's more highly developed intelligences.

Dryden, a nationally acclaimed author, told the researchers that "in producing twenty-two television programs on the world's best learning and teaching methods, and the world's best schools, I can't recall ever running across any student with attention-deficit syndrome" (G. Dryden, personal communication, April 23, 2007). He attributes this in part to highly trained teachers and students who use their own natural talents to learn in untraditional ways.

Dryden's point has been underscored by similar accounts collected from art, music, and physical education teachers. When we approached Angela, a music teacher, to discuss her students labeled with ADHD, she matter-of-factly stated, "I don't know who the ADHD kids are." Michelle, an art teacher, shared, "I don't think I've the same problems with ADHD kids in my class as other [classroom] teachers because art is immediate contact with media [e.g., paint, plaster, paper, and so on]. And students with ADHD often like to manipulate objects." A physical education teacher, Sue Ann, recounted that "because most students with ADHD need to move, I do not have a problem teaching ADHD kids. However, the classroom teachers of students with ADHD come to me weekly, if not daily, to inquire about their inappropriate or off-task behavior. In fact, not only am I not having behavior problems, the ADHD kids are getting the best grades in my class." These teachers, along with many others, spoke to the instructional promise of matching predominant intelligences via a curriculum vehicle in order to ensure the academic success of students labeled with ADHD.

We believe that these anecdotes hint at possibilities that a curricular match can be made by teachers to best serve students labeled with ADHD. As a former physical education teacher, Cynthia encountered the same phenomenon. She shares, "Although I'd received background information on students labeled with ADHD who were in my classroom, I rarely ran into academic or disciplinary problems. I remember one student with ADHD in particular, Sean. A fireball, he would come flying into the gym and upon entering, I'd hear an audible sigh of relief from his teacher. But Sean, in my class, was at his best."

Students with ADHD often go unnoticed in art, music, or physical education. This raises questions such as whether it is the media they use, such as paint, clay, paste, crayons, balls, hoops, bats, ropes, guitars, voices, horns, and rhythm sticks? Are "special" teachers more tolerant of students labeled with ADHD due to class times lasting only 30 to 45 minutes? Are the strengths of students labeled with ADHD in art, music, and PE being tapped? Does the focus improved in these areas provide evidence that students labeled with ADHD have the capabilities necessary for enhanced academic achievement? Is improved behavior and academic performance related to movement in class? Or is it related to an environment conducive to learning hands-on? We'll explore the answers to these questions and more in the chapters that follow. This book reports on promising avenues that can be employed to teach and reach students with ADHD.

Of the hundreds of students with ADHD we've encountered, few have possessed a language-logic profile. In our largest study, a small percentage of boys reported the linguistic (10.5%) and logical-mathematical (7.0%) intelligence as their predominant intelligence. Girls, on the other hand, never reported the linguistic or logical-mathematical intelligence as a top intelligence. New curricular approaches are needed to move students labeled with ADHD from an at-risk to an at-promise perspective. This process begins by looking at each student with ADHD and his or her family individually. This requires making necessary accommodations for individual students labeled with ADHD. It means knowing students' MI strengths so that teachers can successfully bridge the gap between strength and weakness. A comprehensive look at the ways and means to bring students labeled with ADHD to academic promise follows.

# Success at School

PHIL, A FORMER COLLEAGUE with ADHD, has spent his adult life assisting others with the same challenge. He confided to us that, unfortunately, he'd never had a teacher who *changed his life*. As a young student, he thought that since he kept getting Ds, he must be a dummy.

> I'd sit in the back of the classroom and then the teacher walks up and says, "Phil what's so and so?" And I said, I don't know. And she'd say, "*Well,* think about it, hmmm." And I'd just feel so bad.

Chapter 2 attempts to show the hidden potential for all students with ADHD to succeed in school. Research and anecdotes reveal promising avenues with the potential to *change the life* of a student with ADHD. MI cognitive profiles of students with ADHD and their teachers are explored. These dual profiles can open the door to meaningful conversation regarding student and teacher strengths and weaknesses, along with learning and teaching bias. In turn, these joint insights have the power to influence curriculum planning and relationships. To provide a context for such dialogue, the results of our national study on intelligence, achievement, and the self-concept of students with ADHD in MI schools and non-MI schools are reported, and the impact of our research on learning and teaching is discussed.

## ASSESSMENT

*Intelligence*, as defined by Gardner (1999a), is "a biopsychological potential to process information that can be activated in a cultural setting to solve problems or create products that are of value in a culture" (pp. 33–34). This definition emphasizes the creative and practical aspects of an individual's intellectual abilities. It also acknowledges the importance of the person-in-context and the social influences that contribute to the recognition, activation, and development of skills. Intelligence, thus, is not perceived as an immutable, biologically predetermined entity (as is generally presumed by the IQ test), but rather evolves through life with parameters that may shift with time and effort.

The assessment of multiple intelligences for teacher and student can be accomplished in two ways. The determination of personal learning strengths via a MI profile is possible by reflection, observation, and discussion, or by completing the Online Multiple Intelligences Developmental Assessment Scale (OMS). The MIDAS™ may be completed using the two complementary codes on the inside back cover in this book. Refer to Appendix B. The MIDAS™ profile describes strengths and limitations for all eight intelligences. An accurate portrait of the learner with ADHD will emerge, as well as that of the teacher.

### Reflection, Observation, and Discussion

Teachers, although they may not view themselves as such, are by their very nature data collectors in the classroom. As professionals with the opportunity to view students on a daily basis, individually and within a group setting, they are constantly reflecting, observing, and discussing students' strengths and weaknesses. This natural process can be used for the assessment of multiple intelligences.

**Reflect.** The first step in assessment is reflection. The teacher reads the definitions of the eight intelligences that follow and reflects on which two of the eight intelligences best describe the student with ADHD. In addition, a reflection on the definitions of multiple intelligences in Chapter 1 and Appendix C will add further insights.

Building on the work of Gardner (1993a), researchers such as Armstrong (1994), Checkley (1997), Hoerr (1996a, 2000), and Viens (1999) further discussed and identified characteristics of the eight intelligences.

*The student with musical intelligence thinks in sounds*, rhythms, melodies, and rhymes. Often, these students can be seen humming or whistling to themselves, drumming their fingers on the desk, or tapping their hands, feet, or pencils. These are the students who love music class and may play an instrument or sing in a band. Whereas it might seem like common sense, playing background music while students are working in class does not engage the musical intelligence and may actually distract students with ADHD.

While being interviewed, Jacob, a seventh-grade boy with ADHD and a flair for music and fashion, tuned in to the background music in the restaurant and tuned off this researcher. It is important to note that, despite his preadolescent status, his actions were unintentional. He was not trying to be rude, nor was he trying to purposefully listen to the restaurant's background music. His was an in-born response. Musical intelligence is engaged if the student shows the aptitude to think in music, to be able to hear patterns, and to recognize them and or manipulate them.

*The student with bodily-kinesthetic intelligence thinks in movements.* These students use their bodies skillfully, in part or in whole, to create, perform, or solve problems. They may move around, touch things, and gesture. However, it is important to note that, although these students exhibit bodily-kinesthetic intelligence, they should not be identified with the class member best described as fidgety, and often fail to remain still during instruction. In our research, students with ADHD with a diagnosis of predominantly hyperactive reflected the same profile as those without predominantly hyperactive ADHD. Students with predominantly hyperactive ADHD self-reported naturalist and spatial intelligences as strengths. However, bodily-kinesthetic intelligence was a distant third out of eight intelligences reported for all three types (inattentive, hyperactive, and combined) of ADHD. Although some students with ADHD may, in fact, possess bodily-kinesthetic intelligence, it is important for the teacher to reflect on how these students think and not to get "distracted" by more outwardly physical manifestations of ADHD.

*The student with linguistic intelligence thinks in words*. Telling stories or jokes, making lists, writing poetry, and employing an above average vocabulary are characteristics for these students. Students with linguistic intelligence read and write easily. However, being "talkative" or a "chatterbox" is not necessarily indicative of this strength. Students who are bilingual also may not necessarily have a predominant linguistic intelligence.

*The student with the logical-mathematical intelligence thinks in numbers and/or by reasoning*. These students like to question, count, categorize, explain, analyze, compare, explore, calculate, investigate, problem solve, strategize, and/or reason. In class, this is the student who often enjoys math. You may see this student drawn to computers, puzzles, or strategy games. It is important to note that such students are not only those who are attracted to mathematics; this "intelligence is not only about numerical reasoning but, as the name implies, includes logical reasoning abilities that might not involve numbers at all" (Viens, 1999, p. 9).

*The student with the spatial intelligence thinks in pictures and images*. This student doodles and draws, sketches, makes crafts, constructs three-dimensional structures with Legos® or blocks, or is adept at completing puzzles. Such students may appear to be daydreaming. Because spatial intelligence involves spatial orientation and using visual or spatial information, unexpectedly, a blind person may be adept at spatial intelligence. Blind or vision-impaired individuals are experts at maneuvering themselves through space via a cane. They have a great concept of space. Think of the "blind traveler finding the bus stop, undertaking a journey and finding his [*sic*] way back again (quite a commonplace occurrence)" (Butler, 1994, p. 366).

*The student with naturalist intelligence thinks by observing, recognizing, understanding, classifying, and organizing patterns in the natural environment*. These are the students who may bring their rock or bug collection to school. They love the outdoors and are quick to note environmental changes. They are the students most drawn to class pets or plants, and they often enjoy science class. The naturalist intelligence "is not limited to the outside world" (Baum, Viens, & Slatin, 2005, p. 19), and also includes recognition of cultural artifacts or nonnatural patterning activities and classification.

*The student with the interpersonal intelligence thinks socially "by bouncing ideas off other people"* (Armstrong, 1994, p. 27). More than displaying a strong preference for working in a group, these students have the ability to understand classmates and social actions. They often get along with their peers, display empathy, and easily resolve conflicts. They have a talent for easy communication, mediation, and negotiation.

*The student with the intrapersonal intelligence thinks deeply*. Reflective with a strong sense of self, these students can easily identify their strengths and weaknesses and plan accordingly to achieve in school. In class, they can be observed making decisions for themselves, initiating and self-pacing during projects, and journaling (e.g., keeping a diary). These students may also appear to be daydream-ing, planning, and working independently. Although they do not always prefer to work alone, what characterizes them is their ability to recognize their learn-ing preference.

**Observe.** Once a thorough understanding of the eight intelligences has been obtained, the second step is to observe students with ADHD while they work in all subjects using a variety of materials. Observe these students in various settings. Pay attention to the student in structured (e.g., language arts, reading, writing, math, science, social studies, and so forth) and nonstructured classroom settings (e.g., recess, playground, lunch, bus). Watch them outside of class (e.g., music, art, physical education, computers, library) as well. Also review documents (e.g., portfolios, report cards, projects, class work, tests, and so on) and look for students' strengths and weaknesses.

**Discuss.** The third step of assessment is to describe a student's intellectual strengths and to discuss insights with students and their parents. Collegial dialogue can provide teacher teams with a thorough picture of the strengths of a student with ADHD.

During our research, we found that, when parents were asked to read the MI descriptions and pick two of the eight intelligences that described their child, par-ents were able to identify at least one, but often two, of their child's strengths as denoted by the MIDAS™. Discussion questions (e.g., How is free time spent? Pro-vide examples. How are talents displayed?) addressed to the student, parent, and teachers can help determine which intelligences best reflect students' strengths.

During our private practice and while conducting research, we assessed the student with ADHD by interviewing student, parent, and teacher. When speaking with the student, we found that a discussion concerning likes and dislikes, and what the student excelled in or failed at in school (e.g., grades) helped corrobo-rate the MIDAS™ results. The same held true when interviewing the teacher or parent of a student with ADHD. Parents often shared that their child had a long history (e.g., proclivity) of being drawn to the same activities. These were often closely correlated with their child's MI profile and natural proclivity. Though chil-dren possess all eight of Gardner's (1993a) intelligences to a certain degree, they display a natural proclivity at a young age toward one or two of the intelligences that are carried throughout their lives. This was the case with Raul and Liam. For others, their strengths may not be revealed until later.

Raul is an only child who attends to selected tasks for long periods of time. As a child, Raul, exhibited ADHD characteristics as well as characteristics associated with spatial intelligence. His mom remembered "being amazed at his spatial strengths."

> At 18 months, he could do a 24-piece puzzle; at age 2, he could complete a 50-piece puzzle; when he was 3, it was a 100-piece puzzle; and by the time he was in kindergarten, he was up to a 500-piece puzzle, and without much difficulty, I might add. His visual spatial strength was confirmed when he was tested and scored very high in the spatial battery test.

Liam showed a natural proclivity at an early age as well. One of three siblings in his family, which consisted of two boys and a sister, Liam, like his brother, had olive skin and lots of hair. His mother revealed that, as a toddler, he was fascinated with cars.

> I remember our long road trip to Georgia. Liam was 3 and as we were driving he would blurt out, "There's a Buick! Look at the Porsche, Mommy!" and was able to give the make and model of cars. We were all quite impressed! Liam had been collecting Matchbox cars since he was a toddler. As he got older, he really enjoyed putting together those car kits to make small car replicas. His strength continues to be in the naturalist and spatial intelligences and his obsession with cars continued. He now drives a 1992 Volvo. He detailed it, located missing car parts at junk yards, and replaced the old parts. He takes much pride in his car. He just loves working on the car, taking pieces apart, and then putting them back together again.
>
> The authors have examined Liam's academic progress throughout his schooling and, although he has struggled to obtain good grades, he has succeeded and is now in college. Not surprisingly, he is pursuing a career in engineering.

## MULTIPLE INTELLIGENCES DEVELOPMENTAL ASSESSMENT SCALE (MIDAS™)

While traditional IQ tests serve to mark the limits of an individual's "general intelligence," the MIDAS™ describes the course and direction of intellectual growth and achievement potential in specific areas of skill for the eight intelligences. Rather than setting boundaries for a person's capabilities, MIDAS™ offers an aptitude description in several different areas of promise.

The Multiple Intelligences Developmental Assessment Scale (MIDAS™), a valid and reliable MI-based tool, can reveal the strengths (the two top or predominant intelligences) and weaknesses (the two lowest or weakest intelligences) as reported by students with ADHD and their teachers.

### Description of MIDAS™

There are four forms of the MIDAS™ assessment that correspond to four different age groups. One version is for adults, another version is applicable for teens. The last two versions of "MIDAS™–KIDS" are the most relevant to our readers. The "All About Me" MIDAS™ version is a questionnaire that consists of 93 items that are self-completed by students 9 to 14 years old. The "My Young Child" questionnaire contains 70 items and is completed by a parent (or another knowledgeable informant) for children 4 to 8 years old.

The MIDAS™, Teen–MIDAS™, and MIDAS™ KIDS questionnaires are based on MI theory as described by Howard Gardner (1993a). A MIDAS™ profile provides detailed information in three broad categories. It gives a reasonable estimate of the person's intellectual disposition in each of the eight constructs (linguistic, logical-mathematical, spatial, musical, bodily-kinesthetic, naturalist, interpersonal, and intrapersonal) and describes 24 or more skills associated with each intelligence (e.g., instrumental and vocal skills for musical). Third, intellectual style scales estimate a proclivity for innovation, general logic, and leadership. With the aid of a

MIDAS™ profile and interpretative materials, a person can carefully make educational plans that maximize the effective use of strengths to achieve success.

## Completion of MIDAS™

Students with ADHD and their teachers should now complete the MIDAS™ online, using the Web site and complimentary codes found on the inside cover of this book (refer to Appendix B). The MIDAS™ profile and the Brief Interpretative Packet will be attached in a PDF file. Adobe Acrobat Reader is necessary to print the profile. If this program is not installed on the computer, it may be downloaded for free at http://www.adobe.com/products/acrobat/ (click on "Get Adobe Reader"). The online MIDAS™ version takes approximately 20–30 minutes and results will arrive via e-mail upon completion of the MIDAS™. A sample of a MIDAS™–KIDS profile for an ADHD student and an Interpretative Packet are presented in Appendix C.

The MIDAS™ Profile Report consists of three pages. Page one provides a graphic display of the eight main intelligences scales and intellectual style scales. Page two lists the names of subscales hierarchically from highest to lowest. Subscales describe specific sets of skills associated with each of the main intelligences. For example, artistic design, space awareness, and working with objects are three of the spatial intelligence subscales. Page three provides all the percentage scores for the main and subscales. It is important to note that the first two pages of the profile are qualitative descriptions of the respondent's abilities, and that actual scores are not displayed until page three. This arrangement intentionally emphasizes the goal of creating a rich description of the person's MI profile over the categorical labeling of skill levels via numerical scores.

The MIDAS™ is designed to provide an objective measure of the multiple intelligences. "Judiciously administered and cautiously interpreted, a measure inspired by multiple intelligences can be helpful to teachers, students, and parents" (Gardner, 1997, p. 122). With regard to the MIDAS™, Gardner (1997) states, "I consider Branton Shearer's efforts to be among the well-founded ones, with considerable grounding in psychometric procedures" (p. 121). However, both Gardner and Shearer discourage using assessment as an end in itself, for example, for labeling a student as "musical" or "linguistic." Instead, results should be used to personalize the curriculum and instruction for students.

The MIDAS™ is designed to be a thoughtful and systematic survey of the teacher and student's strengths. Questions have gone through a rigorous process of refinement and selection, including qualitative review by subject area experts and have undergone statistical tests. However, it resembles an interview or dialogue rather than an impersonal set of general questions. The generated MI profile is the first step to understanding, rather than a final truth regarding predominant intelligences. After the MIDAS™ profile report is received, the next steps are to complete the Brief Learning Summary and Dialogue and Reflection activities in Appendix C.

Gardner (1993a) believes that individuals' predominant intelligences and the way in which they learn is so natural that forgetting them "is virtually impossible" (p. 386). This was the case with Paul, a fifth grader with ADHD, who exhibited strength in musical intelligence. You cannot miss Paul in a crowd. He is head and shoulders above his fellow class members, which draws one's eye to him. His teacher states, "The minute the music comes on, he 'feels' the dance move, and he immediately starts dancing. He can't stop. He dances all day. He'll hear a piece of music and he goes into dance mode. As an accommodation for Paul, I allow him to demonstrate the moves for the class. Because he has a tough time being third or fourth, I usually let him go first so he won't disturb others' learning. After his turn he is better able to focus on the lesson." His music teacher had the foresight to know that once she acknowledged Paul's strength, he'd be able to continue with his learning.

Through trial and error, she had come to the realization that if Paul's needs were not met, he wouldn't produce quality work. The teacher found a way to meet her need (i.e., to have Paul learn the lesson) and the student's need (i.e., to allow Paul to "shine" and demonstrate the lesson), while taking into account the needs of the class as a whole. The next step, which is undeniably more difficult, is to find ways to teach what is difficult for Paul, by bridging his strength in music to his weakness. This will be further explored in Chapter 3. Recent brain research indicates that abilities may be developed over a lifetime. All of the intelligences can be improved with effort, risk-taking, and motivation, but most importantly, self-awareness. Embracing Gardner's conception of intelligence, along with completing the online MIDAS™ assessment and/or MI assessment via reflection, observation, and discussion, allows for the construction of a preliminary portrait.

The MI profile and portrait of a student with ADHD may be an area that no one has ever detected, let alone honored as "intelligences" worthy of being built upon. Discoveries such as these are especially important to academically struggling students who are at-risk of identifying themselves as "dumb," "disabled," or "slow." It can be a profound experience for students to have their spatial, naturalist, interpersonal, intrapersonal, bodily-kinesthetic, or musical intelligence validated in the presence of teachers, parents, and peers. Moreover, students who exhibited difficulty in reading and math can have these learning challenges detoxified through the special recognition of their other intellectual strengths. After completing the MIDAS™ and reviewing the MI profile, one student commented, "I've never been book smart but I know I'm not stupid. I now have a better understanding of myself in general" (Shearer, 2004, p. 155).

## TEACHER AND STUDENT MI PROFILES

Assessing the MI strengths of the *teacher* of a student with ADHD may be just as important to the student's academic success as having the teacher and student learn the MI profile of the student with ADHD. By knowing the teacher's MI strengths, a fuller understanding of how a MI profile impacts curriculum and instructional choices for students with ADHD can be gained. Often, there is a marked difference in MI profiles between the teacher and student with ADHD. For example, *we found that the strengths in teachers were polar opposites to the strengths of students with ADHD*. This incongruity may lead, at best, to minimal use of teaching strategies, but it can also cause communication conflicts, potential prejudicial grading, and, at worst, avoidance of curriculum and instruction that would allow a student with ADHD to flourish.

Teachers' MI profiles have a profound bearing on instruction, which subsequently impacts student learning. An inherent bias in teaching style arises if teachers' MI profiles are different from those of their students with ADHD. This may affect how students receive knowledge, thus interfering with how students with ADHD learn best. Teachers need to reflect on their instructional delivery, and likewise, students need to understand how they learn best and why they are attracted to particular subjects and repelled by others.

Reflection on past classroom experiences are key. For example, Valerie, an elementary school teacher, stated, "I was not good at teaching activities relating to the spatial intelligence. I did not draw well. Thus, I did not make sketches on the blackboard to convey ideas that could have benefited students with spatial intelligence. My lessons did not include construction-type activities to complement a skill. My students rarely engaged in assembling, disassembling objects, elaborate art activities, or three-dimensional projects. And I certainly never ventured into any spatial awareness–type activities." Not surprisingly, her MI profile indicated that spatial intelligence was her weakest or lowest intelligence. Her avoidance or dislike of spatial-related activities reached back to her days as an elementary student. She remembered many teachers throughout the years assigning a drawing as a complement to an instructional activity, a popular teaching method that is still used widely today. She dreaded having to share her artwork with classmates and, thus, she did not wish to inflict the same "punishment" on her own students when she became a teacher. Unfortunately, what was a punishment for her was a missed opportunity for her students. She avoided what did not come naturally to her as a teacher—namely, spatial-related activities. However, she conveyed that she now realized that the students in her class who had strength in spatial intelligence were not supported.

It is natural to be drawn to what one does well. Normally, talents reflect an MI profile. Yet, what teachers and students do with their self-knowledge (MI profile) is what may make a positive difference in teaching and learning.

## MI Profile of Teachers

The interpersonal and linguistic intelligences are often the predominant (top two) intelligences of teachers. This is a marked difference to the MI profile of students with ADHD (Schirduan, 2000; Schirduan, Case, & Faryniarz, 2002). To foster an understanding and sensitivity toward how students with ADHD best learn, administrators and educators must overcome their bias toward the language-logic profile that is preferred in school and society. Prejudice toward intelligences that are not considered "academic" disenfranchise students with special needs or unique learning abilities, dooming them to educational and, possibly, lifelong failure. Traditional methods of teaching rob some students of learning, particularly those students with ADHD. MI theory spotlights the reason why some students fail. It counters the falsified notion regarding the one best way to teach and encourages the use of curriculum to fit each student's unique cognitive profile instead of undermining what may surface as a predominant intelligence.

When teaching education classes at a college, the authors of this book had students take the MIDAS™ to expose the potential bias that may arise when the profiles of teacher and student differ. Most had the interpersonal and linguistic intelligences as their predominant intelligences. This was not an anomaly but rather a trend found among teacher education students. As would seem reasonable, however, it was not surprising for one of the predominant intelligences to align with declared college content majors. For example, the musical intelligence became predominant among future music teachers, spatial intelligence was highly developed among art teachers, and bodily-kinesthetic intelligence was characteristically found to be a strength among physical education teachers. The personal (interpersonal and intrapersonal) and linguistic intelligences among teachers were confirmed by other studies.

The MIDAS™ was administered to elementary, middle, and high school teachers, all of whom had college degrees. These studies revealed the group mean score and reported interpersonal followed by the linguistic and/or intrapersonal intelligence as the predominant intelligences among elementary, middle, and high school teachers. Although teachers may possess strengths in the personal intelligences—interpersonal (to think about and understand another person) and intrapersonal (thinks about and understands oneself)—and linguistic intelligence (thinks in words), these were often the weakest intelligences in students with ADHD. Generally what has been learned by the authors is that teachers and parents report the language–logic intelligences as major strengths. Students with ADHD rank these intelligences as weaknesses. Specifically, boys and girls with ADHD in SUMIT sites did not perceive themselves as competent in language or math. A small percentage of boys reported the linguistic (10.5%) and logical-mathematical (7.0%) intelligence as predominant intelligences. Girls, on the other hand, never reported the linguistic or logical-mathematical intelligence as a top intelligence. When all the students with ADHD who had participated in our research were studied, the intrapersonal intelligence was ranked last for both boys and girls with ADHD and first for teachers. It's not surprising that teachers possess interpersonal intelligence. The drive to enter the classroom may be related to their belief that they understand and relate well to students.

These research results suggest that, in order to foster that deep interest and desire to help students, one must step out of a comfort zone, teaching via the personal and linguistic intelligences. This may mean success or failure for students with ADHD. Such findings don't imply teaching toward a lesson in eight ways, but rather requires reflection on the part of the teacher on how to best make connections from strengths to weaknesses in students' learning. And while intelligence is not the same as discipline or domain and working or learning style, taking students' strengths into consideration when planning lessons helps to increase student understanding.

The teachers at one school took strengths into consideration and made a group decision to teach from their strength. Teachers plan and teach in teams based on their predominant intelligences (Campbell & Campbell, 1997, p. 15). Teachers with naturalist intelligence contribute to curriculum planning via science, and teachers with logical-mathematical intelligence teach math associated with grade-level curriculum. Imagine being supplanted in an environment where teaching strength came easily and was shared in its delivery by others with the same proclivity. While being comfortable and content, now imagine a student with ADHD supplanted in an environment (e.g., language arts class) that feels unnatural and uncomfortable. Classroom alternatives can be found that fit both teacher and student.

Simple objects, such as a rabbit and a camera, were two objects used in class to make learning feel "natural" for an ADHD student such as Ryan. Ryan fit the textbook description of a student with ADHD. Constantly moving, Ryan was attending to everything *but* his schoolwork, until "Bugs Bunny" arrived on the scene. His teacher shared, "I found that a rabbit helped to calm Ryan, my fourth grader with ADHD."

I would allow the rabbit to sit in Ryan's lap. Ryan would pet the rabbit, and do his work. It was a terrific tool! It helped him focus and I found that if he didn't have the rabbit, he couldn't focus.

Next door, Whitney, a fifth-grade teacher, identified the camera as a potential tool.

Typically, the students with ADHD will rush through their projects, meeting the minimal requirements, and head for the Legos® I have in the back of the room for those who finish early. However, this was not the case with our project using digital cameras. The two students with ADHD in my class were especially drawn to this activity. They were the students in class who were thoughtful in the pictures they took. They did really well.

Whitney, quite by accident, found an activity that came naturally to two of her students with ADHD who have strength in spatial intelligence. The camera allows them to view vistas while teaching them literally and figuratively to focus. On the MIDAS™ for KIDS, students rated the question "Do you often like to use a camera, look at photographs or picture books?" positively. This question reflects just one potential alternative classroom strategy to be used by the teacher of students with ADHD.

## MI Profile of ADHD Students

The naturalist and spatial intelligence profile surfaced among study samples of students with ADHD (Schirduan, 2000; Schirduan, Case, & Faryniarz, 2002). A student with strength in naturalist intelligence such as Quinlan has the ability to understand the natural world, including plants, animals, and scientific studies. His parent reports, "My ADHD son, Quinlan, is a naturalist and has been since he was a toddler."

He would always want to go outside and be into everything. I would give him a stick in the yard and he would be entertained for hours! As he got a little older, he would find a stick and build pretend campfires. He loved to pick flowers and plant seeds and watch them grow—like pumpkins. I remember when Quinlan was in fifth grade, he started building stonewalls all over the yard. I have 4 acres, so there were a lot of stonewalls! As a preteen, he would and still does take care of the yard. He does all the landscaping and is very meticulous—making paths in the orchard, etc. It's amazing! In fact, our neighbors took notice and they hired him to work in their yard! He is now a freshman in high school, very bright, with a 127 IQ, and he still loves activities related to nature, like fishing and camping. He just loves that stuff. Quinlan entered the Agricultural Education Program at his school.

While Quinlan displayed one of the two intelligences that surfaced in the profile we found among ADHD students in our study, Sandra displays the other, the spatial intelligence. A student with spatial intelligence has the ability to think in pictures and images and to perceive the visual world accurately. This intelligence involves the capacity to think in three dimensions, work with objects effectively, create artistic designs or craft activities, and or assemble things.

Sandra's story offers a glimpse of a student with ADHD who has spatial intelligence. Sandra, like some other study participants with ADHD, was initially reserved when we first spoke to her, but her demeanor quickly changed when we began talking about her strengths and what she does well. Sandra has a strong interest in art, a proclivity that has its roots in early childhood. Her daycare provider noticed her ability right away and marveled at the control Sandra showed when using crayons.

> She'd be very selective with colors and she would place one color next to another, *not* placing one over another. She had a great ability to stay within lines. If it was a sketched picture that she was just filling in, [she was] just very aware of the colors and how she wanted them placed. It seemed she had already thought about how she wanted them placed on the paper versus some children [who] just seem to pick up any color and just start scribbling. (Schirduan, 2000, p. 155)

There are a number of indicators that Sandra works effectively with objects (a spatial intelligence criterion). Sandra's parent described this skill as her "picking things up, creating, making things."

> She was able to hold a pencil at a very young age. She was also able to maneuver and handle scissors at quite an early age and able to cut quite well. So her fine motor skills I felt were really in-tuned [above average]. (Schirduan, 2000, p. 15)

Parents and teachers should honor their students' cognitive profile. However, this was not the case for Susan. Hers is a story that reveals a missed opportunity in that her identified skills could have been used as a springboard to ascertain her learning difficulties. Outwardly, Susan, a third-grade student with ADHD, was beautiful with long blond hair and brown eyes. At home, Susan was experiencing a strained relationship with her half brother, and at school, she lacked academic self-esteem and felt little self-worth. Susan's mother dismissed her daughter's proclivity toward the naturalist intelligence at a young age because "it comes so easily to Susan . . . I just find with her love of nature and animals that is something that has been there since she was very very young." When asked "What is she most successful at during school?" Susan's mother responded, "That's a tough one." In school, Susan received mostly Cs. Science, however, revealed a different side of Susan. In this subject, she received As. Nonetheless, her teacher stated that overall Susan is a low average student. Even Susan perceived herself as a poor learner. When asked "What kind of student are you?" she sheepishly admitted, "Not really smart, 'cause I saw my report card and it's sorta bad" (Schirduan, 2000, p. 150; Schirduan & Case, 2004, p. 92; Schirduan, Case, & Faryniarz, 2002). There was never any thought on the part of the parent or the teacher to bridge her abilities in science to other academic areas and, thus, Susan remained trapped by her negative portrayal of her learning ability.

### Impact of MI Profiles on Teaching and Learning

Any understanding of how a student with ADHD best learns must include his or her MI profile to enhance the student's educational opportunities and options.

Simple awareness of the predominant intelligences is not enough. In order to guide students to successful learning experiences, educators must *use* the intelligence profile. The profile aids in understanding the ways in which a student seems to learn more easily. Ultimately, though, it must be determined how best to use identified strengths to help a student become successful in other academic endeavors. For example, at school, a curriculum that is sensitive to a student's predominant intelligence, such as Caroline's, empowers that student by teaching to understand concepts through strengths, not weaknesses. Caroline's parents requested a consultation to help prepare their vivacious daughter for the transition from middle school to high school. They were concerned with social adjustment issues in adolescence, as well as inconsistent academic performance. Caroline, a student with ADHD, had exhibited interpersonal intelligence (thinks by bouncing ideas off other people) and spatial intelligence (thinks in images and pictures) in middle school. She revealed a preference for schoolwork that tapped into her interpersonal intelligence. One of her favorite school assignments involved interviewing people. The report was on the history of U.S. currency. "I met with a coin dealer to get people's input. . . . I love interviewing people," said Caroline.

Caroline and all other students have intellectual strengths and preferred learning and working styles. Understanding this allows teachers to motivate students to greater accomplishment, personal satisfaction, and lifelong learning. Teaching style stems from an MI profile. Just as important, an MI profile provides individuals with knowledge regarding why certain teaching activities may seem rewarding or tiresome and frustrating. This insight may help educators make informed curriculum decisions. It may also explain why teachers find certain students exhausting or a pleasure to teach. Personality conflicts that occur between teacher and student may simply be a mismatch of intellectual approach and style.

Understanding a student's predominant intelligences and natural proclivities and acting on that information requires effort on the part of the educator. Although uncovering the MI profile of a student with ADHD is important, labeling a student with the naturalist intelligence, for example, is not as informative as noting the different ways in which naturalistic interests are demonstrated. As Hatch (1997) noted, "We must take into account a constellation of factors—what intelligences they possess, their interests in and knowledge of particular fields, and the contexts in which they live and learn" (p. 26).

While examining a student's intellectual profile, a teacher should not "track" a solitary intelligence. Instead, such information should serve as a vehicle for further exploration into other competencies (Gardner, 1993a). In that way, the profile becomes a tool for students to understand themselves better, enabling them to use that knowledge to extend their understanding and skills. Early intervention is important in the development of an individual's intelligences. Given the appropriate resources and bridging strategies, any "normal individual can attain impressive competence in an intellectual or a symbolic [e.g., linguistic, numerical, gestural, pictorial] domain" (Gardner, 1993a, p. 316).

> "Different minds learn differently and that's a problem for many children, because most schools still cling to a one-size-fits-all education philosophy. . . . [T]hese children struggle because their learning patterns don't fit the schools they are in" (Levine, as cited in Gorrell, 2002, paragraph 1).

Levine's comments resonate with students with ADHD.

## ADHD STUDENTS IN SCHOOLS USING MI THEORY (SUMIT) AND "NON-MI" SCHOOLS

In order to evaluate students with ADHD in different educational settings, elementary and middle school students in our studies were drawn from Project SUMIT at Harvard University, as well as those schools that have not yet formally embraced this curriculum theory. Our studies disclosed a naturalist and spatial intelligence learning pattern among students with ADHD that does not fit the language-logic learning pattern of most schools.

### MI and Academic Achievement for Students with ADHD

While it has been seen that some students with ADHD have not done as well as their peers on standardized tests and fall below grade level (Zentall, 1993), students with ADHD who attended SUMIT sites achieved average success (e.g., grades on report card) as reported by their teachers (Schirduan, 2000).

The Teacher Perception of Achievement Level was the instrument used to answer questions regarding the achievement level of students with ADHD. Teachers of students with ADHD were asked to rate their students' current level of achievement. Achievement level was defined as the most recent report card results. Findings indicated that *students with ADHD in SUMIT sites attained an average achievement level.*

Teachers were asked questions about retention, grades skipped in school, difficulty with reading and math, poor grades, and special education services (e.g., learning disabled, gifted classes). Students with ADHD in SUMIT sites appeared to be achieving at higher levels of success than previously reported. This showed promise for students with ADHD, revealing that the majority of students with ADHD in the study at SUMIT sites have not been retained in school, nor were they relegated to the special education classroom. Simply put, students with ADHD achieved success at SUMIT sites. It may be that teachers in SUMIT sites were teaching weaknesses (linguistic, logical-mathematical) via strengths and that this form of instruction is compatible with students with ADHD intelligence patterns.

This is in keeping with Sternberg's (1996) findings that "students performed significantly and substantially better when the form of instruction was at least partially compatible with the students' pattern of abilities" (p. 22). Imagine the academic successes for students with ADHD when instruction is compatible with their MI profile. This is especially pertinent, given Barkley's (1992) statement that "almost all ADHD children referred to clinics have been doing poorly at school" (p. 20).

### MI and Self-Concept of Students with ADHD

Although naturalist and spatial intelligences were the predominant intelligences of students with ADHD, *the personal intelligences (intrapersonal intelligence and interpersonal intelligence) were among the lowest reported.* Students participating in these studies consistently rated intrapersonal intelligence and interpersonal intelligence among their areas of weakness. These intelligences focus on the individual's self-knowledge and positive relationships with others. Such intelligences are important to school success and present challenges to ADHD students. Barkley (1992) reports that, upon entry to school, "an emerging pattern of social rejection [appears], if not earlier, in over half of all ADHD children because of their poor social skills" (p. 25).

"The intrapersonal intelligence is the key intelligence. . . . [I]t positions us for success. . . . [C]onversely, a weak intrapersonal intelligence means that we will continue to meet frustration and failure. . . ." (Hoerr, 2000, p. 43). For the student with ADHD, a weakness in the intrapersonal intelligence does not allow for the identification of weaknesses in academic and social realms. "The point is that having a weakness isn't nearly as much of a problem as not knowing what the weakness is. If you don't know where you are weak, how can you systematically improve?" (Hoerr, 2000, p. 43).

Problems as a result of this conflict may arise between teacher and student with ADHD, as well as between the student and peers. As difficult as it is to teach students with ADHD it can be even more difficult to be their classmate. Al, an adult with ADHD, shared a story concerning Mikie, a student with ADHD and a confirmed "computer whiz." He used this anecdote to describe teachers' reaction to Mikie.

> When he [Mikie] tried to answer a question one day, the teacher finally yelled at him. "Quit disrupting us" and she just yelled at him. . . ." Al commented further that "ADD people have the unique ability to stand on that last nerve . . . we never take no for an answer . . . we push and push and push and push. . . . [W]e negotiate everything . . . nothing is done the first time you've ever asked it and we just push . . . and so maybe he had just stepped on the last nerve until she had just flipped. . . . I don't know . . .

Interpersonal sensitivity is a key skill to success and survival in the classroom. Students with ADHD have "unique" abilities. It takes a mindful teacher to bring them forth to build upon their weakness.

Self-concept goes hand in hand with academic progress (Damico & Armstrong, 1996). "Lack of confidence is the intangible at the core of educational problems experienced by so many of our children" (Howard, 1990, p. 12). Unfortunately, many students with ADHD face academic difficulties and low self-esteem (Braswell, Bloomquist, & Pederson, 1991).

Teachers can build positive self-esteem in students with ADHD (Purvis, Jones, & Authement, 1992). In conjunction with academic content, teachers can instruct students in ways that provide them with a sense of themselves as learners. "It is within the curricular area that students acquire self-concepts" (Rosselli, 1998, p. 247). Problems with academic self-concept can be linked to formal education particularly at the formative elementary level. The influence that a teacher has in shaping the self-esteem of students with ADHD cannot be underestimated.

Brock, a sensitive, introspective client in our private practice, was a student who often got lost in his thoughts. He is a student with ADHD, and he told us about his trying school experience.

> In fifth grade, it [ADHD] got worse and the teacher didn't help either. She said I was lazy and I didn't want to learn. She was a b***h! She made me feel like a loser and like I couldn't do anything right. It took everything I had to get through fifth grade.

Such feelings have been addressed by Levine (n.d., paragraph 12), who advises that "From the moment a child gets out of bed in the morning until . . . safely tucked in at night, there's one central mission: the avoidance of humiliation at all costs. . . . [B]e so careful not to subject them to public humiliation" (paragraph 1). Lowered self-esteem, frustration with content delivery, and diminished learning on the part of students with ADHD all lead to school failure.

"Effective education programs for AD/HD were the most difficult treatment modality to be found through the public school system," state Cantwell and Campbell (as cited in Hawkins, Blanchard, & Brady, 1991, p. 53). Piers (1984) summarized psychoeducational interventions for students and concluded that "indirect attempts (where the program was not directly identified as having the goal of enhancing self-concept) appear to be somewhat more successful than direct attempts . . ."(p. 84) in improving student's self-concept. However, our study found that an elementary school curriculum that enacted MI strategies may actually improve the self-concept level of students with ADHD (Schirduan, 2000). The primary tool used to measure self-concept in the study was the Piers-Harris Children's Self-Concept Scale (PHCSCS). This questionnaire consists of 80 items and assesses self-concept in students between 8 and 18 years of age. Piers (1984) defines *self-concept* as "a relatively stable set of self attitudes reflecting both a description and evaluation of one's own behavior and attributes" (p. 1). Students with ADHD in our study at SUMIT sites completed the PHCSCS. Student responses were combined into cluster scales, which provided a detailed assessment of specific dimensions of self-concept, as well as an overall score reflecting a more generalized feeling of self-concept. The *students with ADHD in SUMIT sites generally reported average self-concept* overall, as well as in areas related to intelligence, school status, behavior, physical appearance, anxiety, and happiness.

Our study found discrepancies between teacher and student perceptions scores. Teachers rated their students level of self-concept lower than the student-completed PHCSCS self-report. Essentially, students rated their own self-concept higher than their teachers' student ratings.

A possible explanation for this is that students with ADHD often are unaware of their poor social skills, failing to understand social cues that classmates or teachers send. This inevitably leads to poor relationships, limiting the good interpersonal relationships that are one of the keys to academic survival for students, with or without ADHD.

Kevin, a small and somewhat sad second grader with ADHD, exemplified a student who displays poor school relationships. He reported low self-concept on the PHCSCS, but when interviewed, he appeared supremely self-confident. An interview with his mother revealed that she, too, overexaggerated his abilities and stated that he does well in everything. His teacher maintained that Kevin was an average student. The questions related to school life indicated low self-concept. His current and former MI teachers rated Kevin as having a low average self-concept and commented, "interpersonal intelligence—that was one of his problems—just getting along with his peers. I don't think Kevin knows how to be a friend" (Schirduan, 2000, p. 181).

The area that teachers and students with ADHD agree on is popularity. Statements on the PHCSCS included "evaluation of his or her popularity with classmates, being chosen for games, and ability to make friends. Low scores on this scale reflect shyness, lack of interpersonal skills, or personality traits that tend to isolate the student from others" (Piers, 1984, p. 39). Students with ADHD reported this dimension in their responses to the PHCSCS and during interviews as their *lowest* area of the six major areas within general self-concept.

It has been reported that "children with ADHD have some of their greatest difficulties in adjusting to the demands of school" (Pfiffner, 1995, p. 206). Self-esteem echoes academic success, or lack thereof (Damico & Armstrong, 1996, p. 25). Our research found a correlation between achievement level and self-concept in students with ADHD in SUMIT sites that was moderate yet significant. Moreover, the correlation between intellectual and school status and self-concept was high and significant. The use of an MI curriculum may not only facilitate learning, but potentially could hold the key to alleviating the poor self-concept of students with ADHD.

## A Comprehensive Look at the ADHD Student MI Profile

The predominant intelligences of students with ADHD should not be generalized. The use of reflection, observation, and discussion with prior teachers, teacher team members, and parents is strongly encouraged. However, there may be trends in the MI profiles of ADHD students. The two most notable are spatial and naturalist intelligence.

**ADHD Student and Spatial Intelligence.** Although there have been no prior studies investigating students with ADHD in light of MI theory, a connection between ADHD and strengths in spatial intelligence has been suggested by Armstrong in earlier research (1987), which was raised later in Schweitzer's research. Schweitzer, a psychologist and researcher, studied photographic images and brain scans of individuals with ADHD. She conducted a study on adults with and without ADHD as they performed math problems. When the brain scans were examined, she found that the two groups processed information differently. The men without the disorder "seemed to hear the auditory prompt and talk themselves through the problems using words" (Fine, 2001, p. 27). These study subjects used the middle regions of their brains that are linked with processing verbal strategies. The men with ADHD performed math problems by visualizing images in their mind. They used the occipital regions of their brain, areas associated with visual processing, to perform the math. The men with ADHD told Schweitzer after the test that "they pictured images in their heads—for example, a chalkboard with numbers written on it—to help in doing the calculations" (p. 27). Hence, individuals with ADHD exhibited a preference toward the spatial intelligence when conducting math problems.

Like the men with and without ADHD, Silverman (2002) noted that some individuals are visual-spatial-oriented while others are auditory-sequential learners, concluding that "the visual-spatial learning style describes about one-third of the students in a regular classroom" (Silverman, 2002, p. 332). Hence, teachers need to incorporate spatial learning activities for students, such as visualization or guided imagery. Visualization is an effective teaching strategy for students with ADHD, and represents a spatial instructional technique. Best defined as the process of representing learned material, visualization relies on images to assist learners in understanding content meaning.

Visualization takes practice. We suggest that teachers first try visualization among students with ADHD in conjunction with an easy, nonthreatening activity (e.g., teaching how to make a peanut butter and jelly sandwich or imagining the perfect vacation). Students are instructed to close their eyes and form a mental image. Once visualization is mastered, the student with ADHD is instructed on how to use it as a study technique. Students with ADHD can be asked to visualize notes placed on the chalkboard, or to play a movie in their mind to remember information in class when completing homework or as a recall mechanism on tests.

Owen, a former client, was experiencing difficulty in home and school. Having moved out of state from his mother's to his father's residence, Owen's family problems and lack of motivation in school was reflected in poor grades. Owen displayed a strong preference for academic work that tapped into his spatial intelligence. While both Owen and his father stated that history was an area of difficulty, Owen illustrated how he learned history through visualization. "I'll picture things, for example, if we're studying the French Revolution . . . Louis the 16th. I'll picture something. . . . I'll have a picture of him in my mind, even though I haven't seen him . . . [and I'll visualize] the castle and peasants [to help me learn]" (Schirduan & Case, 2004).

Owen drives home Silverman's (2002) point that "it is absolutely certain that some of your students—perhaps the ones you aren't reaching, are visual-spatial learners" (Silverman, 2008, Visual Spatial Resource, paragraph 3). She coined the term *visual-spatial learner* to describe the talents of students who think in images. Visual learners get the big picture. They remember what they see, yet they often forget what they hear (Silverman, 2002).

**ADHD Student and Naturalist Intelligence.** The student with naturalist intelligence understands the natural world, including plants, animals, and scientific studies. "This intelligence has to do with observing, understanding and organizing patterns in the natural environment. A naturalist is someone who shows expertise in the recognition and classification of plants and animals" (Campbell & Campbell, 1997).

Eve, a third grader with ADHD, displayed a strength in naturalist intelligence. Learning is difficult for Eve and, as a result, she would often disengage from the classroom. Shy and exhibiting difficulty in finding the right words to answer our questions, Eve talked insistently about nature, exclaiming, "We got to raise the butterflies . . . from a little larva and it grew into a pupa then an adult and then a butterfly. We watched it. I mean a chrysalis then a butterfly. It was a painted butterfly" (Schirduan, 2000).

As with all eight intelligences, an interest in the natural world appears at an early age. This was also the case for Karl, a student with ADHD and strength in the naturalist intelligence. His grandmother explained that Karl loved animals to a fault.

> One day, as a little boy, while Karl was walking in the woods (backyard), he heard some noise and followed it. He found three baby kittens about 2 weeks old. He took them home, found a great *big* box and placed nice soft blankets way at the bottom of the box. He bought a baby bottle and formula at the pet store and made a hole in the box to hold the bottle to feed them. He kept them safe and warm and fed. All by himself! After a few weeks, when the kittens could now eat "regular" cat food, he found homes for two of them and kept one. Karl has loved animals since he was a baby.

Years have gone by and he still has that cat. Karl still loves animals. If there are animals around, I always know where to find him. You would think his large physique would deter animals from approaching him, but it doesn't. When Karl picks up a kitten, it literally gets lost in his arms. He wants to be a veterinarian when he grows up.

Karl takes refuge in the woods behind his house. Students with ADHD need natural settings to be restorative. "Results indicated that children function better than usual after activities in green settings and that the 'greener' a child's play area, the less severe his or her attention deficit symptoms" (Taylor, Kuo, & Sullivan, 2001, p. 54). This may be related to the two types of attention that students use: voluntary and involuntary attention. Voluntary attention, which is also referred to as "directed attention," is when the student with ADHD must deliberately pay attention to a task (e.g., word problems: If a car is going 80 miles per hour, how far will it have gone in 60 minutes?). It requires sustained attention, which is not innately easy. After prolonged use, directed attention becomes fatigued (Kaplan, 1995). Hence, the student with ADHD gets tired and attention suffers.

According to James, involuntary attention, on the other hand, is "easy and does not require effort" (as cited in Taylor, Knor, & Sullivan, 2001, p. 57). Involuntary attention plays a role in recovery of fatigued directed attention. Nature draws on our involuntary attention. Kuo and Taylor (2004) found that "nature experienced in a wide variety of forms—including wilderness backpacking, gardening, viewing slides of nature, restoring prairie ecosystems, and simply having trees and grass outside to be linked to superior attention, effectiveness and effectiveness-related outcomes" (p. 1,580). One can imagine science class including such activities as viewing slides of nature, taking a walk to observe and record the change of seasons, or planting seeds in the spring. The far-reaching benefits of nature for students with ADHD is exciting. One teacher, Mamie, a self-declared "nature enthusiast" and someone with a science background, recounted:

> I am often asked to teach a science lesson when I visit schools. A favorite lesson of mine to teach is about the red wriggler, better known as worms. Oftentimes, there is no green space to be had in a city, and even in suburban areas, few people garden. Many students have never ever seen a worm, let alone touched one. Worms are ideal because these small living animals can be held in your hand, they can be touched, they are relatively hardy, so students can "handle" them a bit, they don't bite, and they are fun to observe. I remember this one boy, Tony, he had ADHD. He was a real problem. He could not focus, he was all over the place. I let him play in that dirt for hours. I am not exaggerating! He was focused, well-behaved, he was gentle with the worms, responsible, etc. You know, I have taught the worm lesson to many students throughout the years. I have observed that most kids really take to it, but the teachers will comment that students that usually give them trouble are very involved and I notice that their demeanor changes. The ADHD kids seem to love any science lesson I teach.

While Kuo and Taylor (2004) advocate for students with ADHD spending time after school and on weekends outdoors as a treatment to reduce ADHD symptoms, we ask, why wait until after school? Why not reap the benefits of the impact of physical activity in an outdoor space before school begins? Nancy, a physical educa-tion teacher, began an indoor walking program for students at her school. She states that students would arrive early every morning and walk for 30 minutes each day before school began. The benefits were quite evident in students with ADHD. Since LA (language arts) is taught the first 90 minutes of the day, and the walking pro-gram began mid year, the LA teachers immediately commented at the inception of the walking program, "it's a lot easier to teach them (students with ADHD). They are calm and ready to start their day." Taylor, Kuo, and Sullivan (2001) report that students function better than usual after spending time in green settings. In fact, the greener the area, the less severe the symptoms associated with ADHD.

An outdoor walking program is in keeping with what has been termed *atten-tion restoration theory*, which "suggests that natural environments assist in recov-ery from directed attention fatigue in part because they draw on involuntary attention rather than directed attention" (Kaplan, 1995). Students with ADHD such as Eve, Karl, and Tony may prefer activities related to the naturalist intelligence because these demand less directed attention. If such therapy is planned and imple-mented, students with ADHD are supplied a reprieve before entering into a sub-ject area that they may not prefer and that may require directed attention.

Unfortunately, science often gets brushed aside at the elementary school level. Since the advent of No Child Left Behind (NCLB), teachers tend to focus on the three Rs—reading, writing, and arithmetic, not science and nature. Parents also limit their child's outdoor exposure. Linda tells us, "we have a river in the back of our school. One day I took my students out on a nature walk. We began our walk and then came to a clearing in the woods and one of my students, David, a meek and mild child, quiet as a mouse, who rarely spoke in class, said, 'Oh, is this na-ture?'" Madison, an elementary school teacher, shared how an urban first grader, Maria, blurted out in amazement, "Am I dreaming?" when exposed to the woods on a nature walk taken behind the school. She explained that a lot of (urban) kids can't go outside in their neighborhoods due to potential dangers.

Science and spending time outdoors may be an afterthought for teachers and parents. One parent, Claire, explained that "although we live in a rural commu-nity surrounded by woods, a lot of folks refer to it as 'cow town.'"

> One day, my daughter, Annette, a friendly, relatively athletic middle schooler, invited her friend Robin over, who I am told watches way too much TV. Now mind you, Robin also lives in our community. My daughter suggests to Robin that they take a walk in the woods. They go off and upon their return, I hear Robin say, "I've never done that before." She was referring to taking a walk in the woods! She is 12 years old, lives in a rural community surrounded by woods, and has never taken a walk in the woods before, and I was astounded. You know we look to our parents on how to act and if children don't see their parents enjoying nature, respect-ing nature, connecting to the land, I fear what lies ahead.

While educators are focusing on NCLB, Gina McCarthy, Commissioner of the De-partment of Environmental Protection in Connecticut wants students to enjoy nature and connect with the land. She began the No Child Left Inside Initiative that attempts to get people outside and into state parks and forests (Thompson, 2007). Her sentiments that children don't spend time outdoors playing, climbing trees, or riding bikes are echoed by Richard Louv (2005). Louv remembers un-structured outdoor play as being "standard for me as a hyperactive child growing up in the rural Midwest. I fondly recall digging forts, climbing trees and catching frogs without concern for kidnappers or West Nile virus." He maintains that kids are disconnected from the natural world.

The adage "what becomes normal is what you live" is clear from what one parent shared about Margo, a passive and obedient child:

> During a visit to our farm, a cousin who lives in New York City saw I had a jar of mealworms on our piano. Curious about it, Margo, who was in first grade, investigated. As I placed a mealworm on her hand, Margo's face lit up. Her mom's facial expression was one of disbelief and disgust. To thwart off any negative feelings mom may potentially transfer to Margo, I had to look her right in the eye, and with a wide grin, shaking my head up and down, I said, "Aren't they fascinating?" I encouraged Margo to follow her curiosity about mealworms in hope that she'll form her own opinion about the natural world. You see, what becomes normal is what you live.

Some parents, such as Lydia, actively try to surround their children with nature.

> I've always appreciated nature and tried to instill a love of nature in my kids . . . but in our single-minded society raising two middle schoolers [in a community] where what you have and where you go loom large among peers, it's not easy. This was all too evident when returning from our annual trek to the mountains and our children adamantly refused to utter a word of this to friends and dreaded the age-old question posed by teach-ers, "What did *you* do on your summer vacation?" During this week, we live on an island without electricity, working toilets, or most of the creature comforts. Without reservation, I can honestly say that my children abso-lutely love going each year. Yes, they tell me "no one else does it for their vacation," but it mystifies me and saddens me that the thought of sharing their connection to nature created such a visceral reaction.

For the student with ADHD who exhibits a preference for the naturalist and spatial intelligence, environmental exposure can act as a curriculum tool by pro-viding visual stimuli and whole picture perspective. This is a necessary study skill that is needed by visual learners in general and by students with ADHD in par-ticular. "Nature inspires creativity in a child by demanding visualization . . ." (Louv, 2005, p. 7).

Exposure to the natural environment may also incite the bodily-kinesthetic intelligence, a distant third–rated intelligence that is found to be strong among students with ADHD. Bodily-kinesthetic intelligence involves the use of hands for manipulating objects, and is often associated with the tactile learner. Amy L. Ritter, a researcher in Dr. Kuo's lab, who holds a keen interest in ADHD and the preva-lence of a tactile learning style, states, "Natural environments are restorative for children with AD/HD, and this is possibly due to the makeup of those environ-ments (e.g., natural environments have a lot of manipulatives, opportunities for hands-on learning, and more immediate/tangible consequences, etc.)."

Students with naturalist intelligence have keen sensory skills (e.g., sight-visual, touch-kinesthetic). Moore (as cited in Louv, 2005) explains that "natural settings are essential for healthy child development because they stimulate all the senses and integrate informal play with formal learning. . . . [M]ultisensory experiences in nature help to build the cognitive constructs for sustained intellectual development" (p. 85). The student with ADHD and the naturalist and spatial intelligence profile may be drawn to these intelligences because nature, which stimulates the eighth intelligence, also stimulates the spatial (visual beauty in nature) and kinesthetic (there are many tactile outlets in nature) intelligences.

Classroom discourse is embedded in the educational philosophy and learning preference embraced by the teacher. This may be problematic for students whose predominant intelligence is incompatible with the way a teacher instructs or with academic and societal trends regarding intelligence preference. Delivery of instruction is not always compatible with the way in which students learn best and often models the predominant intelligence of the teacher rather than complementing the predominant intelligence of the student with ADHD. Consequently, educators consistently reteach skills using the same mode of instruction, though students may continue to experience limited mastery.

Gardner (as cited in Jordan, 1996) states, "we have not been cognizant of the ways in which basic inclinations of human learning turn out to be ill-matched to the agenda of the modern secular school" (p. 32). Sadly, the delivery and organization of instruction for students with ADHD—indeed, for many students—remains unchanged.

One must take into account not only a student's MI profile of intelligences and related fields, subjects, and domains, but also characteristics associated with ADHD. In all the LD evaluations reported by physicians, Duane (1988) reports that reading disability was the most common obstacle. He noted that students with reading difficulty had an aptitude in math, art, and the sciences. His findings are in keeping with our own in light of the pattern of predominant intelligences (natural and spatial) identified in students with ADHD. Hence, using the naturalist and spatial intelligences to help students with ADHD in reading and math is important, and will be the focus of Chapter 3.

In Chapter 3, we will discuss how teachers can capitalize on a student's MI profile. Using anecdotes, connections will be made from the intellectual strengths of a student with ADHD to possible curricular implications. For example, Eve's naturalistic ability to discern patterns of life and species of life (e.g., stages of butterflies, identifying species of butterflies, and ability to discern life patterns of a butterfly) might easily translate into discerning patterns in math. The focus of the next chapter will be to discuss ways to teach math, reading, and writing via the strengths and preferences of students with ADHD.

# CHAPTER 3

# MIndful Teachers:
# MIndful Curriculum and Instruction

MINDFUL TEACHERS AND A MIndful curriculum employed to instruct students who present a broad spectrum of predominant intelligences are not only vitally important for classroom success, but may be imperative for the achievement of students with ADHD. Students who have shown academic initiative and have experienced countless scholastic disappointments represent a school system failure. Working to achieve MIndfulness to ensure the success of these students empowers students and teachers alike.

## BEING MINDFUL OF THE STUDENT WITH ADHD

It is hard *not* to be MIndful of the students with ADHD in your class who exhibit classic characteristics of inattention, impulsivity, and/or hyperactivity and other traits that are often comingled with ADHD. Teachers describe these students as difficult to teach. They are the students who blurt out answers before the completed question, bounce out of their seat, and are inattentive when provided with classroom direction.

### Time-Tested Techniques

Often, teachers of students with ADHD seek council from other school professionals. The advice given may be conventional: Provide a quiet, distraction-free place to work; place the student near the front of the classroom, and preferably next to a positive role model. Although this advice may, perhaps serve as a beneficial first step, it may not suffice. Students with ADHD are considered the most "frequently encountered problem in the regular classroom. . . . These students not only experience academic and social difficulties but often disrupt classroom activities and others' learning" (Francis, as cited in Dyson, 2000, p. 3). Additional steps may need to be taken to manage inattention, impulsivity, and/or hyperactivity. MIndful teachers address basic characteristics of ADHD first, then instruct.

### ADHD Devices

"Carly drove me crazy at the beginning of the year," Madelena, a first-year, first-grade teacher, explained. Carly is "tall and thin" when compared to her classmates, a body type that suits her boundless energy.

She could not sit still. She was always off-task and distracting to her classmates. It was hard to get anything done! Since we have an ADHD [consulting] team in our town, I asked them for help. The occupational therapist recommended a "Move N Sit Wedge®" seat cushion. It is placed on the student's chair. It is filled with air and has nubs on the seat. It allows her the wiggle room she needs, but doesn't slide off the chair. The team also suggested I place thick rubber bands, Thera-Band®, around the legs of her chair to allow Carly to kick the bands as she swings her legs. This allows her to release some energy without making noise. Finally, I placed a piece of Velcro under her desk to satisfy her sensory need to touch. These devices have been a tremendous help to me. She is now able to sit with just enough wiggle room to stay focused on the task at hand.

Like Carly, Sam, a third grader, also had success with the "Move N Sit Wedge®" seat cushions, which are wedge-shaped pads, inflatable by mouth. He also was provided with a weighted vest. Sam was described by his teacher, Eden, as "a very active student." He had "difficulty maintaining focus for any period of time." His weaknesses in reading and math required the provision of additional assistance. Sam was strong in interpersonal intelligence. Even though it was considered a risk, the kindergarten teacher decided to have Sam assist in the kindergarten room. Twice a week, Sam assisted the younger students in math. It turned out to be a great success. The younger students looked up to the third grader who was their math helper. Sam took his weighted vest to the class and explained that the vest was his "thinking vest," and then began to wear it with more regularity.

Others echo these sentiments. Irene says, "I have seen success with Move N Sit Wedge® seat cushion, which affords a little bit of movement so that larger, extraneous movements (e.g., squirming, sitting on edge of chair, falling out of chair) are averted." However, some students with ADHD may need large gross-motor movement. One colleague, Donald, who has ADHD and counsels those with the disorder, suggests affixing PVC piping to elevate a desk so that the student with ADHD is standing during instruction. This allows the student with ADHD to move freely during class time. Another alternative to the PVC piping is to assign two desks in the back of the classroom and allow the student with ADHD to change seats when the urge to move arises.

More conventional alternatives for large gross-motor movement include running an errand for the teacher, getting a drink of water, or sharpening a pencil. It is not advised to punish students by removing opportunities for movement such as recess and physical education.

Students with ADHD often benefit from gross-motor movement. Candice, an elementary teacher, tells of her success with Issaih. "Last year, I had a student, Issaih, and Issaih was bright, interested, and quick to make connections. However, he found it very difficult to sit with us in whole group without some exaggerated rolling on the floor, flopping down in the middle of things. One thing that teaching in an MI school allowed me to try included [incorporating] frequent motor breaks. In our school, we use a research-based movement sequence called 'Brain Dance®.' Issaih was able to take a break with this on his own [when he felt an excessive urge to move]."

In an attempt to release energy, Chapman-Booth (1998) suggests allowing students with ADHD to pace in the back of the classroom. She also suggests having students keep small objects in their desks if it is not too distracting to others. Martha Jean, a veteran teacher, has found success when using small objects with her older ADHD students. She tells us she "noticed the most predominant theme among students with ADHD that she worked with to be distractibility," and she believed it "inhibited their ability to focus and if they are not focusing, they can't learn."

Distractibility seems to show up as physical manifestations. For example, Martha Jean reports that her learners often talked incessantly, rocked back on their chair, or tapped their pencils. She needed to find a way to allow them to release this need while not distracting others' learning. One thing that worked particularly well for her was pipe cleaners. Being able to pick one up, twist and bend it, form a shape, or attach it to other pipe cleaners proved to be a popular, nonobtrusive distraction. Another tool was a balance disk. Whenever there was a need for motion, the student could stand on this rocking, stationary disc. If she was teaching at the board, they could rock quietly without distracting others.

Betty, an occupational therapist (OT) we interviewed, found a stationary disk to be successful with active students who may need a little extra help learning a skill.

> I often use this activity at the beginning of an OT session when I see that the child is unfocused and in high gear. It is a simple activity that I have found has elicited focus, calming, and organization to a child. I have them sit and bounce as vigorously as they need while still remaining safe on a therapy ball. They are instructed to listen for the word *go*, then start bouncing. I then have them listen for the word *stop*, and after stopping bouncing, I ask them a simple question (e.g., name a color, number, food, animal, etc., or spell a spelling words, relay a math fact). She continued, stating that "this exercise enhances focus and attention by requiring the focus on an auditory cue (stop/go). It maintains that by having the student come up with an answer and also by stimulating the vestibular and proprioceptive systems through the bouncing.

Another teacher, Rose, shared that she has used a smaller therapy ball for an activity she dubbed "steamroller." She defined this activity as involving the "rolling of a therapy ball up and down a child's back, leg, and sometimes head with deep pressure to elicit calming and, hopefully, increased focus."

The sense of touch elicited a calming effect for Chuck, a student with ADHD in the third grade. His teacher, Dina, reported that his "MI profile is the musical and bodily kinesthetic intelligences. He is always on the *move*."

> He is like a top—you could feel his heart beating out of his chest. He is quite a challenge, but a lot of time what worked well was if I was in close proximity to him. He responded well when I had contact with him: I would rub his back, have my arm around him, and this seemed to calm him down a bit.

Research confirms that teacher proximity helps maintain student attention (Gardill & DuPaul, 1996, p. 90). Gardill and DuPaul (1996) suggest standing next to students with ADHD when providing directions.

Calm can come by counting. A cognitive exercise may involve counting to reach perspective. One respondent, Seth, revealed:

When I am rushed and fidgety, instead of feverishly rushing to get something done when I'm on a time limit, I've found if I count how many seconds a task takes me while I'm doing it, it slows me down when I realize, through the counting, that my perception that the task is taking too long is not true, that I really am accomplishing it rather quickly.

## Tackling Transitions

The counting of a clock helped Laline with her inattention. An immigrant from Cuba, Laline is a fourth grader with ADHD who has the bodily-kinesthetic and visual spatial profile. Given Laline's behavioral issues, to keep her on task, her teacher "displays a huge digital clock on the smart board."

I will say, you have 2 minutes to put away your folder and join me on the rug. This is a digital clock and can count up. Laline watches the clock like a hawk and *always* completes the task before time runs out. Because Laline is a visual learner, this technique works quite well.

Robert, like Laline, also battles inattention during transition time. To help him stay focused, his teacher utilizes his strengths, evidenced from his MI profile. Robert "loves to dance. So, I use music in class to help him 'move and groove' to the next activity."

I play "Cockatoos, Count by Twos," by Hap Palmer. As he moves to the music, I noticed that it helps him to stay focused. So, for example, the class needs to clean up from a project and then line up by the door by the time the song is over. I play the song and he knows the song so well and can predict how much time he has before the music stops and he is to be in line. It's quite remarkable. He will know at certain intervals in the song how much time he has to accomplish certain tasks before the next part of the song and eventually when the song ends and he is expected to be in line.

Teachers often use music to help ADHD students transition from one activity to another. One teacher, MaryAnn, reported, "I have adapted the lyrics to this one song 'Yes I'm ready,' written and sung by Barbara Mason, that seems to really work. The lyrics I adapted are":

"Are you ready?" (I sing it and they all make sure they are attentive and in line).
    They answer, "Yes, I'm ready" "To go outside (me)," "To go outside (kids)," "To go outside, right now (all)."
    I use music a lot when they are off-task.

Students with ADHD have difficulty not only with transitions, but also with changes in school routines and daily schedules. Behavioral change may occur at the following times: when the student enters or exits the classroom, during lunch-room, or while on the playground.

Changes from classroom teacher to a substitute or between classrooms may also result in off-task behavior. Heightened awareness and subsequent prompts by the teacher to stay on-task can assist the student with ADHD with transitions and changes in routine. For example, consider the following prompts: verbal prompt—"eyes on me," visual prompt—use the sign for "pay attention" in sign language, music prompt—sing their name, interpersonal prompt—ask the student to find a person who is facing forward, bodily-kinesthetic prompt—stand near the student.

## Teacher Tips

Advance notice to students with ADHD as to when a change in routine will occur is helpful in combating off-task behavior. A copy of the upcoming class schedule may serve this objective. For the student with ADHD who has strengths in the spatial or naturalist intelligence, Beth Robelia's (1997) description is relevant:

> It can be scary for a person with ADHD to be removed from their regular routine. It's hard for them to organize things in their head (if their brain was a TV screen it would look like they were channel surfing every 6–30 seconds), so they need to have exter-nal structure. (p. 52)

Beth suggests pattern planning to assist with maintaining routine and struc-ture, whereby each day takes on a pattern. For example, on Mondays at 8:45 when you arrive, you hang up your coat and backpack, sit down and begin board work. At 9:00, we have morning meeting, at 9:15 is language arts, at 10:00 is physical education.

Zentall and Lieb (as cited in Gardill & DuPaul, 1996) "observed decreased levels of activity in both hyperactive and normal children in a structured condition" (p. 90). Often, best practices benefit all students, including those with or without ADHD.

Amanda, an MI teacher, takes a visual approach to maintaining structure via classroom rules. She says, "no students are officially diagnosed with ADHD in my pre-K classroom. However, the characteristics associated with ADHD are oftentimes seen at a young age."

> These students often benefit when I use lots of visual prompts in the classroom. I use pictures (visual prompts) of students doing things expected in the classroom. If some children are off-task at morning meeting, I'll ask, "What does a good morning meeting look like?" Show me with your bodies. When a child is not following the group rules that we made to-gether as a class, I might bring her to the "Ways We Take Care of Our-selves, Each Other, and Our Classroom" poster that the class creates in the beginning of the year. Here, the child will see pictures of kids in the class caring for each other (hugging, helping a friend with putting on a shoe), cleaning our room at clean-up time, and caring for themselves (raising hand at group time to speak). Seeing their pictures, and seeing that they helped make (and sign) this poster, helps bring the child back into the group norms that she agreed to be a part of. These are responsive class-room techniques that help create a healthy, positive class environment.

MIndful teachers address inattention, hyperactivity, and impulsivity in practical ways and *move* outside their comfort zones. If conventional efforts fail, they attempt something different. However, while a weighted vest may work for one student and a Move N Sit Wedge® seat cushion allows wiggle room, students with ADHD may be too self-conscious using them, with risks to self-esteem outweighing the benefits. Students will respond differently to these techniques and MIndful teachers vary their practices to find the perfect fit.

Undeniably, even for MIndful teachers, some students with ADHD are probably some of the toughest students to teach. Many "have trouble picking up subtle social cues, and suffer socially since they cannot seem to stop talking or hold back derogatory statements. They are infamous for saying exactly what they think" (Robelia, 1997, p. 51). Inattention, impulsivity, and hyperactivity, as well as other traits, must be addressed in that "the disruptive behavior displayed by students with ADHD frequently interrupts the concentration of their peers . . ." (Gardill & DuPaul, 1996, p. 89).

Knowing the strengths of students with ADHD can make all the difference. Diego, a first grader with ADHD, was often in a time out or being asked to leave the classroom due to his disruption. Diego, having immigrated with his parents from Mexico, spoke little English. His classroom teacher, Wanda, shared that he was unable to write his name or identify colors. He recognized only four letters of the alphabet. Diego's art teacher, Gwen, conveyed that, surprisingly, Diego could tell her the colors of the pet lizard housed in the art room and what it eats.

> I heard him tell another student that the pet is nocturnal! He remembered this fact from last year! He is just so mesmerized by the pet. He can be disruptive and a real handful. Nothing seems to motivate him. Nothing except our classroom pet, that is. He gravitates toward animals. I am able to get Diego to focus on the task at hand if I reward him with, say, a digital picture of him with the pet. Before this, Diego would not complete the art task and he did nothing. Now that I have been able to tap into his strength in the naturalist intelligence, I can get him to accomplish art tasks, incorporating the pet as a tool when necessary . . . whether it is drawing a pet or using his fine-motor skills to cut a picture of it out [writing about the pet, etc.].

As an extension and springboard to teaching hard-to-reach concepts with which Diego is struggling, his teacher, Wanda, can use the pet to create a book to learn letters, letter sounds, sight vocabulary, and so on. The possibilities are innumerable.

Diego's talents could have been neglected and never realized if not for the insights of Gwen, his art teacher. His experience, sadly, may be the exception. Caron Mosey (2002), an adult with ADD, describes her experience:

> As I progressed through school my mother recognized a teaching style used by most of my teachers. Mom's theory is that there are two kinds of children: children who have their learning nicely wound up in a circle, and children who have their learning in a square. Most kids are circles, and as teachers instruct, they teach as if all children are circles. They go round and

round in their teaching, teaching to the needs of the circles. But some kids have their smarts tucked into the corners, and as teachers are going round and round, they miss out on those children.

Mosey (2002) goes on to say that "kids with their smarts tucked in the corners are the kids like me, the AD/HD kids" (paragraph 13). For students such as Diego, the failure to discover his corners can easily result in academic failure.

Treatment programs for students with ADHD may entail one of four approaches: medication management alone, behavioral treatment alone, a combination of both, or routine medical visits. Multimodal treatment studies often echo the following review: "long-term combination treatments . . . in some areas—anxiety, academic performance, oppositionality, parent–child relations, and social skills—the combined treatment was usually superior" (NIMH, 2007).

The treatment choice to medicate a student for symptoms of ADHD does not come easily. Parents agonize over this choice. Although medication is often found to improve characteristics associated with ADHD, such as attention impulsivity, as well as personal interactions, academic recovery has not been met with similar success state Rapport, Denney, DuPaul, and Gardner (as cited in Miranda, Presentacion, & Soriano, 2002). Furthermore, "Simply medicating children without teaching them the skills they need to improve their behavior and performance, is not likely to improve the children's long-term prognosis" (Pelham & Gagney, as cited in Miranda, Presentation, & Soiano, 2002, p. 226).

In contrast, the decision to incorporate nonmedical strategies for students with ADHD comes more easily to parents. While parents and teachers may not always agree on the approach, the sheer number of choices among strategies provides an avenue to consensus. Choosing a comfortable strategy in conjunction with parents, teachers, and support staff is key. Consistency in the application of the strategy is also important. Teachers should first identify the ADHD student's problem area and then, via trial and error, choose a technique that best suits their students' needs, keeping in mind that no two students with ADHD are alike.

Teachers are often told to provide a quiet, distraction-free area for quiet study for the student with ADHD. And that's what Rosalyn, an elementary teacher, found quite by accident with one of her students with ADHD.

> In the lower grades, we have writer's workshop and it can get kind of noisy in my room. One day during writer's workshop, I was in my office, which is enclosed by glass but separate yet adjacent to the classroom, and a student with ADHD tendencies came to me to ask me something and immediately said, "Wow, it's so nice in here." There was the humming of the vent and this boy always has difficulty writing, so it occurred to me that perhaps he would do better with his writing in this environment. So I took a paper out, placed it on a table in my office and told him to write and complete the assignment. He wrote so much better, and afterward, the boy said, "Miss Holden, I work a lot better this way." I decided that I needed to create the same environment for him in the classroom.

Not all students with ADHD need, want, or should have a quiet area, which was the case with Isabella.

I never struggled much in elementary school. I memorized everything and that seemed to work. Once I attended middle school, I found the school-work to be challenging and I couldn't focus as much. My dad, who also has ADD, would create this really quiet study area at home for me to do my homework. But it didn't help. You see, he was the one who needed the quiet environment to study. I, on the other hand, need lots of noise to concentrate. I know that may sound like a contradiction, but in my mind there are six things going on at once to distract me from doing my home-work. So I found that if music is playing, the TV is on, and family members are talking around me, I am able to quiet my mind enough to focus on homework. It is as though what others would call a "distraction" (e.g., music or TV) would occupy some of the six things going on in my mind to allow me to concentrate and complete my homework.

No two individuals, even within the same family, are alike. "Recognize that ADD/LD is neurological and beyond the control of the student" (Chapman-Booth, 1998). Address the core symptoms of inattention, impulsivity, and hyperactivity before seeking a multimodal approach. "Lack of consistent improvement beyond the core symptoms leads to the need for treatment strategies that utilize combined approaches" (NIH, 2000, p. 189). Finally, as Chapman-Booth (1998) admonished, "stop attributing students' poor performance to laziness, poor motivation, or other internal traits."

## MINDFUL TEACHERS: MINDFUL PLANNING FOR THE ADHD STUDENT

This section begins with a teaching anecdote. The intent is for the reader to reflect on his or her teaching philosophy. An inventory is provided to aid in revealing the extent to which MI is or is not a part of your curriculum. The next section offers lesson plans that are designed with the ADHD student in mind. Examples of how MI can be incorporated into lesson planning are provided. This section con-cludes with ways to introduce MI theory to your students is presented.

### MIndful Teachers: Philosophy of Teaching MI

Teachers have the ability to foster or harm a child's self-esteem with a simple as-signment. The following anecdote reveals the devastation one former teacher, Lisa, recalled from her elementary school years.

The assignment was to draw flowers. We were instructed on *how* flowers were to be drawn. Red flowers, green stems, a leaf to each side, just so, all in a row. That's not the way I saw flowers, but I did as I was directed. We were given the flower drawing assignment again. [This time] I drew what I saw when I imagined flowers. I ended up sitting on a tall chair with a dunce cap, a witch-style hat with the word *dunce* written on it, on my head. Well, that about did it for me. I spent the rest of the year on that chair, arms folded defiantly across my chest. I missed recess too, but no one was going to tell me . . .

It's almost unfathomable to imagine the humiliation that this 4-year-old kindergartener experienced, and equally difficult to accept that some teachers continue to practice this arcane ritual. However, it happened to Lisa, an education student. Future teachers were asked to describe someone who inspired them to become teachers. Lisa shared, "as a 4-year-old, I could tell time and read. [However,] I flunked kindergarten. My parents didn't really know why . . . [and] I was too young to explain. By the end of second grade, I was reading ninth-grade books and doing algebra. . . . I remember it and my second-grade teacher as if it was yesterday." Her story takes a foreshadowing turn:

> First grade was uneventful, then second grade. *What a teacher!* She had the energy and enthusiasm of a group of children on their way to recess. She liked us! Every day we [students] got to talk to her, just her and me. School was great. Looking back, it was my second-grade teacher that inspired me to teach, [and] to make a positive difference in a child's life. To help them find their potential and unleash it. I count myself blessed to be able to do this.

To envision being that second-grade teacher, a teacher who so deeply touched the life of a 7-year-old and changed her forever, requires that a teaching philosophy be developed that will serve as a compass for guiding decision making. "When a person adopts a particular theory, s/he takes on a set of beliefs concerning what questions about learning are valuable, what methods for studying these questions are legitimate, and what the nature of learning is" states Miller (as cited in Hamilton & Ghatala, 1994, p. 6).

A teacher's philosophy surfaces in classroom discourse, curriculum, and instruction. Psychologists and educators repeatedly champion the belief that classroom teachers should focus on students' strengths rather than their weaknesses (Armstrong, 1994; Gardner, 1993a). MI theory helps us do that. A teacher who embraces MI theory may incorporate curriculum and instruction that is sensitive to students' strengths, their predominant intelligences. Teachers who follow MI theory as part of their philosophy empower students by recognizing their students' unique intelligence profile and thereby assist underachievers by teaching hard-to-reach concepts through their strengths.

Researchers found normal and superior IQs among students with ADHD in lieu of underachievement in 91% of the sample, according to Weiss, Minde, Werry, Douglas, and Nemeth (as cited in Hawkins, Blanchard, & Brady, 1991, p. 53). Yet, students with ADHD fall behind their peers academically. Even the use of labels such as ADHD isolate and fragment children, as well as affect a child's "self-concept and overall achievement" (Smerechansky-Metzger, 1995, p. 12). "Handicapping conditions [such as ADHD] are socially constructed . . . 'Who am I?' shapes 'Who I can become" (Reid & Barton, as cited in Poplin & Cousin, 1996, p. 11). LD students feel "isolated, victimized, devalued, and oppressed" (p. ix). This was true of Deron, a sensitive, self-conscious middle schooler and former client with ADHD, who shared that, beginning in second grade, his teachers described him as "Confused, slacking off, forgetful, lazy, in his own world, unorganized, and impulsive."

Do problems among students with ADHD reflect misalignment of their profile of intelligences with the language-logic profile emphasized in school? Do problems reflect poor teaching or poor choices when choosing a philosophy of teaching?

"As educators, our responsibility lies not in explaining differences in young children or labeling and diagnosing differences, but in responding to those unique differences in the classroom by supporting students and utilizing their strengths" (DuCharme, 1995, p. 582).

Schools continue to fragment students' skills, penalizing students who are not proficient verbal and math learners. Multiple intelligences perspective represents "a paradigm shift because it changes the way we look at students and their potentials. As a result, we view our roles and responsibilities quite differently" (Hoerr, 1996b, p. 8).

## Mindful Curriculum

Gardner (as cited in Checkley, 1997) stresses the nexus of multiple intelligences and a curriculum focused on understanding. His theory originated from those elements that are valued in the world. "So, when a school values multiple intelligences theory the relationship to what's valued in the real world is patent. If you cannot easily relate this activity to something that's valued in the world, the school has probably lost the core idea of multiple intelligences, which is that these intelligences evolved to help people do things that matter in the real world" (p. 11). Blind obedience to the traditional ways of teaching is the result of erroneous historical argument or of having "what happens in schools happens because that is the way it was done in earlier generations, not because we have convincing rationale for maintaining it today" (Gardner, 1993b, p. 199).

The body of courses that are taught in traditional schools are listed in a report from Perie, Baker, and Bobbitt (1997), which states that the time spent teaching the four core subjects—language arts, math, science, and social studies—from the years 1987–1988 to 1993–1994 has remained relatively unchanged. Public school teachers in grades one through four continue to spend 68% of their time teaching these four subjects.

These four core subjects, along with delivery of instruction, is well entrenched in tradition. Willinsky (as cited in McCormick, 1994) states that "it has been estimated that 'basal' reading 'programmes'—books, or 'readers' designed to teach children reading in the United States . . . are used in 90 percent of all reading classrooms for 90 percent of their instructional time (p. 163). An atmosphere of past practice pervades and few "question the tenets of their intellectual predecessors" (Garrett, 1994, p. 9).

A fundamental core problem with the traditional enacted curriculum in public schools may be that curriculum often cloaks itself in only two of the eight intelligences—linguistic and logical-mathematical intelligences. "As long as schools operate on an essentially linguistic modality that gives place of privilege to a kind of literal, logical, or mathematical form of intelligence, schools limit what youngsters can learn" (Eisner, as cited in Hearne & Stone, 1995, p. 441).

MI curriculum can make a difference for underachievers. Campbell (1992), a third-grade teacher in Washington, developed a classroom program based on the MI theory. He found that in addition to improvement in academics, three areas of concern with students with ADHD—behavior, self-confidence, and motivation—also improved, and that many students state "they enjoyed school for the first time" (p. 201).

While students possess all eight intelligences to varying degrees, schools don't always value those students who are adept in spatial, musical, interpersonal, intrapersonal, naturalist, and bodily-kinesthetic intelligences. Preoccupation with linguistic and logical-mathematical ability as a society is manifested by the "widespread use of, and over reliance on, IQ Scores and measures in determining school placement. [This has] diverted our attention from other kinds of intelligence that reside within every child" (Hearne & Stone, 1995, p. 349).

"When significant discrepancies exist between their primary intelligence and those valued in American schools children may become identified as learning disabled" (Kugelmass, 1996, p. 257). O'Brien (as cited in Cooney, 1995) argues that "instead of expecting the child to be ready for school, the schools should be ready to meet the needs of individual children" (p. 164).

## MIndful Planning

The inventory in Figure 3.1 is intended to aid the teacher in identifying missing intelligences in your curriculum.

## MIndful Instruction

Identification of the predominant intelligences of students with ADHD allows teachers to select appropriate pedagogical practices. Knowledge of the profile of intelligences is helpful for teaching hard-to-reach skills by bridging their strengths to their weaknesses. In short, teachers could implement instructional interventions appropriate to the individual student with ADHD. However, when many teachers were students, they were never "exposed to alternative teaching methods . . . no wonder we are more comfortable using the linguistic and logical strategies that were practiced on us" (Emig, 1997, p. 47).

MIndful instruction includes implementing the following suggestions by Pfiffner and Barkley (as cited in Gardill & DuPaul, 1996): "students with ADHD appear to respond better to frequent feedback with immediate and highly salient consequences, one-to-one instruction situations, increased supervision, the use of novelty, and the presentation of numerous opportunities for active responding. In contrast, infrequent and delayed feedback with minimally salient consequences, as well as group instruction, less supervision, and familiar repetitive tasks tend to intensify ADHD symptoms" (p. 90).

Fast-paced instructional approaches appeal to the student with ADHD. Henry, an adult with ADHD who coaches ADHD students, recollected that when teaching students with ADHD, "talking faster" helped students learn more, pay attention, and retain more information. He also recommended instructional tasks be "short and fast."

Russell, a middle school math teacher, uses fast pacing and believes "that a timer in math for students with ADHD would be beneficial because it limits the amount of time (e.g., 3 to 5 minutes) to complete a task (e.g., math facts). Once the time is up, the teacher can check that all students understand. It's not important whether the student completed two or ten problems. What is important is that it allows the teacher to check for understanding for all students. It allows the student with ADHD a manageable amount of time to direct his attention to the task at hand." To maintain improvements for your student with ADHD, Chapman-Booth (1998) suggests the provision of immediate feedback to the student with ADHD, no matter how small the accomplishment.

**Figure 3.1.** A Personal Teaching MI Inventory

Describe the general rate of frequency during a typical week over the course of a marking period that your students engage in the following activities:

| Linguistic: | 0 | 1–2 | 3–4 | Daily |
|---|---|---|---|---|
| reading | — | — | — | — |
| writing | — | — | — | — |
| public/persuasive speaking | — | — | — | — |
| other: | — | — | — | — |

| Spatial: | 0 | 1–2 | 3–4 | Daily |
|---|---|---|---|---|
| imagining | — | — | — | — |
| drawing/design | — | — | — | — |
| constructions/crafts | — | — | — | — |
| other: | — | — | — | — |

| Logical-Mathematical: | 0 | 1–2 | 3–4 | Daily |
|---|---|---|---|---|
| critical thinking | — | — | — | — |
| cause and effect analysis | — | — | — | — |
| calculating | — | — | — | — |
| estimating | — | — | — | — |
| problem solving | — | — | — | — |
| other: | — | — | — | — |

| Interpersonal: | 0 | 1–2 | 3–4 | Daily |
|---|---|---|---|---|
| cooperative learning | — | — | — | — |
| understanding human behavior | — | — | — | — |
| interpersonal problem solving | — | — | — | — |
| social analysis | — | — | — | — |
| role-playing | — | — | — | — |
| other: | — | — | — | — |

**Figure 3.1.** (continued)

| Intrapersonal: | 0 | 1–2 | 3–4 | Daily |
|---|---|---|---|---|
| personal reflection | — | — | — | — |
| self-assessment | — | — | — | — |
| journaling | — | — | — | — |
| activity log | — | — | — | — |
| meta-cognition | — | — | — | — |
| feeling responses | — | — | — | — |
| goal setting, strategic planning, monitoring, self-correction, post-reflection | — | — | — | — |
| other: | — | — | — | — |

| Musical: | 0 | 1–2 | 3–4 | Daily |
|---|---|---|---|---|
| singing | — | — | — | — |
| instrumental work | — | — | — | — |
| musical appreciation | — | — | — | — |
| other: | — | — | — | — |

| Bodily-Kinesthetic: | 0 | 1–2 | 3–4 | Daily |
|---|---|---|---|---|
| movement activities | — | — | — | — |
| hands-on/projects | — | — | — | — |
| role-play/skits | — | — | — | — |
| gestural cognition | — | — | — | — |
| dance | — | — | — | — |
| other: | — | — | — | — |

| Naturalist: | 0 | 1–2 | 3–4 | Daily |
|---|---|---|---|---|
| animal care/behavior | — | — | — | — |
| plants and agriculture | — | — | — | — |
| ecological awareness | — | — | — | — |
| scientific thinking (observation, data collection, pattern awareness) | — | — | — | — |
| other: | — | — | — | — |

**Learning Styles.** For our purposes, learning style, simply defined, is the student's preferred method of learning. Three learning styles that we address are auditory (listening), visual (seeing), and kinesthetic/tactile (doing/touching). Once the learning style of the student with ADHD is identified, you'll know his or her preferences, and classroom methods can be adapted.

First, the visual learner may prefer to sit in the front of class to better view materials and the teacher. This student may understand new information via the teacher's facial expressions during instruction. The student often maintains eye contact.

Second, the auditory learner prefers verbal instruction. This student may participate by engaging in classroom discussions, or may sit quietly and "absorb" it. This also may be the learner who may not maintain eye contact with you, but hears everything.

Third, the tactile or kinesthetic learner prefers a classroom teacher who employs a hands-on learning approach. Kinesthetic activities might have a student using broad arm sweeps (large gross-motor movement) and writing a name in the air. Writing a name with a finger on the back of another student is an example of a tactile activity. The evaluations of students with ADHD seen at the National Reading Diagnostics Institute in Naperville, Illinois, reveal that students with ADHD "need to engage in gross motor (large-muscle) activity to learn best" (Linksman, 2007, paragraph 1). Pauline, an administrator at an MI school, noted that upon her observations of students with ADHD in different grades, she noticed that "direct engagement, movement, manipulatives, and technology" represented key instructional methods. With regard to manipulatives, Sylvester, an art teacher, maintained that he didn't "have the same problems with ADHD kids in my class as other teachers because art is immediate contact with mediums. And students with ADHD often like to manipulate objects."

Martha Jean, who discovered that her readers liked to manipulate objects in reading, underscored the manipulation of objects as an instructional tool. What she found for reading practice is that "learners with ADHD have more interest in doing hands-on activities."

> In my class, modifications of the LIPS® (Lindamood Phonemic Sequencing) have worked especially well. These activities to practice their phonemic awareness were visual and kinesthetic. Students practiced matching sounds to colored blocks. They moved or changed the blocks according to whether the new sound they heard replaced or moved the previous sounds. This is an essential component, which is connected to phonics. I was glad to see that students with ADHD were willing to do this practice, with enjoyment and focus.

Wilson (as cited in Louv, 2005, p. 72) suggests that students with the naturalist intelligence have keen sensory skills (e.g., sight-visual, touch-kinesthetic, hearing) and, thus, may benefit from a combination of sensory skills during lessons. Given that the top intelligence among students with ADHD in our study was the naturalist intelligence, sensory activities with students with ADHD are crucial.

Elaine, a special education teacher, hypothesized that the removal of a sense may also benefit students with ADHD. "In science, we conducted an experiment to make students more aware of disabilities."

We decided to isolate one sense at a time and document the results. For example, to isolate the sense of sight, one student was blindfolded while his partner scripted what s/he heard, felt, smelled while sitting in the woods. They just sat and listened and wrote. It was a real calming activity for all students. It made me think of the student with ADHD. My guess is that by decreasing one sense (seeing) would result in increasing (e.g., listening) the concentration and focus of the student with ADHD. I would think the ADHD student would be concentrating so hard on the task at hand and what the teacher was asking. I would think they would have to compensate (e.g., seeing) and use more of the other sense (hearing). I also believe that, since students were accountable to their partner, there was a level of responsibility and expectation.

Students with ADHD may be auditory, visual, or kinesthetic, or may have a combination of these three learning styles. Learning style is not equivalent to intelligence. Gardner states:

> Learning styles [and working styles] are claims about ways in which individuals purportedly approach everything they do. If you are planful [working style], you are supposed to be planful about everything. If you are logical-sequential [learning style], you are supposed to be logical-sequential about everything. . . . Multiple intelligences claims that we respond, individually, in different ways to different kinds of content, such as language or music or other people. (Cited in Checkley, 1997, p. 11)

For a specific instructional lesson, identify the predominant learning mode of your students. Once this mode is recognized, it's possible to employ and maximize it to enhance student learning. For general instructional lessons, it has been ascertained that some percent of the school-age population remembers what is heard; more recall well visually the things that are seen or read; and most benefit from touching, hearing, seeing—a multisensory approach to learning. For example, many must write or use their fingers in some manipulative way to help them remember basic facts; other people cannot internalize information or skills unless they use them in real life.

**Working Style.** Krechevsky (1994) developed a list of working styles to describe students' approach to tasks, how they interface with materials. Students may be easily engaged, reluctant to engage, confident, tentative, playful, serious, focused, distractible, persistent, frustrated by activity, impulsive, reflective, apt to work slowly, apt to work quickly, conversational, and quiet (Krechevsky, 1994, pp. 207–209). To obtain a listing of working styles along with definitions and determine a student's approach to a task, refer to the work of Project Spectrum (Krechevsky, 1987).

Working styles are often activity dependent. This means that if a student with ADHD is strong in the naturalist and spatial intelligences, then you may see a working style of "focused" or "easily engaged" during a construction activity, while the working style may be "distractible" "impulsive" and "reluctant to engage" when reading.

Students with ADHD can come to learn their working style and develop an understanding of tools that can help them develop task commitment. Jemal, a student with ADHD, makes lists—lots of lists. His approach to a task would be considered "planful." He states, "lists have helped in terms of completing tasks."

> I take a task and break it down into more manageable parts. I then place a box next to each part. I find it rewarding to check off each box as I go along. This helps me to complete the task.

Chapman-Booth's (1998) work speaks to Jemal's planfulness. She suggests that instructions be broken into short, sequential steps, thus dividing classwork into "mini-assignments" for the student with ADHD. Hence, the application of a writing assignment for a student with ADHD in the classroom might follow from the example of Linda, an elementary teacher with a wide grin and inviting personality.

Linda believes that "a lot of students with ADHD have great ideas but find it difficult to get it down on paper. That held true for Terry, a third grader with ADHD in my class."

> I use a graphic organizer in writing. It has seven story parts, seven story boxes for each part (setting, character, problem, etc., a story planner, a place to draw pictures, etc.). Terry was having a tough time completing the graphic organizer. What worked best for her was to have her verbally tell me what was happening in the story. For example, she might say, "I was very excited." I would then make four lines and she would write her words on the lines. She would need constant assistance, but I found that scaffolding is key to help her become an independent writer. Seven story parts: setting, problem, reaction, goal, attempts, outcome, ending.

Finding the "goodness of fit" in how students with ADHD learn is a goal of every MIndful teacher. Teachers in our study found a "goodness of fit" between curriculum and instruction, since the students with ADHD in MI schools do better academically and socially. Sternberg (1996) also found that "students performed significantly and substantially better when the form of instruction was at least partially compatible with the students' patterns of abilities." (p. 22). Tanksley (1994) found that behavior, attendance, and academic achievement improved when different learning and teaching strategies were designed around a student's interests and learning style.

## LESSON PLANNING FOR ADHD STUDENTS

Jones (as cited in Bete, 1997) states,

> Metaphorically the room represents the topic to be taught; the doors represent the different entry points students may use to enter the room or topic. Multiple entrances are provided to accommodate the individual differences among students. All entry points share equal validity and use different intelligences as the initial means of learning a topic. (p. 17).

The above framework follows a five-step procedure. First, students enter the room via their predominant intelligence. "Each entry point consists of activities, lessons or learning centers that highlight a logical-quantitative, narrational, foundational, aesthetic or experiential way of perceiving and processing information" (Jones, as cited in Bete, 1997, p. 13). Second, students study the topic through the other four entry points. Third, students work cooperatively with classmates (e.g., to gain new insights). Fourth, students synthesize the information they have gathered (e.g., to reflect). And fifth, in what can be used as an assessment tool, students teach learned knowledge to others (e.g., to encourage further exploration) and apply to new topics.

Campbell and Campbell (1997) discuss five ways that teachers can apply MI to the classroom: lesson designs, interdisciplinary curriculums, student projects, assessments, and apprenticeships. MI theory "gives teachers a complex mental model from which to construct curriculum" (Campbell & Campbell, 1997, p. 19). MI theory permits room for maneuver, but also adheres to a shared philosophy that acknowledges that students have unique cognitive profiles.

With lesson design, teachers can use MI as an entry point. In math, for example, addition can be taught traditionally through paper-and-pencil exercises that employ logical-mathematical intelligence, or it can be taught through another intelligence, such as the bodily-kinesthetic intelligence where the students role-play the addends and sum. Another "door" could be spatial intelligence. Students extend both hands in front at eye level. Then they bend fingers to represent the nine times tables. For example, "9 × 2 = 18" is represented by bending only the ring ("2") finger of the left hand, palms outward, which leaves "1" finger to left and "8" to the right.

The above examples are specific, but more general means can aid ADHD students' learning through an MI curriculum. A classroom's set-up may allow students to choose from eight learning centers or "stations" that represent the different intelligences. Choice is another means for delivering instruction that is MIndful of different intelligences. Students can choose or request how they would like to learn a lesson. Parental involvement may also aid teachers in constructing MIndful curriculum and homework can become a new avenue for incorporating the intelligences.

Second, with interdisciplinary curricula, teachers can coordinate lessons so that each discipline is represented. When teaching at the elementary level, a group of teachers might adopt an interdisciplinary approach to a second-grade unit on Russia. In physical education, Russian games and dancing were seen, satisfying the ADHD students' need for gross-motor and bodily-kinesthetic movement. In art, students were immersed in a Russian artistic experience, using small ceramic pieces as manipulatives. This served the ADHD students' need for tactile expression. Science lessons were concerned with examining the species evident on the Russian landscape. A broad subject can easily be broken into specific skills intended to address all of the ADHD students' predominant intelligences.

Broad student projects allow learners to draw on many intelligences and cover information in greater depth. Because many vocations in the workforce require a project-oriented approach, asking students to engage in projects at school prepares them for the work they will encounter in the workforce.

Assessments provide students with a means to "demonstrate their higher-order thinking skills, generalize what they learn, provide examples, connect the content to their personal experiences, and apply their knowledge to new situations" in their student projects or coursework (Campbell & Campbell, 1997, p. 18).

Finally, apprenticeships represent the broadest stretching of a student's learning, not only providing mastery of a skill over time, but also integrating skills as a whole, as opposed to the more traditional breakdown of discrete skills. This allows the ADHD students to utilize their energies by employing problem-solving skills and task commitment to an ever-changing challenge under the guidance of an expert.

## MI Lesson Planning

It is not necessary to incorporate all the intelligences in a single lesson plan or learning unit. However, many teachers have mentioned that designing projects in such a way results in a very powerful learning experience. If two or three intelligences in a lesson are used and appropriate for the topic, then the learning for the majority of students may have been reached. Long-term learning units or weekly lesson plans can be structured so that each intelligence is recognized, addressed, or activated periodically.

A misconception in the application of MI theory, according to Gardner (as cited in Checkley, 1997), is that "everything should be taught seven or eight ways. . . . [T]he point is to realize that any topic of importance, from any discipline, can be taught in more than one way" (p. 10). The advantage of the often-used linguistic and logical-mathematical intelligences approach is that a large amount of information may be conveyed efficiently. However, those students who do not have the language-logic profile may fail to learn. Furthermore, the quantity of material covered does not guarantee quality of understanding. Understanding, the crux of curriculum, can be assessed whenever the information, concept, or skill is used to solve "real-world" problems or create meaningful products.

## Lesson Plan Format

Examples of how MI can be incorporated into lesson planning are provided. This section supports lesson plans designed with the ADHD student in mind: ADHD environmental factors (e.g., sit in front of classroom), ADHD type (e.g., inattention), ADHD learning style (e.g., touching/doing), and ADHD MI profile (e.g., naturalist and spatial).

We've created a lesson plan format to reflect Gardner's image of how a lesson might look by borrowing his metaphor of a room with five doors. The room is the topic. Each door represents different entry points that may be used by students to enter the room. Many doors are given to accommodate individual differences and to personalize lessons. No single entry point is more valuable than another. The student's predominant intelligence is used as an initial means of learning a topic, the "door of their choice, gaining access to the topic through their dominant intelligence(s). Each entry point consists of activities, lessons or learning centers that highlight a logical-quantitative, narrational, foundational, aesthetic or experiential way of perceiving and processing information." (Jones, 1997, as cited in Bete, 1997, p.18). See Figure 3.2. The lesson plan format can be adapted to accommodate your needs. The lesson plan format has a familiar look. It includes entry points, grade, subject, title or topic, anticipatory set or setting the stage, goals and objectives, materials, procedure, assessment, and reflection.

This lesson plan is designed for the student with ADHD. Therefore, within the lesson plan format, there will be entry points that include the type of ADHD, environmental factors, learning and working style, and MI profile. There is a section called "Tips" where you can reflect on insights or trouble areas.

**Figure 3.2.** MI Lesson Plan Template for the ADHD Student

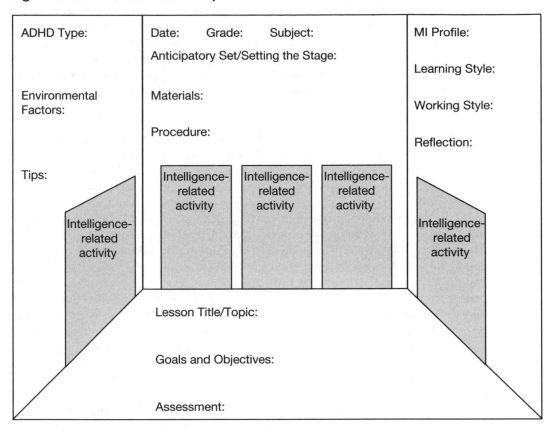

To illustrate, say that a teacher is presented with Zachary, a tall, long-limbed student with ADHD who says, "I have been referred to as 'twitchy,' given my high energy level. At times, my energy level interferes with my ability to concentrate on my work." The teacher would determine that Zachary presents as "combined" in the area marked "ADHD Type."

Under "Tips," a teacher might write, "difficulty with transitions." This was the situation with Anthony, whose current teacher, Kimberly, reported that she introduced "a floor drum, having a class drummer, and putting 'John' and 'Anthony' on the drum to create a beat to accompany many class experiences, including transitions such as going to parent pick-up and buses. This integrates curriculum such as drumming syllables in our names. It also seems to relax both of these students, who often appear nervous and excited and need frequent refocusing. Being able to surprise these two with a curriculum-based, but inviting, song also helps them to re-engage, move in a positive way, and enjoy being with our class."

### Introducing MI Theory to Students

**Human Intelligence Hunt©.** To help students become acquainted with the eight intelligences, an intelligence hunt written by Thomas Armstrong (1994)

provides a meaningful learning experience. Teachers would distribute the list of tasks in Figure 3.3 and explain that there are two rules: First, the students must perform the task and initial the "hunter's" task sheet. Second, the students must acquire eight different sets of initials. Finally, the first person done shouts "Gardner!"

The authors have conducted the intelligence hunt on many occasions. Depending on your audience, you can adapt the above list. For example, animal prints can be used with older students and pictures of animals can be shown to younger students.

**MI-Inspired Unit Plan.**  Another way to introduce MI theory to students is to ask them to describe the intelligences they use on a daily basis (see Figure 3.4). Gardner's MI theory provides educators with the means to employ a curricular intervention for students with ADHD. Hearne and Stone (1995) ask if art, music, [and physical education] were valued in our society, as opposed to language and math, would we have a different group of students labeled LD (p. 441)? Smagorinsky (1996) asks, "Why do schools value one type of product (writing) over other types of products (drawings, dances, musical scores)? This value is primarily based on traditions; schools have historically valued linguistic performances . . ." (p. 11). Hearne and Stone (1995) assert that "we must begin to address the failures of traditional deficit models and their abysmally low 'cure' rate" (p. 439). With reforms such as MI theory, "we are left to contemplate the field of learning disabilities and perhaps the existence of learning disabilities as a verifiable phenomenon . . ." (p. 447). The feeling of academic failure follows students with ADHD into adulthood. "Who among us enjoys being in a setting in which we fail?" (Hoerr, 1996a, p. 36). Yet ADHD students experience frustration and failure on a daily basis, which infringes on their educational and career choices.

The next section presents general MI strategies to be used with students with ADHD. This general approach can apply to *all* subjects with which the student with ADHD is having difficulty.

Difficulty in one area may often be successfully overcome by rerouting a task through an individual's more highly developed intelligences.

**Figure 3.3.** Human Intelligence Hunt

Find someone who can:

____ Whistle a few notes from Beethoven's Fifth Symphony.

____ Stand on one foot with eyes closed for at least 5 seconds.

____ Recite at least four lines from any poem learned.

____ Draw a quick diagram explaining how an electric motor works.

____ Briefly share a dream that occurred in the past 2 weeks.

____ Complete this numerical sequence: 36, 30, 24, 18, ___, and explain the logic behind it.

____ Honestly say he is relaxed and comfortable relating to other people during this exercise.

*Source*: Armstrong, 1994.

*Note*: To add the naturalist intelligence, which has been omitted from the list above, simply show an animal print, and add the line "____ Identify this animal print."

**Figure 3.4.** Multiple Intelligences–Inspired Unit Plan

---

**Objective:** To be able to identify the MI and how they are used in school and life

**Outcomes:** Students will be able to:
   1) Name and describe domains of the eight intelligences.
   2) Describe their MI strengths and weaknesses.
   3) Describe uses for MI in studying or in the community.
   4) Identify the intelligences related to occupations.

*Linguistic:*

Write your own MI descriptions.
Read MI work descriptions aloud in class.
Brainstorm and list MI strategies.

*Spatial:*

Create a web diagram of the eight intelligences.
Design posters in the room that reflect the intelligences.
Draw a "logo" for each intelligence.
Visualize yourself as a person famous for his or her skill in each intelligence.

*Musical:*

Find popular songs with lyrics that incorporate the intelligences.
Make rhyming, rhythmic couplets for each intelligence.

*Logical-Mathematical:*

Analyze a job or task and estimate how much of each intelligence is required.
Graph the MI profiles of classmates.
Classify the MI words.

*Bodily-Kinesthetic:*

Learn gestures for each of the multiple intelligences.
Role-play and mime MI occupations and ask peers to guess which intelligence is being presente

*Interpersonal:*

Interview a family member who is strong in each intelligence.
Practice "listening for understanding" as you think and share about one another's profile.
Role-play that you're the boss at a big company and are hiring eight people for jobs.

*Intrapersonal:*

Journal and reflect on your MI profile.
Design an action plan for using your strength to study, go to college, or just have fun.
Think how it feels to be weak in your particular area. What can you do about it?

*Naturalist:*

Investigate how animals are good at the different intelligences, e.g., birds are good at singing.
Conduct a survey of crops in the area and the jobs associated with them.
Discover the intelligences of a farmer or scientist.

---

According to Gardner (1992):

> We now know that individuals have very different kinds of minds, that they learn in different kinds of ways, and that they can even demonstrate their knowledge and understanding in characteristic ways. Because these findings are quite well established . . . we are challenged to find the optimal means to address each child, and to remain ever-vigilant to new and better ways to educate that child . . . (p. 48)

## MINDFUL INSTRUCTIONAL STRATEGIES FOR ADHD STUDENTS

Learning new information can occur easily or can require substantial effort. There are many factors that influence successful memorization and the acquisition of new skills. Learning requires attention, concentration, and effort. *How* we choose to study can make a great difference. Understanding that there are different ways to study and to practice new skills can aid in the construction of a study plan that fits the goals of the task. The MI profile can provide useful clues as to which strategies may be the most effective. The highest profile scores are often the best-developed abilities and will facilitate new learning. The next learning and study strategies may match the requirements of the material to be learned.

**Musical.** Use rhyme, rhythm, and repetition. Notice how the words sound. Repeat it until you can hear it clearly and it sounds just right. Does it "ring true"? Make a musical beat to it. Sing it to yourself. Make up a song lyric that explains it. Study with pleasant music, a metronome, or with perfect quiet. Say it out loud, sometimes slowly and sometimes quickly. Emphasize the accent or the voice inflections.

A physician treating Jonathan for depression referred Jonathan to us. He was a small, quiet, but friendly fifth grader who exhibited a clear strength in the musical intelligence. Cheerful when talking about music, his proclivity appeared at an early age.

> My mom said I was blessed with a good voice. . . . [A]s a child, I sang with a cassette playing. . . . [I]n third grade, I was in the church choir. . . . At school, I was her [music teacher] "star pupil" . . . I played flute in school. . . . [M]usic was my favorite subject . . .

Jonathan stated that he "hates" language, French, and social studies. He was counseled to listen closely for the rhythms and sound patterns used when his teachers explained these subjects. For example, the lesson plan "Using Word Syllables to Create Rhythmic Sentences©" (Miller, 2006), designed for students in grades three to eight, demonstrates how to use one word with one or multiple syllables to represent rhythmic patterns. In this lesson, you are forming the rhythmic patterns. Jonathan could, for example, learn French words by assigning note values to each word grouping (e.g., one-syllable words would be a quarter-note value, two-syllable words would be two eighth notes in value, and so forth). As an adaptation to this idea, Jonathan would listen closely to his French, language, and social studies teachers in order to decipher rhythm and sound patterns spoken during lectures. This attention would serve to help him learn the material.

While musical intelligence is not engaged by playing music in the background, Jonathan may simply be happier having background music and, thus, more open to learning. For some students with ADHD, music might be too distracting, especially in light of the fact that many individuals with musical intelligence tune in music, even background music. This was the case with Jacob, another student with ADHD, who exhibited musical intelligence as his predominant intelligence. We were in a restaurant and he tuned in the background music and tuned off this interviewer. His actions were unintentional. He was not trying to be rude, nor trying to purposefully listen to the background music. His inclination came naturally.

**Bodily-Kinesthetic.** Do it three times for practice. Use "hand-over-hand" demonstration. Touch, walk, and talk to keep attention focused. Write it large or over and over again. Dramatize to get a "feel" for it in your bones. Hold on to it and use gestures. Play and move through it step-by-step, like a mime. Tinker with it; build a model. Explore it with your hands or move through it in imagination. Be patient as it moves through you. Take "movement" breaks often.

Described by his parents and teachers as having "ants in his pants," John was a third grader with ADHD in a MI school. John's strength was in bodily-kinesthetic intelligence. When we interviewed his teacher, Kelly, she described a lesson taught on directions—north, south, east, and west, and stated, "If I moved him, I got him." Of the learning style and instructional methods applied, John finds most success with a hands-on approach. "When he's with us, [John's with us . . . ] and he's with us much better when there's more activity [active learning] going on in the room. . . . [W]hen I can do that and get him actively involved in the learning, John's with us" (Schirduan, 2000, p. 170).

**Logical-Mathematical.** Question, count, categorize. Ask why and how. Explain it step by step. Analyze it. Experiment with it. Find a pattern that is new or fits. Explore the possibilities. Test an answer logically. Collect, compare, and critique. Strive to understand—how, why, and what!

Mark, a former client with ADHD, received weekly counseling sessions to address disparities between his poor grades in school and his good scores on tests. "Mark was a great math student," maintained his father. During Mark's free time, he often engaged in activities related to math, especially video games involving logic or strategy. Mark asserts that he's "pretty good [at video games]." While describing a particular video game to us, Mark stated, "you play it out in your head . . . [I play out all the scenarios] and thought that was the only way it could be [to win the game]." Mark liked to learn best by "figuring it on his own first," and reported that, as a child, he easily learned math and has done well in math.

He does not, however, do well in social studies. He could benefit by applying his logical reasoning ability (which does not have to include numbers) in social studies. For example, in the social studies lesson Box and Deliver© (Dunlea, 2006), students use logic and strategy (logical-mathematical intelligence) to practice longitude and latitude plotting skills, mapping skills, and reasoning abilities for practical use. The game uses maps, and students choose a location and deliver a product as quickly as possible to its destination. Along the way, hazards and problems may arise (weather, road conditions, construction, and so forth) and students must think quickly to find alternative routes.

**Spatial.** Show it three times to yourself. Demonstrate it all at once so you get the "big picture." Watch, visualize, and sketch. Think of a simile, metaphor, or even an exaggerated or odd picture. Make notes with different-colored pens. Use page layout or shapes for note taking. Make "visual maps" to organize new information. Take photographs, video, or make a graph. Add attractive personal style or decorations. Daydream or make a movie in your mind. Create a cartoon, picture book, or sculpture. Organize information in a colorful, spatial layout. Place new information on labeled shelves in imaginary kitchen cupboards, or on a workbench.

Jack's mother was concerned with her son's failing and near-failing grades and sought our help. Jack's strength was in spatial intelligence. In one session, he came to us with an impressive art portfolio spanning many years. Happiest when drawing, painting, and doodling, Jack, a confident and budding artist, proclaimed, "I used to draw a lot. . . . [M]iddle school was the height of my doodling." We decided to put his doodling to work. He now incorporates idea sketching (Armstrong, 1994) into classroom notes. He takes notes in class, leaving a column free on the right side of his notebook to draw the key point or main idea being taught. Regardless of the subject matter, he has now been able to mobilize his strength in drawing and bridge it to an area of weakness. In this way, he was able to sustain his attention in class.

**Linguistic.** Take detailed notes. Write an outline. Make a list or checklist. Repeat it three times to yourself. Make up memorable abbreviations. Make up an exciting, odd, or scary story. Explain or teach it to someone else. Preview, question, read, review, and test. Listen, question, outline, and explain. Talk about it into a tape recorder and review it.

Josh, a sixth-grade student with a predominantly inattentive type of ADHD, was a self-described "debater." A former client, his predominant strength is in linguistic intelligence. His linguistic strength appeared in school and home contexts. Josh's mother mentioned her keepsakes of his work from his elementary school days. "He did a first grade report on tigers" that she saved. "Josh shared a poem published in a magazine." Josh stated that as a "little kid [I] wrote stories . . . short and long." Articulate and loquacious, Josh received good grades in language. Nonetheless, according to Josh, math "is quite painful."

Josh might find math more pleasurable if he can make connections between his strengths and weakness, as in the lesson plan on Venn Diagrams© (Dalke, 2006). The point of this lesson is to introduce students to the idea of comparison through Venn diagrams by comparing two stories. Josh may benefit from his teacher placing math facts and problems within a language framework. The teacher may also try to incorporate problems that involve language, such as word problems, to bridge his strength to weakness.

**Interpersonal.** Study in a group. Have classroom discussions. Understand why it's important to someone else. Teach it to a friend until he understands it. Join a team in competition or in cooperation. Study with a partner. Create a lesson plan to teach it to someone else. Teach it so even a child could understand. Listen just to learn, without questioning or interrupting.

Carol, a former client and middle school student with ADHD, has cognitive strengths in the areas of interpersonal intelligence (thinks via discussion with others) and spatial intelligence (thinks in images and pictures). Carol showed a preference for schoolwork that tapped into her interpersonal intelligence. Carol and her mother were both cognizant of her difficulties with French. Carol's mother stated, "She does struggle with her foreign language." Carol concurred, "I don't like French . . . the genders confuse me." However, when Carol was allowed to employ her interpersonal intelligence by engaging in a game of charades to learn French verbs she found success. "I believe I got a 98 on that [French] test just because of the charades" (Schirduan & Case, 2004).

**Intrapersonal.** Ask what you already know about this. Ask how this agrees or disagrees with past experiences. Why is it important for you to know it? What is your opinion about this information? Ask what you don't know or need to know and how to find out. Work alone at it. Stop to reflect often about this information. Challenge yourself to learn it. Test yourself. Visualize yourself in an occupation that uses this information. Convince yourself that you will be a better person by learning it. Learn it just for yourself. Learn to catch when your mind is wandering and bring it back to task.

Donna, a sixth grader with ADHD, had made progress in school following her ADHD treatment, which combined medication and outpatient counseling. However, her parents continued to have concerns that Donna was not yet fully utilizing her strengths. It was decided to administer the MIDAS™. She evidenced a preference for schoolwork that taps into her intrapersonal intelligence (to think about and understand oneself, reflect and monitor thoughts and feelings). For example, in language arts and writing courses (which Donna's father reported as her least favorite subjects), Donna described a favorite school memory: "[In language arts/writing] we had to do projects [about our life] . . . from birth to now . . . pictures of self . . . write and explain a big event each year . . ." She continued, "it was fun to show the class. . . . [I]t was cool to see other people and what happened in their life." Donna did well in writing once she was able to apply her intrapersonal intelligence.

**Naturalist.** Observe something carefully and identify patterns. Record and organize data in a system that makes sense. Imagine or build a "living model" that shows relationships. Consider how the information fits into the natural world. Discover how it has developed over time and look for growth. Imagine how you are cultivating the knowledge to feed your mind.

Suzanne was a reserved, compliant, and very sweet study participant in the third grade. Like many students with ADHD, she admitted that reading, spelling, and math proved difficult in third grade. On her most recent report card, science was the only subject in which she recieved an A. Childhood experiences revealed an interest in science, which still extends to the present day. Her mother explained, "she has a great love of nature, animals, the outdoors."

> Where we used to live, we had to go over a crest of a hill to get down to the house, and there would be the most spectacular sunset . . . and she would say let's stop and look at the sunset or look at the moon, you know, and we'd be there for a long time just looking . . . so she's really learned an appreciation for nature. . . . She has a natural love for animals [too] she just goes right over to them. . . . Her favorite show [on television] is a nature show.

When interviewed, Suzanne's responses teemed with examples of her interest in natural forces. She enjoyed scientific inquiry. One example she provided was when her teacher conducted an experiment with electricity. A class demonstration was held where the class all held hands and made a circle. The teacher explained that electricity flows in a closed circuit. She demonstrated by squeezing the hand (which represents a pulse) of the person next to her. That person continued by squeezing the hand of the person next to him and so on. Then she gave each child a wire, battery, and light bulb and asked them to make the bulb light. When told how much Suzanne had taken away from the demonstration, the teacher remarked, "Suzanne was the first kid to do it. . . . I can get her to smile when I call her Professor Sue."

Suzanne's talent in the naturalist intelligence and positive feelings toward scientific inquiry are evidenced from her teacher's remark that Suzanne "doesn't get frustrated in science when we do experiments where the other children do get frustrated" (Schirduan, 2000).

The general philosophy guiding the implementation of an MI assessment encourages the development of *all* the intelligences, building on particular areas of strength and using these strengths to overcome areas of underdevelopment. Good teachers have been using many of the instructional strategies associated with MI for years. However, an assessment of student intelligences increases the likelihood of reaching more students in less time. Moreover, the choice of strategies when the MI profile of a student with ADHD is known can mean the difference between success and failure, especially for a student with a limited attention span. There is no "one right way" to implement MI. Chapter 5, "Study the MI Way," also has an extensive list of study strategies that teachers can apply at school.

The next section presents teaching anecdotes in reading, writing, and math to illustrate how MI can be applied to elementary and middle school students with ADHD. The strategies that follow stem from the success that MI and traditional teachers have found when teaching ADHD students how to read, write, and compute, and can be adapted to the curriculum objectives and grade level being taught. Where appropriate, a brief mention of theory and research will accompany the anecdotes. A synopsis of suggested strategies for students with ADHD will conclude the reading, writing, and math sections, respectively.

## TEACHING READING, WRITING, AND MATH TO ADHD STUDENTS VIA MI

Traditionally, the "three Rs"—reading, writing, and arithmetic—have been used to explain the triptych of a basic skills-oriented instructional program. Although schools have expanded to include the arts as an additional skill, as well as focusing on more procedural "R"-related skills, such as representing material, relating content to other learnings, and employing reasoning skills, it is still impossible to progress successfully through the educational system without these original basics. However, it is very possible to teach reading, writing, and math to ADHD students via the multiple intelligences.

### Reading

Causes of reading problems vary. For example, students may miss a step in the reading process (e.g., letter-sound relationships), or may have differences in learning styles, low self-esteem, lack of motivation, learning disability (Linksman, 1995), and variations in MI profiles. Solutions to the reading problems presented should be MIndful and comprehensive. MIndful strategies for aiding the reading process (e.g., vocabulary) appear next.

We have found that many of the ADHD students with whom we have been connected have strength in the naturalist intelligence and spatial intelligence. Subsequently, the MI profile of many teachers in our studies indicates a "weakness" in the naturalist intelligence. For ADHD students, a teacher like Patty would be a gift. Patty, a tall, thin, astute, middle-aged woman, gave freely of her time and gave us a mother's and teacher's perspective on the natural world.

> My friends were extremely interested in my thirst for knowledge about the natural world. I always showed their children what I showed my kids. They were thankful that I took the time and interest to do this, since they would not have gotten their hands dirty. Nor would they have had the enthusiasm to engage the kids and show them this was an exciting adventure, and they could do it, too. The hardest part of sharing my interests in nature is helping the adults overcome their disgust of things natural. I don't want them to negatively influence the enthusiasm and curiosity of the children. I find that bringing colorful, nonfiction books and magazines [into the classroom] help to show why science is so important in everyday life.

ADHD students are often drawn to science. The natural world does not have chairs constraining them. Classroom rules such as the raising of hands do not constrict spontaneity. Students are engaged, the interest level is high, and their time is spent observing, touching, and manipulating objects. They are free to make noise, move around, make a mess, and be creative. The natural world provides an environment and subject well suited as a classroom for students with ADHD.

If you can't beat 'em, join 'em. That's an adage that could easily be assigned to Billy's teacher, Kat, an unlikely candidate to stray from her predictable teaching ways. Billy displayed typical ADHD symptoms and had a normal IQ, but was not doing well in reading. Test results indicated that he was above average in intelligence and had no learning disability. Kat stated that both she and Billy's parents were concerned.

> Billy showed no interest in the anthology stories presented in class and often stared out the window. He had been diagnosed with ADD, but did not receive any services from the special education team. One day, the special education teacher was in the classroom assisting some identified students and noticed Billy. There was a wild turkey outside the window and he was *fascinated*. A suggestion was made to use that animal to interest Billy.

Kat continued sharing with us how she was able to differentiate reading instruction and eventually learn a new curricular method to help other students with the naturalist intelligence. She stated that "books were obtained from the library, sites were found on the Internet, art projects were set in place with the visual/spatial [art] teacher, and Billy began his 'research.'"

> Using these tools hooked him into learning about the wild turkey. As time went on, he investigated other animals and I realized that others in the

classroom were also naturalists. I changed my approach to reading, and the other students also showed more enthusiasm in learning to read using material that interested them. Not only did Billy benefit, but the entire class. [As a result,] I was having more fun teaching.

When Billy's teacher altered her curriculum approach to reading through personalizing to a naturalist intelligence, it generated enthusiasm for teacher and student alike. Using material that interests students with ADHD (e.g., turkeys/science) is vital to gaining and maintaining their attention and interest.

Quick Reads© is a program that gratifies students' interest in science and provides ADHD students with short and fast instruction.

> QuickReads by Dr. Heibert are exactly that—short texts to be read quickly and with meaning. The QuickReads program consists of different levels and each level contains three books, and each book contains many many texts. These texts support automaticity with the high-frequency words and phonics/syllabic patterns needed to be a successful reader at a particular grade level. Additionally, with topics in two subject areas: social studies and science (e.g., life science, geography, and earth science, physical science, etc.), texts in the QuickReads program encourage meaning and comprehension. Curriculum-embedded nonfiction texts in science and social studies are not only interesting but fun for students. (About QuickReads, 2006)

Danielle, a distinguished teacher with 30 years' experience who works at an MI school, commented on how QuickReads works for students with ADHD.

> Fluency is crucial to reading comprehension. Therefore, I use QuickReads to improve fluency. I believe that these short passages are key to improving fluency. My experience has been that if students know they are going to be timed, they do better. It allows them to focus for a certain amount of time, and a specific task (e.g., punctuation). The QuickReads are not easy or hard, since it is on their instructional level. It is not a test. I think students with ADHD especially feel "I can do this for a short period of time."

Melanie, a reading coach at an elementary school in the South, also advocates for the use of the QuickReads program.

> When working with struggling readers . . . as a reading coach, I've observed the engagement of students who compete with themselves to improve their fluency score. Additionally, we have found that the text of the reading passages is at an appropriate level of difficulty. The students really want to read! When struggling readers reread a passage with fluency (speed, accuracy, and expression), you should see the expression on their face!

Ann, a short, soft-spoken special education teacher, states that she's worked with the print version and technology version of QuickReads.

> As a special education teacher, I think QuickReads is a really good program and I've seen a big improvement in student's reading, especially with fluency. What I've found with my students who have learning issues is that, whether they use the technology or print versions, they were more

engaged and on-task due to the small size of our reading groups, the attention, often one on one, I am able to provide, as well as the social studies and science content of QuickReads, two subjects these kids are often pulled from.

Keeping interest high and selecting reading content to match the MI profile of the student with ADHD is key to teaching reading. If students exhibit the spatial intelligence, they may benefit from the work of Jeffrey D. Wilhelm (2004). In his book *Reading Is Seeing*, Wilhem uses comic books, graphic novels, and picture books with elementary and middle school students. Students with ADHD and the spatial intelligence will be able to "see" the connections evident within the text, and the pictorial displays will capture their attention in a way that black and white text might not.

Literature Circles by Harvey Daniels is a reading program that can be used to serve the learning style of students with ADHD. The use of small groups, choice of reading material, natural conversations, and "liveliness" could act as an enticement to ADHD readers. In addition, the roles and responsibilities associated with Literature Circles can be adapted to the MI strengths of student with ADHD. Literature Circles rely on small groups of students who gather to discuss stories in-depth. Collaboration is at the center of this approach, where conversations about books invite personal connections, digressions, and open-ended questions. Roles can be assigned according to the MI strengths of the student with ADHD. For example, the role of illustrator (draws a picture related to the reading discussion) can be assigned to a student with strength in spatial intelligence. Someone with strength in the interpersonal intelligence is best served in the role of discussant (develops questions for the group to discuss), or passage picker (chooses a selection that the group rereads and discusses because it is interesting, informative, and so on). The role of vocabulary coach (chooses words that are difficult or used in an unfamiliar way) or summarizer (prepares a brief summary of the passage read that day) should be reserved for someone with preference for linguistic intelligence.

The role of connector (finds a connection between the story and another book, event in their personal life, or the outside world) can be allotted to someone with strength in intrapersonal intelligence. A student with ADHD who has strength in logical-mathematical intelligence may be given the task of travel tracer (tracks and charts the movements of characters). Finally, the student who displays the naturalist intelligence may act as an investigator and or private detective to find the specific elements that led up to the story's conclusion.

Peg, a newcomer to the field of education, uses Literature Circles with Cal, a third-grade ADHD student who exhibits the naturalist and interpersonal intelligences, and who would be good in the role of an observer, investigator, or even graphic locator. His teacher shares that Cal "is very much into nature. He is constantly bringing in animals. He has so much knowledge about animals and nature. If we go to recess, he is the one observing birds in trees, following the path of a caterpillar, collecting leaves and rocks. He reads well below grade level. He also has problems completing his work."

However, for Cal, this is not the case since his involvement with Literature Circles. Peg continues, "in Literature Circles, you typically work in small groups and assign roles to students in the group."

A student's responsibilities might include making a personal connection in the reading (intrapersonal intelligence) or summarizing a passage (linguistic intelligence), or drawing a picture (spatial intelligence). Cal had a prearranged engagement and had to miss school one day. He was upset because of his responsibility to the group for Literature Circles. He was very concerned and told his mom he just "had" to bring his work to the group. It is the social aspect (e.g., interpersonal intelligence, in this case), I believe, that motivates Cal and helps him to achieve in reading.

Context is important to the student with ADHD. Wilhelm (2004) found that, given boys' reading habits, it was the setting and geographic locations that were important "to the boys' engagement with reading" (p. 74) about topics and settings that are familiar. Cal's involvement in the group and search for patterns could pave the way to his summarizing the story based on the other students' findings. This role might also support his developing self-esteem as a reader and provide him with evidence of his ability to complete a task responsibly.

A chronic complaint that Peg and many teachers make regarding students with ADHD is incomplete work. Through the employment of Literature Circles, Cal's teacher told us that she found a way to address his reading difficulties and poor work habits.

Danielle and Melanie chose QuickReads, and Ann and Peg chose Literature Circles, all with the intent of improving students' reading skills. Improved work habits and enjoyment of reading material were positive consequences of these instructional approaches for their students with ADHD.

Clifford J. F. Morris, too, found positive results with an instructional approach. He is a special education teacher who reported his experience when asked to modify instruction for a number of his students. "Among numerous other learning limitations, their overall reading scores were located approximately two grade points below their chronologically aged grade-four peers." Morris explained that it was his responsibility to "upgrade their overall oral reading, reading comprehension, and cursive writing skills." In his estimation, these students had "continuously encountered numerous academic and social problems learning to read via conventional classroom ways, [so] it became my task to find an alternate way for them to do reading." He selected a remedial language program from the Carlos reader (readability level 3) of the Merrill Reading Skill Text Series, explaining that "the Merrill series represents a logically planned supplementary skills reading program."

The rationale behind selecting this program was to provide exciting program materials that would steadily upgrade word decoding, oral reading, vocabulary development, reading comprehension, phonics, and practical study skills—in short, overall language development. All of my special or "exceptional" learners were limited in most of these areas. The Merrill program achieved these objectives by providing carefully devised, systematic, skill development exercises based on interesting and motivating one-page stories. The Carlos reader represented just one of the many readers in the program.

This teacher then employed a "remedial grade-four reading program with interesting stories—specifically, a reader with one-page episodes that would be motivating, short, and easy to read. The Carlos reader was not only at their read-ability level but seemed practical, in that within every episode, a little boy called Carlos continued as the main character and hero."

Clifford told the story of Carlos, the hero:

One Saturday morning, while with his mother at her place of work, a little boy called Carlos convinced her to let him purchase and bring home an old rusty and broken-down robot. After repairing the "piece of junk" to its original form, Carlos decided to train the robot to be his personal assistant. He thus labeled the robot MOSH (short for "My Own Special Helper"). In each of the 42 stories of this reader, Carlos tries, usually unsuccessfully, to train MOSH to complete many household and neighborhood chores. My students easily identified with the contents of these stories! The five steps I used were:

Step I:   Reading aloud to students
Step II:  Word search puzzles as a spelling aid
Step III: Selecting an interesting story
Step IV:  Constructing hand puppets
Step V:   Videotaping a puppet show

As an end to the project, Clifford described the project's conclusion: "After a class party where they watched the video, each student walked out of the class-room. Each of them received their own personalized copy of the video. That even-ing, their parents watched them read . . . on TV!"

Clifford summarized his experience utilizing this program by stating that "Overall, I felt that the activities approached four of Gardner's eight intelligences, namely linguistic-verbal, bodily-kinesthetic, visual-spatial, and interpersonal intelligence."

These teachers discovered what worked for their students with ADHD inten-tionally and unintentionally. Their successes stem from MIndful curriculum and instruction, specific accommodations made for students with ADHD (e.g., provide a note taker), their learning style (e.g., tactile) or working style (e.g., reluctant to engage, inattentive), preference for instruction (e.g., short, fast), or MI profile (e.g., naturalist, spatial).

Lynn, a tall, young, elementary school teacher with high energy, observed that students with ADHD do best in reading when their learning characteristics are accommodated.

I find that my ADHD students thrive in my Reading Groups. We use Junior Great Books®. It is discussion-based literature, very rich literature. Every student has a book and I read along with the class. At the end of the story, each student writes his/her own question from the story on a post-it note. We now have 30 questions to discuss! I often ask the initial question for discussion to begin the group. The students with ADHD love it because it's all discussion and high energy. Students can "blurt out" their thoughts and ideas without having to raise their hands during this group discussion.

In addition to our research (e.g., naturalist or spatial intelligence profile), "research" conducted in classrooms by teachers of students with ADHD offers a number of instructional avenues. Linda Kreger Silverman (2002), in her book *Upside-Down Brilliance: The Visual-Spatial Learner*, states that many students "with AD/HD are probably visual-spatial"(p. 218). She contends that if your student with ADHD is a visual-spatial learner, he or she may have a difficult time mastering phonics. Hence, Armstrong's approach to phonics may assist the teacher with instruction of phonics.

Armstrong (2003) offers "another approach to sound–symbol correspondence that is visually based called the 'Gattegno's Words in Color reading program'" (p. 44). In this program, each of the phonemes is assigned a color. For the student with ADHD and spatial strengths, they might be able to master 40 colors versus 40 sounds more readily.

With regard to learning style, Silverman states that students who are "[visual spatial learners] tend to be sight readers." (Kreger Silverman, 2002, p. 289). Thus, learning sight vocabulary may be mastered with more success than phonics.

Another approach to sight vocabulary for the ADHD student with bodily-kinesthetic intelligence might be appropriate. Jillian, an MI teacher, reported that Eric, her ADHD student, had exhibited strength in the bodily-kinesthetic intelligence, but was "weak in the linguistic intelligence. Specifically, his sight vocabulary." To assist him, she "set up a hopscotch game. I would take sight vocabulary words and place them on the hopscotch pad. He had to toss the beanbag and, as he jumped, read the words. We would do it numerous times, of course, but using bodily-kinesthetic-related activities one on one or when he worked in small groups worked best. He responded better to academic tasks when I use his MI profile."

If students with ADHD prefer learning sight words to phonics, the following ideas next on Whole Word Reading Instruction may prove beneficial (see Figure 3.5).

Still another approach to vocabulary can be taught through music. Elizabeth, a music teacher in her mid-40s who was teaching in an MI school we visited, recommended incorporating musical intelligence for students with ADHD as an aid to learning vocabulary.

She provided an example from her own instruction: "When we are learning a song such as a ballad, a story, I'll place the entire lyrics of the song on charts. We'll go through each verse to discuss any words the students don't know. We discuss the meaning of the words and then I will ask for antonyms and synonyms. I have a vocabulary chart of the words for the song on the board."

Elizabeth also spoke about blending of language arts skills with musical intelligence. She stated that she works with language arts skills with comparing and contrasting with stories/songs.

> We read two versions of the story Joseph and the Overcoat (one is by Phoebe Gillman). We then compare and contrast both stories. We discuss what is different, what is the same, etc., and then I taught them the song. The songs from both stories are different as well, so we will compare and contrast them as well as discuss the song in terms of order (what items were made in which order from Joseph's overcoat etc.).

Specific skills are required for teaching reading (e.g., phonics, sight vocabulary, comprehension, and so forth). If a student with ADHD has strength in the spatial intelligence and/or has the visual-spatial learning style, the visual-spatial reading techniques in Figure 3.6 might be useful.

**Figure 3.5.** Whole Word Reading Instruction by Betty Maxwell

Be sure that the child can retain a visual image. Some children with ADHD perceive in a blink, but have poor short-term visual memory. Play games, such as "I Spy," with eyes closed. Encourage taking "memory snapshots" of favorite words.

Build a large sight vocabulary. Label things. Use picture dictionaries. Have a Treasure Box of great words. Sylvia Ashton-Warner gave children their own pile of words—whatever they wanted to learn. "Treasure Boxes" with favorite words aid the sight word process. It is important to learn lots of sight words, which become stored in visual memory and are available for analytic phonics.

Play games with Treasure Box words. Pull two or three random words and make a silly sentence. Pull three to five words and use in a story. Sort 12 words into categories. Any category will do, such as words with double letters, seven-letter words (five-letter, four-letter), action words, words that make pictures in your mind, words ending in "y," words with only one vowel, words with letters all the same size [for example, "a, o, r, s" and "P, O, U"], words with letters that go below the line ("g, j, p, q, y"). Have the children make up their own categories.

Pin words behind people and play "Guess the Word." Others see the word and can answer yes or no questions.

Small, bland words that are not easy to visualize (e.g., "the," "went," and "over") can be learned in fun, colorful phrases, such as "The monkey went over the bridge."

Make pictures for phrases, such as "over the bridge," "into the dragon's mouth," "behind his back," "the King of Slobs," "for ME!," etc., to help learn Dolch [high-frequency word list] reading vocabulary.

After you read a story aloud, play "Word Hunt" on a couple of pages. Ask the child to find an interesting word—never a bland word such as "for," "of," "the."

Have all the children make their own books. They can cut out or draw pictures, then dictate captions. Staple the pages together into books. Have fun reading these books.

After the children are reading a bit, use Treasure Words for analytic phonics. Have them sort words into categories such as Same Beginning Sound, Same Ending Sound, Rhyming Words, Silent E Words, and so on. Can they make a silly sentence or tongue twister out of some of the words?

Discover word patterns. These will often be rhymes. On the board, play games that substitute beginning or ending sounds. Rather than teach short vowel sounds (which are hard for VSLs [visual-spatial learners] to learn), teach a rhyming word or a word from the same "family." Remember that these children are good at recognizing patterns, love seeing relationships, and have a superb sense of rhythm, but are poor at memorization.

Teach consonant blends through silly tongue twisters: "Please play on the planet, Pluto," "Greedy Greta eats green grapes," and "Spray the spruce with sprinkles in the spring," Read the Dr. Seuss alphabet book to the children, then have them make up tongue twisters of their own.

Teach Greek and Latin roots, prefixes, and affixes. See if the students can find these parts of words in the additives on cereal boxes, in dictionaries, in books with Latin names of animals and insects, in medical books, at the zoo, or at a botanical garden.

Accompany reading with visualization techniques to assist children in learning to spell words they want to use in their creative writing.

*Source*: Silverman, 2002, pp. 289–291.

**Figure 3.6.** Visual-Spatial Reading Techniques

Use a sight approach to reading rather than relying solely on phonics.

Silent reading is preferable to oral reading. Ask comprehension questions and allow students to find answers through reading silently at least part of the time.

Teach them to use their finger as a visual guide in reading. It keeps them from jumping from word to word around the page.

Use a frame that shows only one line of print at a time.

VSLs respond well to poetry. Use rhyme and rhythm to enhance reading.

Offer them books—even adult-level ones—in their areas of interest. Gifted VSLs can often find answers to the questions that pique their curiosity in very advanced books, even if they can only decode a fraction of the words.

Give them books with lots of pictures—even comic books.

Don't require them to read every word on a page. Instead, encourage them to make a photographic imprint of each page. Ask them where on the page they can "see" a particular idea in their mind's eye.

Try using enlarged print.

Teach them work patterns, roots, and affixes, and decoding as puzzle solving.

Use books rich in visual imagery (e.g., *The Chronicles of Narnia* and *Harry Potter*) to enhance interest and ability in reading. (*Be aware that some visual-spatial learners may need initial help in learning to visualize.*)

*Source*: Silverman, 2002, p. 293.

For ADHD students with strength in bodily-kinesthetic intelligence, Margie, an elementary teacher, discovered that Lucy Calkin's reading technique "talk and turn" served as a positive instructional tool for her student Andrew. Margie reported that the class was studying Greek mythology and was using the "talk and turn" technique. She explained that "you read aloud a story and at a pivotal point in the story you tell the students to 'talk and turn.' Students turn to the person next to them and talk for a minute or so. Students may make predictions or inferences or discuss a question I pose."

When addressing how this method helped with Andrew, she continued, "One day, I read Hercules to my students. Andrew was enthralled with the story." He has ADHD, strengths in the interpersonal and bodily-kinesthetic intelligences, and demonstrated the bodily-kinesthetic intelligence in reading.

He is a leader in class with a powerful personality. He was listening [to Hercules] very closely and would be completely still. It was as though he was in another zone. We got to one part of the story, where Hercules went down to Hades and had to get past a three-headed dog and Hercules was wrestling with the dog. As I read, I could see Andrew crouching and listening, his body writhing. It was at this point that we had "talk and turn." Andrew, still in the moment, leapt forward and did a forward dive roll! It was exactly what happened in the story when we continued reading. Andrew was able to use his body as a tool to understand what was happening in the story, then predict via his body movements how the fight would play out. It was amazing! This happened not once, but many times with different stories.

Other teachers might have curtailed Andrew's classroom acrobatics, but Margie applauded. Andrew's understanding of the story was witnessed in his attentiveness as well as in his bodily movement. Margie's open-mindedness is in keeping with Levine (n.d.), who states, "The biggest mistake we make in life is to treat everyone equally when it comes to learning (Levine, 2007, paragraph 7)."

From our research and anecdotal findings, the pattern recognition ability associated with the naturalist intelligence can be activated to enhance academic skills such as reading, writing, and math.

The student with ADHD with naturalist ability is able to identify and recognize patterns. This skill plays a pivotal role in academic performance. For example, patterns can be found in both reading (e.g., word families, and so forth) and writing (e.g., "i" before "e" except after c). Kreger Silverman (2002) states emphatically that "Math is not about memorization or drill or speed. It's about patterns: seeing interesting relationships between numbers" (p. 302). Students with naturalist intelligence have skills in observing, recognizing, understanding, classifying, and organizing patterns in the *natural environment*. These students can transfer this ability to the learning of *reading, writing, and mathematics.*

To aid in the learning of phonics, the phonemes can be, as Armstrong (2003) noted, initially introduced as nature sounds such as the "oo" sound an owl makes (hooo! hooo!) to teach the "oo" in *tool* (p. 126). Sight vocabulary can also be taught through an exercise that has the class walk outside and label elements in nature, such as rocks, trees, flowers, brooks, and so on. These elements can be integrated into a writing prompt response where students complete the sentence "On our walk today, I saw . . ."

In our work we have gathered many successful strategies that are linked to an anecdote, researcher, or particular instructional methodology. These reading strategies that we've ascertained from our research and work with ADHD students and their teachers and parents include the following:

- Match the MI profile to general strategies for teaching any skill (refer to the section on MIndful Instructional Strategies for ADHD Students earlier in this chapter).
- Bring color to learning details. (For example, Katie, a former client, used her favorite color to highlight the main ideas in class notes, her second favorite color to highlight supporting details, and her third favorite color for specific dates and times. It was her way to prioritize information.)
- Bring colorful (i.e., visually pleasing) and nonfiction (e.g., science as in QuickReads) materials to reading.
- Consider task novelty to sustain attention (Zentall, 1996).
- Seize teachable moments (for example, Billy's teacher, Kat, used his interest in turkeys to enhance reading skills).

- Pair the student with a stronger reader and good role model.
- Incorporate phonics and syllabic patterns needed to be a successful reader (e.g., QuickReads).
- Create small reading groups to work on specific skills such as comprehension (e.g., similar to the technique used by Melanie, the special education teacher from the South).
- Implement short reading passages to keep attention and improve fluency (e.g., Reading Coach, QuickReads).
- Divide assignments into chunks so work is managable and success attainable.
- Incorporate technology and use computer and print versions of stories.
- Allow students to choose reading material (e.g., Literature Circles).
- Allow students to choose whom to read to (READ—the Reading Educational Assistance Dog program—involves reading to pets; Armstrong, 2003).
- Assign MI-related roles to reading (e.g., a student with strength in spatial intelligence might be assigned as illustrator and may draw a picture related to the reading).
- Choose materials within the ADHD students' zone of proximal development. In other words, choose developmentally approriate material (e.g., Reading Coach used QuickReads, multilevel readers, which allow students to compete with their own score).
- Take advantage of a peers' influence to improve the reading skills of the ADHD student (e.g., Cal succeeded when he was responsible to the group with Literature Circles).
- Find a "good fit" between reading programs and ADHD characteristics (impulsivity, hyperactivity), such as students' high energy and need to share answers (e.g., Lynn, a teacher who chose Junior Great Books® reading material, allowed students to "blurt out" answers).
- Teach sight vocabulary using games or physical activity. Keep the vocabulary words mastered in a notebook or create word or pictorial flash cards or a word bank (e.g., Jillian created a hopscotch game to teach vocabulary).
- Approach a concept, subject matter, or discipline in a variety of ways (e.g., Elizabeth used music to teach the reading skill of comparing and contrasting stories in *Joseph and the Overcoat*).
- Present opportunities to choral read to increase the self-image and comfort levels of all readers (e.g., Lynn demonstrated this using Junior Great Books®).
- Foster listening skills as the teacher reads (e.g., Margie used the teaching technique "Talk and Turn" with Literature Circles).
- Build background and context for reading (Wilhelm, 2004).
- Suggested readings include *Reading is Seeing* by Jeffery Wilhelm, *The MI of Reading and Writing* by Thomas Armstrong, and *Upside-Down Brilliance: The Visual Spatial Learner* by Linda Kreger Silverman.

To gain greater understanding of the underpinnings of successful reading and writing strategies used with ADHD students, refer to cited research and anecdotes.

### Writing

Writing goes hand in hand with reading, and many students with ADHD may find writing a challenge. As with reading, the MI profile of the student with ADHD should be considered when writing activities are assigned.

Feinberg (2007) describes Lucy Calkins's work, which advocates writing workshops with students and providing students with a writer's notebook, where they put into words what they observe, think, and feel. Mary, a cheerful, oversized woman willing to try just about anything to reach her students, explains Calkin's writer's notebook: It is where "a student with ADHD would keep a notebook with them, on them. The ever-present writer's notebook, which the ADHD student can touch, hold, think about it, manipulate it, just might have the 'physical' presence to encourage a student with ADHD to write more." An affinity for short tasks in writing may also assist the student with ADHD. Mary comments further, "I think students with ADHD may do better in writing when the teacher can break down a task into chunks. For example, asking the student to think of the main idea and three supporting details. Then writing is a 'doable' task for an ADHD student."

The use of a graphic organizer presents another way to "break down a task into chunks" and make writing a doable task for the student with ADHD. Traditional graphic organizers with boxes (e.g., for the setting, characters, and so forth) can be used to assist in writing, or something such as tracing a hand may do the trick. Martha Jean says that her students with ADHD may be "more creative writers than the other students in my class."

> They have all these interesting ideas in their heads, but they just can't seem to get them on paper. So to help with organizing their ideas, [I do] a technique with them using their right hand. First, they trace their right hand onto plain paper, where they will write "Introduction, Supporting Paragraph 1, Supporting Paragraph 2, Supporting Paragraph 3, and Conclusion" on each finger. Your essay is on your hand and you can take it with you whenever you write. The thumb is the introduction. It is a short, but important part of the essay. Your pointer, middle, and ring fingers follow. These three fingers are longer, like your supporting paragraphs. Remember that these fingers are separate, and the details for each need to be clear and apart from one another. Last is the short pinky. It is similar to the thumb, but different, like your conclusion. When you touch the pinky to the thumb, it makes a circle. When you write your conclusion, and wrap it up, you come full circle by commenting about what you set out to do in the introduction.

Rebecca, an elementary school teacher, relayed the techniques she used with Max, an ADHD student who was experiencing difficulty with writing. Rebecca has taught at every elementary grade level (kindergarten through eighth grade) within the last 9 years. She explained that Max, a second grader, had strength in the logical-mathematical and interpersonal intelligences. His area of weakness was writing.

> At the beginning of the year, he would literally break down and cry when he had to write. I decided to tap into his interpersonal skills. Since he is

very social and likes to talk a lot, I found that with his writing, he had great ideas. Verbally, he could tell me so many things. So what I decided to do was to have him verbally tell me or a classmate his story. I would then write four sentences from our discussion, and he would write four sentences. I weaned this down to my writing two sentences, then one sentence. He can often write independently now. Writing was his biggest hurdle to overcome. I am so proud of him and the progress he has made since the beginning of the year!

Another teacher, Ralph, revealed how he had helped Robert, a sixth grader with ADHD in his class. Ralph explained that Robert had strengths in the spatial and bodily-kinesthetic intelligences. His weakness is reading comprehension and figurative language.

He is a concrete thinker, very black and white, so when it comes to thinking and writing abstractly, it can be difficult. However, when he used his body along with visualization, he found success. For example, we were reading a passage from a novel about World War I. It described the dive bombers as "swarming like hornets." When I asked him, "What do you think that looked like?", Robert acted it out using his body to make the connection. He was acting out the passage as I read. He really got into it. Robert's arms and hands were extended like the wings of a plane, his body swayed, he was making the sounds. I didn't have a picture of the dive bombers, but I could tell he was visualizing it in his mind. He would occasionally look up as if viewing it on a screen, etc. I could tell he was able to picture it the way the author wrote it, using similes, etc.

Through the use of his body as instructional tool, Robert "was able to make the connection and went on to write a dramatic paragraph using metaphors and similes. It was very effective." Ralph explains that "I could tell how effective it was by the way Robert felt when he read the paragraph he wrote. Furthermore, he included details such as 'the siren was at 130 decibels,' etc." Ralph informs us that "Of course he would prefer to describe it in detail in a very concrete manner, but using his spatial and bodily-kinesthetic intelligences, he found success in writing abstractly, figuratively."

Wilhelm (2004) has found that visualization improves key comprehension skills and improves test scores in reading. "Imagery and visualization treatments have achieved demonstrable success in various kinds of studies of the most intractable instructional problems around improving reading" (p. 16). Wilhelm notes that visualization is used for "seeing patterns" of details across a text or texts to discover complex implied relationships. He further states, "even cursory use of instruction supporting visualization improves scores on standardized tests" (p. 16).

Improvements in reading and writing or language arts became a dual goal for one elementary school art teacher who sought newer ways to reach all her students. Sherri, an art teacher whose colleagues describe her as "thinking and sleeping art," made the decision to broaden her instructional focus.

I integrate art and language using stick puppets. For example, students choose a character from a story and make a puppet. Next they draw the character's clothes and props, etc., and color and cut them out. This fulfills an art standard. Then students draw a sketch of the setting of where the character lives and attach it to the back of the puppet theater. At the puppet theater, they verbally tell a story. Finally, they will get together with other students and their characters and make up another story. When the students return to class, they write down their stories.

Illustrating the steps needed prior to writing helped all of Sherri's students, but was particularly helpful for students with ADHD and the spatial intelligence.

Yolanda, also an elementary art teacher, not only employed spatial intelligence to help students with ADHD write well but also took into account their fidgetiness.

Part of my job is to go into classrooms. I incorporate art when I can to complement the classroom teacher's lesson. One day, I noticed during a writing lesson that the first graders wouldn't look up at the board to refer to the parts of a story when writing. I also noticed that first graders need to touch things, especially the students with ADHD. So I designed Writing Spools® to assist students when writing. There are four wooden spools on a rope. The first spool has a sticker of a person (character); the second spool has a sticker of a tree (setting); the third spool has the words *first, next, then, finally*, and *oh no*!; the fourth spool has a Band-Aid on it (solution to the problem). The student moves the spools from left to right as s/he completes each part of the story. The students enjoy using them. In fact, I was told they request to use them.

Kent, a middle school art teacher whose students follow him around as if he is the Pied Piper, combined art (spatial intelligence) and writing (linguistic intelligence) via the Writing Spool®. This lesson uses a painting entitled *Watson and the Shark* by John Copely. For the student with ADHD who has the naturalist *and* spatial profile, this art lesson appeals not only to the student's strength in spatial intelligence but also magnifies attention due to its natural content and visual excitement. Kent describes his instructional use of this painting by explaining to students that this "was a story of a shark attack that was made into a painting."

I briefly tell the tragic story and place a large image of the picture on the board. Of course, we discuss the historical painting from an art perspective, but then I go beyond the lesson and integrate a writing activity. I ask them to write about the picture, describe the day. I give them each a Writing Spools.© The student moves the spools from left to right as s/he completes each part of the story. We then gather on the rug at the end of class and students read and peer review (via spools and rubric) stories.

Kent also employs an effective approach to teaching writing concepts (beginning, middle, and end) using art pictures or paintings.

I place a picture of a landscape up on the overhead. I "walk," if you will, through the painting with them. I teach the writing concepts to a story— beginning, middle, and end—via a painting. I have students write a story as they walk through the foreground, middle ground, and background of the painting. I literally divide the painting into three sections and make lines on the overhead transparency. Depending on the grade, the students are expected to write a paragraph or one sentence for each section of the painting. I encourage students to use *all* of their senses (What do you see?, Can you taste anything in the picture?, etc.) when writing the story. I believe every sense you have is a cognition, and you will remember a story or any skill for that matter more easily if you incorporate the senses.

Students with ADHD who exhibit poor writing skills rarely use descriptive words and frequently overuse selective words when writing. Teachers must look to the MI strengths of their students with ADHD to address these writing problems.

Carmel was described by her teacher, Julia, as an ADHD student who was "having difficulty using more descriptive words in her story writing."

I had the student use her strength of bodily-kinesthetic intelligence to act out her sentences/character actions. As she acted out the sentences, I had her tell me what she was doing. Then she sat down and wrote what she had acted out, remembering the words and phrases she had said aloud. This helped her to elaborate by adding description to her sentences. I believe supporting the student with a multiple intelligence approach made a direct improvement in her next scored writing prompt. Her next writing prompt assessment improved two points (on a scoring scale of two to 12).

Carmel's teacher described how other teachers of students with ADHD could improve student writing through the use of following technique.

The original sentence was "The boy went home."

The rewritten sentence was "The sad boy slowly walked down the dirt road toward his house, kicking up dirt as he walked." The student acted (bodily-kinesthetic) the sentence out and realized that it did not contain many details. So I proceeded with asking the student one question at a time. After I asked the question, the student would act it out, and then we labeled the action with words. The first question was "How did the boy go (went) home?"

The student acted the "went" out and then labeled the action with the word *walked*. The second question was "How did the boy walk?" The student acted out and then labeled the action with the word *slowly*. The third question was "Where was the boy slowly walking?" The student acted out and then labeled the action with the words *his house*. The fourth question was "Why was the boy slowly walking?" The student acted out and then labeled the action with the word *sad*. The fifth question was "What did the boy slowly walk on?" The student acted out and then labeled the action with the words *dirt road* and added *kicking up dirt*. Together, we organized and added words for the prepositional phrases and adjusted them so that the sentence would flow.

In explaining how this same student with ADHD tended to overuse some typical words such as *said* and *went*, Julia explained how she employed the following technique.

First, I had the student change her voice to say the word *yes*, and we recorded all the different ways she could say it (loudly, softly, happily, mad, frustrated, angry, etc). This helped her add *loudly* to her sentence, so it now read "She said loudly." Then we continued on to replace the word *said* with other synonyms, such as *thought, whispered, replied, reflected, spoke, cried, shouted, exclaimed, verbalized*, etc. Her classmates added other "replacement words" to the list as well. The ever-growing list of words was kept on a wall chart so that students could add words as the year progressed.

MIndful teachers differentiate instruction based on the needs of their students with ADHD in different subjects. The writing strategies gleaned from the above anecdotes are listed next. These strategies were found to be successful in the classroom. Some of these techniques can also apply to reading (e.g., visualization).

- Match the MI profile to general strategies to teach any skill (refer to the section on MIndful Instructional Strategies for ADHD Students earlier in this chapter).
- Complement ADHD characteristics and writing (e.g., Mary suggests that the student with ADHD have a writer's notebook on his or her person that can be touched, held, and manipulated).
- Establish a graphic organizer to break down tasks and teach, for example, story parts such as setting, character, problem, and so forth.
- Teach writing standards and help students get organized by tracing and visualizing their hand (e.g., Martha Jean has her ADHD students trace their right hand onto plain paper, where they will write "Introduction, Supporting Paragraph 1, Supporting Paragraph 2, Supporting Paragraph 3, and Conclusion" on each finger. She then tells them, "Your essay is on your hand and you can take it with you whenever you write").
- Pair students for modeling or dictate stories (e.g., Rebecca dictated Max's story).
- Scaffold learning for the student with great oral stories to written stories by providing very explicit and active assistance (e.g., Rebecca, a teacher, writes four sentences, and her student, Max, writes four sentences).
- Use visualization for reading, spelling, and writing.
- Dramatize a story, and then write (e.g., Robert closed his eyes to visualize a reading passage about dive bombers swarming like hornets).
- Incorporate Writing Spools® for students to reference and manipulate (e.g., to assist students when writing the character, setting, sequence, solution, and so on, Yolanda used writing spools).
- Bring art to teach writing concepts of beginning, middle, and end (e.g., Kent used paintings with landscapes to teach students how to write a beginning, middle, and end to a story).
- Act out sentences or character actions to assist with descriptive writing (e.g., Julia, Carmel's teacher, coached Camel to use her bodily-kinesthetic intelligence strengths to write what she acted out).
- Create a wall chart of student-initiated words to replace overused words when writing.
- Allow students to use a computer to type versus hand-write.

**Math**

Math is a problematic area for students with ADHD, according to the teachers we queried. However, teachers suggested that ADHD students with spatial intelligence, bodily-kinesthetic, and musical intelligences and related activities can use these skills to complement math objectives taught in the classroom.

Marguerite explained that her fourth-grade student with ADHD, Patricia, was strong in the spatial intelligence and weak in the logical-mathematical intelligence. Marguerite believed that "pictures and manipulatives were key to teaching place value and regrouping." Marguerite described Patricia as "an impetuous wired student [who] was just not getting it." She recalls the day she "took out the manipulatives, the base 10 blocks, to do the regrouping. It was like night and day. She finally got it!"

Ana, like Patricia, was having trouble with place value. Ana's teacher described her as "a fourth grader with ADHD who has the interpersonal and spatial intelligences as strengths." Ana's weakness was in math, but her teacher discovered that Ana "does better with geometry because that involves the spatial intelligence." The teacher identified Ana as especially weak in numbers.

> Ana has a lot of trouble understanding place value, and I worked with her in a small group. Well, the group got smaller and smaller as each student grasped placed value, until Ana was the only one left! When I was able to bridge her weakness, math, to her visual spatial strength, she finally "got it"!

This teacher helped Ana's learning by using manipulatives supplied by Education Technology, which "makes a color-coded manipulative to teach place value."

> There are color-coded place value arrows/cards with expanded notation, 10-sided colored cubes—each represents a different base 10 value. Because she was able to manipulate it, visualize it, match it, and take things apart and put them back together, she found success.

Bridging weaknesses to strengths cannot be underestimated. Nor can teachers of middle schoolers underestimate their student's self-interests at this stage of development. To illustrate, one middle school teacher, Ben, found that he was able to maintain students' attention when focusing on preadolescents.

> I used self-portraits to get my middle school students interested in art and math. Portraits use a lot of math. You actually measure quite a bit in a self-portrait. You measure between the eyes, etc., as well as graph, plot, and intersect lines, etc. Our faces, all of our faces, are quite similar, but if you move a line ever so slightly, it dramatically changes the look of a face. Students find this amazing. After showing them the same face with different hair, skin tones, etc., we then study the famous portraits to see if the artist used measurements in his/her pictures.

Spatial intelligence can be used to aid the student with ADHD in understanding math. Dana, an art teacher, noted that, through collaboration with colleagues as well as an interdisciplinary approach, she aids student learning in mathematics. She explained, "I attempt to complement lessons taught in the classroom when I can."

> I find that collaboration among colleagues and integration of disciplines can have a profound effect on a student's learning. For example, the classroom teacher was teaching about measurement. Some students got it, others did not. Some students passed a quiz on measurement, others did not. However, after teaching a lesson about nonstandard units of measurements using the eraser on a pencil, I was told they *all* got 100% on their next quiz. In the lower grades, students use nonstandard measurements before using standards of measurements such rulers, etc. I ask students to hold a pencil at arm's length. Artists will often do this to gain perspective when painting and drawing. Then, using the head of the eraser, measure an object in the room—say, for example, the soap dispenser—and tell me how tall/long (or the number of pencil heads tall) that object is. Let's say it is 4 eraser heads long. I then have them predict how tall/long the paper towel dispenser is, using the new nonstandard unit of measure, the soap dispenser. They are able to predict that the paper towel dispenser is 2½ soap dispensers long. The students instantly took to this measuring activity. I believe these types of integrations between art and math at a young age pave the path to learning more difficult math, like algebra.

Heidi, an athletic and outspoken physical education teacher, stresses the importance of movement, and addresses the need for students with ADHD to have an environment where they can release energy.

> One such place is our climbing room. One example in which we can help the ADHD student in math is to integrate BK [bodily-kinesthetic] with math at our climbing wall. I meet with classroom teachers to choose math problems, which are then color-coded according to grade level. So a first grader may be working on addition or subtraction facts while a fourth grader may be working on a story problem. At times, the students create the math problems for the climbing wall in their classroom. Math problems are placed on 3 x 5 index cards and then placed on the climbing wall. The students work in pairs; one student spots another while s/he is working on a math problem. After the student transverses the climbing wall from left to right, s/he stops and does a math problem. It is also possible to incorporate the physical features of the climbing wall into the math problem as well. An example of an addition problem might be to ask a second grader who just traversed seven steps from left to right might be asked to repeat this move from right to left and write the sum down.

Heidi also found success when using activities related to the bodily-kinesthetic intelligence to teach multiplication tables. "Students can also complete the multiplication tables through physical movement by completing curl-ups, push-ups. They role a pair of dice and then multiply, add, or subtract the numbers; and then do one of the warm-ups, curl-ups, push-ups, toe-touches, jumping jacks, etc."

Art, physical education, and music teachers are often well suited to an inter-disciplinary approach. A music teacher stated, "I often integrate music with other subjects."

> For example, I will play a note a particular number of times (in a rhythm) on the guitar or piano. I will then say to my class, "Count the times you hear the notes," and then I'll play another little tune and again I will ask them to count the notes. Finally, I will ask them to add or multiply two [sets of notes I play] to come up with a sum.

This music teacher, McKenna, outlined another music lesson that can be used to teach math.

> I will place a group of eight rhythms on the black board. I will then play three of the eight rhythms. The students will, after listening for the rhythm and timbre, will then have to, first, decode the rhythm to figure out which one it is; next, decipher which order I played the rhythms in to obtain the three-digit number, e.g., 135. It's . . . challenging. I repeat this three times.

One elementary school teacher, Suzy, described how she worked in collaboration with the school's tutor to address students with ADHD problems in learning mathematics.

> Our school's tutor [Jane] found that we had some kids who did not know their multiplication tables. She taught the tables to them in songs like "Mary Had A Little Lamb" and "Row, Row, Row Your Boat." She also incorporated hand gestures to go with them. My two students would *never* have learned them if they hadn't had that type of instruction. Now I sometimes see them moving their fingers and singing the songs to them-selves. That's okay. I know that they'll eventually get further than that and won't need it, but for the harder ones, they may use it all their lives."

Music can be used to address the characteristics of ADHD (inattention, im-pulsivity, and/or hyperactivity) before beginning a math lesson. For example, Janice, an elementary school teacher, explained that she teaches younger chil-dren and uses music to gain the students' attention. She has found that "different tones are good to gain kids attention, especially the two boys in my class who have ADHD tendencies."

> These boys especially like the thumb symbols. I hit the symbols on my thumb and middle finger together and the tone goes for a long time. The students' job is to listen and then, when the tone stops, it is time for the teacher to speak. I find it gets them refocused.

Millie, a teacher, suntanned with a thick French accent, also uses music to gain the attention of students with ADHD. "I use a xylophone to gain the atten-tion of all my students [including those with ADHD]. I play a tune on the xylo-phone and students stop and listen and hum it back to me. I then give the directions to a task." The above two techniques gain the attention of students with ADHD via music so the ADHD student can begin to focus on the lesson. Unquestionably, students with ADHD have difficulty staying focused. This, in turn, impacts their learning. A special education teacher who was interviewed maintained that she finds that all students, including those with ADHD, do not necessarily have difficulty with learning as they do with staying focused. "Not staying focused impacts their ability to learn. I've also found that if I can boost their self-confidence, for example, by providing a leadership role for them to assume, they perform better academically." To improve inattention, Kreger Silverman (2002) suggests that the teacher "Call on them as often as possible during class discussion. Interaction really keeps them focused, and waiting their turn is difficult" (p. 236).

As with inattention, impulsivity is a barrier to learning that many students with ADHD need assistance to overcome. One teacher observed that students with ADHD "rush through their work." This was the case with Oscar, whose teacher made the decision to employ his strength in math to graph and chart areas often associated with his work habits (e.g., rushing).

> I believe Oscar's ADHD impacts his executive function in terms of impulse control. For example, he has strengths in the logical-mathematical and linguistic intelligences. Ironically, his weakness is reading as well. He has a big problem with reading comprehension. He is reading twice as fast as he should be. At this age, he should be reading about 100 words a minute. He reads 90–160, when timed that is! If I don't time him, he reads even faster! He just races through the text. That is how he approaches everything. Because his strength is logical-mathematical intelligence, I use charts and graphs to help slow him down with his reading. We will practice with two short passages a day. We then highlight 10 vocabulary words he can focus on when he reads. He likes the challenge of "solving a problem." The problem he needs to solve is to figure out how to slow down to attend to punctuation, etc., to reach our goal of 100 words a minute. The visual graphs and charts help, but he still needs a lot of coaching to become an independent reader and comprehend what he read.

From the above teacher anecdotes, it is possible to develop strategies to teach students with ADHD mathematical skills. The following are possible math strategies generated from our work to use for students with ADHD:

- Use manipulatives (e.g., Jane observed her students using their hands to learn multiplication).
- Display pictures and graphics to represent math concepts.
- Find and use color-coded manipulatives (e.g., Ana learned place value only when she was able to manipulate it, visualize it, match it, and take things apart and put them back together).
- Make personal connections to learning (e.g., Ben used self-portraits to teach students math skills such as graphing).
- Provide math readiness skills prior to teaching math concepts expected to be mastered (e.g., Dana, an art teacher who takes a multidisciplinary approach to learning, used nonstandard measurements (such as paper-clips) before using standards of measurements such as rulers to teach the skill measuring).

- Combine math and movement to release energy while learning math facts and problems (e.g., Abigail teaches Jeremy the multiplication tables through physical movement).
- Work in pairs (e.g., Heidi uses a climbing wall and asks pairs of students to create and solve math problems).
- Find patterns to teach multiplication (e.g., McKenna, the music teacher, will play some notes and ask students to add or multiply two [sets of notes] to come up with a sum) or recognize patterns.
- Use mnemonics or songs (e.g., Jane used the song "Row, Row, Row Your Boat" to teach math skills)
- Use a timer (e.g., Russell suggests that students with ADHD may perform better for shorter periods of time).
- Use a computer to reinforce math skills (e.g., Captain's Log software).

During our gathering process in finding ways to reach and teach students with ADHD, we heard stories that were outside of mainstream education, such as the elimination of food dye in diets for ADHD students or the use of chewing gum to help the student with ADHD focus on a math test. Programs such as Captain Log, which we'll read about next, may help with academics or Brain Dance by Ann Green Gilbert may help with a writing score. These tools were seen not only to assist students with ADHD with academics but also to improve ADHD characteristics. We do not dismiss these claims, but instead allow the reader to lay claim to any alternative strategies that may improve the issues that MIndful teachers face everyday when teaching students with ADHD.

We spoke to an educator who uses traditional (e.g., medication) and alternative (e.g., Captain's Log, computer software) approaches. Dr. Russell works with students with ADHD and tells the story of Derek. On the intake form, Derek's parents mentioned Derek's lack of concentration, difficulty following instructions, and hyperactivity as their main concerns. His parents believed that his poor grades were due to his inability to concentrate. After a thorough evaluation, he was diagnosed with combined-type ADHD.

Dr. Russell used the MIDAS™ along with other assessment tools, and Derek was found to have the interpersonal, naturalist, and spatial intelligences as his strengths. Dr. Russell explained that "aside from traditional treatments such as medication and behavioral therapy, the main intervention that was used was a software program called Captain's Log® by Brain Train."

It is gamelike software with lively graphics. One can create a customized training plan. The program gives instant feedback, and Derek had a lot of success using it. There are many games and levels, with the ultimate goal for Derek to improve memory, attention, mental processing speed, impulse control, and listening skills.

Derek used the program at home 2 hours a week for 1 year. He also trained at our office 3 hours a month, using Play Attention® for attention training and multiple intelligence–like software games. His parents were vigilant and made sure he practiced at home, which wasn't a problem. Along with the gamelike assignment, the software appealed to Derek's strengths in spatial intelligence. As a result of this software, along with traditional treatments for ADHD, Derek made great strides in his reading and math. He is now getting As and Bs. As an added bonus, his behavior also improved!

In sum, once a student is properly evaluated and diagnosed with ADHD, the MI profile determined, and learning concerns identified (e.g., fluency when reading), then traditional (e.g., medication), time-tested (e.g., sit in the front of the classroom), and MIndful (e.g., Move N Sit Wedge® seat cushion, visualization) strategies can be chosen to improve learning.

The MI profile of many of our students with ADHD was the naturalist and or spatial intelligence. One significant teaching tool to gain immediate results surrounds the general patterning abilities of the student with ADHD and strength in the naturalist intelligence. Thus, for MIndful instruction in reading, use syllabic patterns, word families, and finding patterns of textual details to aid student learning. To instruct in writing and spelling through the use of patterns use grammar's "silent *e* rule": when a one-syllable word ends in *e* and has the pattern vcv—vowel-consonant-e—the first vowel is pronounced and the *e* is silent. Math patterns can be used as well (e.g., multiplication, the multiples of 5 end in 5 or 0, and so forth).

For the student with ADHD and spatial intelligence, a promising instructional tool to gain immediate results are visualization techniques. When teaching reading, visualizing text is a proven way to improve reading comprehension and can change a passive reader into an active reader. (For example, have the student visualize the images he or she read, etc.). To instruct in writing, the student can visualize pictorial information to guide the writing process. Visualization can serve as a prewriting activity. The visualization of math can aid comprehension through having the student construct bar graphs, charting 100 objects, using an abacus, and inventing three-dimensional objects.

Placing our findings on profiles of students with ADHD aside, "We do what we do and decide what we decide because of beliefs that this teaching 'move' will work in this situation with this child or this group. Being unaware of our theories means we cannot test them" (Wilhelm, 2004, p. 20). MI theory provides a MIndful theoretical framework for MIndful instruction that we invite you to "test" with your students with ADHD, no matter where their strengths reside.

An underlying assumption of this book is that traditional schools cater to a language-logic profile. Students with ADHD, who do not have a language-logic profile may languish in schools. Formal education does not have to be an unsuccessful experience for students with ADHD. They can flourish with the help of MIndful teachers and MIndful instruction.

# MIndful Curriculum and MIndful Schools

DAN, A STUDENT WITH ADHD who was frustrated with his past school experiences, shared, "I remember being told to sit quietly with my hands folded, feet together, and eyes forward. Which part of this sounds like a creative [MIndful] environment? If you guessed none, you get an A."

Unless thinking about the curriculum is reframed, answers to teaching students with ADHD may result in a host of traditional solutions that have little to do with how students learn best.

Chapter 4 has dual objectives. It argues that school leaders (e.g., teachers, administrators, and coordinators) should adopt MI theory to benefit individuals with ADHD. Its second objective is to provide a workshop model for professional development in the areas of training in ADHD, managing behavior problems in students with ADHD, raising test scores, strengthening students via the personal intelligences, leading the transition from IQism to MI, and staff development toward an MI-inspired school. Brief examples of schools implementing MI theory within the United States and abroad are offered.

## MINDFUL CURRICULUM AND INSTRUCTION: A PARADIGM SHIFT

MIndful curriculum and instruction demands a shift in pedagogy, a shift that entails a strengths perspective, personal connections to what is being taught, and "manageable" content curriculum. Perhaps, in tandem, we may also see schools improve and students learning, understanding, and synthesizing subject matter.

### Curriculum Rooted in MI Theory

Teachers can be provided with training in curriculum rooted in MI theory to benefit ADHD students. This can be illustrated with the case of Jonah, a heavyset child with an even disposition, who was an elementary student with ADHD and strength in the naturalist intelligence. In Jonah's words, he likes "science the best." His interest in science emerged during an interview when he corrected my choice of words (I said *explode* versus *erupts*) as we discussed volcanoes. His parents confirmed his interest in science, especially animal care, which mirrored his home life, which was filled with domestic pets. Yet the following comment revealed that his teacher did not recognize Jonah's interest in this area. She stated, "science just gets thrown in. . . . I haven't had an opportunity to see him [observe him] in that respect . . . science you know with everything else we're doing, science kind of like gets a couple units but it gets thrown in there . . ." (Schirduan, 2000, p. 171).

## Personalize Education

Teachers can personalize education for students with ADHD to promote achievement and motivation. Personalization comes in as many forms as there are students. It can be found in decoding structural analogues between strengths and weakness, or simply identifying high-interest subject matter for the student with ADHD. For example, Stephanie, an elementary student with ADHD, innately connected her two predominant intelligences (naturalist and spatial intelligence) in science. Her interest in earth science was depicted in her painting of flowers and construction of a snow scene. Her curiosity regarding animals was echoed in her art projects, which depicted varied examples such as a penguin, cat, and butterfly keepsakes. Animals dominated her portfolio, which her mother shared with us. Recognizing her predominant intelligences had the potential to heighten Stephanie's interest level in teacher-directed activities. Often disorganized and careless in her schoolwork, Stephanie's art showed purpose and care for color, line, directionality, layers, and shading. Her teacher describes this as "phenomenal" (Schirduan, 2000, p. 159).

Teachers personalize education by using what interests their students with ADHD. This is done with the hope of sustaining attention in areas that may be less appealing to the student with ADHD. The ultimate goal is to get students closer to completing an assignment, handing in homework, and having their talents recognized and stretched.

Interestingly, in one sample surveyed, teachers and students were asked their perception (with no MI assessment) of strengths in the ADHD student and to name a predominant intelligence. Teachers of students with ADHD and the students themselves reported spatial intelligence as a predominant intelligence for the students with ADHD. This is an important finding, because once a teacher reflects on the strength of a student with ADHD, this identified strength can be bridged to other weaker areas. This curricular bridge can then serve as a springboard to create an action plan for the learning of new material.

MIndful curriculum leaders train teachers to be curriculum brokers and to make connections between predominant intelligences and curriculum to improve learning outcomes. Gardner (1993b) wrote about finding structural affinities between domains in which a child has strengths and domains in which the child has weaknesses. He suggested using an area of strength as an "entry point" to an area of difficulty (p. 206). For example, a child whose predominant intelligence is linguistic and whose weakness is logical-mathematical intelligence may be introduced to learning math through story.

In addition to entry points, a teacher can find structural analogues. A student can be taught traditional subjects by "exploiting those structural analogues that exist across domains customarily thought to be disparate" (Gardner, 1993b, p. 207). Employing a story for the bridging to logical-mathematical learning, the teacher may notice this student doing better with story problems than with math facts/algebra because there is language. This is an inherent structural analogue to word problems.

This was the situation with Manuel, an ADHD middle school student who had a lot going on in his life. A bright, tall, handsome, athletic boy, Manuel had a full social life. However, his parents and teachers reported that Manuel was not achieving at the appropriate level. Manuel had strength in the spatial intelligence and preferred geometry to algebra because geometry, unlike algebra, tapped into his spatial intelligence.

Jim was a small boy with glasses, big blue eyes, and a wide smile with dimples. A fifth grader with ADHD, Jim described himself as a "nerd." Jim's MI profile showed strengths in many areas, but his predominant intelligences were spatial and musical. Talented in piano and saxophone, when asked how he learned to play piano, Jim responded, "One of the most challenging parts in playing music is reading music and music is all about pattern recognition." Patterns are part of the structural analogue to spatial and musical intelligences.

> When you read music, you have to quickly interpret the interval between two notes, simultaneous (chord) or in a series (melody). . . . Regardless, you have to quickly translate into what note you play next and pattern recognition becomes inbred . . . the whole keyboard in piano is laid out spatially in patterns and you translate the pattern sheet music onto the patterns you see on the keyboard.

Just as tastes in music differ from person to person, so do individuals' natural proclivities. "We are not all the same . . . we do not have the same kinds of minds. . . . The heart of the MI perspective . . . [honors] differences among human beings . . . any uniform educational approach is likely to serve only a minority of children" (Gardner, 1995, p. 208). The main result of personalization is that teachers recognize each student's unique profile of intellectual strengths and limitations. This is different from a deficit-centered perspective that identifies weaknesses and subsequently attempts to overcome them directly without considering how other strengths might be usefully employed.

## Education for Understanding

"Schools attempt to cover way too much material, and superficial understandings (or non-understandings) are the inevitable result" (Gardner, 1995, p. 208). Education for understanding directs educational pursuits to the passions of students. Essential reading, writing, and math skills that are necessary to be productive members in society are then honed within selected topics of study.

Sylva (1992) contends that the "long-term effects of early education are mediated by enhanced educational aspiration and motivation, not cognitive skills per se." MIndful curriculum leaders provide a curriculum where students have the opportunity to explore the eight intelligences ensconced in a myriad of disciplines or domains. Once students find success, they are better able to bridge to additional areas and understandings.

Keep in mind that no class requires skill in only one area. In fact, the more forms of intelligence that are brought to class projects and studies, the more enhanced the overall performance and the performance of students with ADHD.

## MIndful Curriculum Leadership

MIndful curriculum leadership encompasses a way of leading toward school improvement by taking into consideration student intelligences as an at-promise phenomenon. Differentiating the curriculum to meet the needs of students has been explored through a variety of pedagogical avenues, and yet curriculum leadership has not inched beyond the accountability features of the prevailing standards-based movement. Normally, these connections have been linked to statewide testing mechanisms, begging the question "Does the school curriculum reflect and embody current state-imposed curriculum standards?" This is essentially backward, failing to take into consideration the student's interest or intelligence.

Henderson and Hawthorne's (1995) notion of a pedagogically centered curriculum practice is defined as having "the primary focus of the curriculum be on the well-being of the child as learner" (p. 53). MIndful curriculum leadership is the practice that takes place in classrooms and is intended to have teachers base their curricular decisions on the intelligences of the child.

The seven paths to MIndful curriculum leadership (Schirduan, Case, & Faryniarz, 2002; Schirduan & Case, 2004) offer practical suggestions regarding how school leaders can be MIndful of student intelligences and use student strengths to promote success.

First, MIndful curriculum leaders can be administrators, teachers, and school coordinators who provide a curriculum rooted in MI theory. MIndful curriculum leadership advocates that curricular attention be paid to the differing cognitive profiles and needs of all students. Imagine a student with strength in the musical intelligence attending a school where the day begins with music. An opportunity to excel is presented to this student for 30 minutes every day. Imagine the impact on the rest of this student's day. Then imagine, if you will, this same student attending a school 5 days a week, 200 days a year, 40 weeks a year, where music is played only once a week.

Second, administrators should examine the ADHD populations and be aware of the bias toward the language-logic profile in schools. Such reflection would foster an understanding and sensitivity toward how students with ADHD best learn, and would honor the predominant intelligences that these students bring to the classroom setting. In this way, administrators have the opportunity to change their own minds about which students present problems as learners or potential discipline problems.

Third, MIndful curriculum leaders honor students' cognitive profiles and aid teachers in becoming MI assessors to describe strengths and limitations. Teachers must examine the connection between the onset of academic problems for students with ADHD and students' profile of intelligence. Are these problems reflective of the misalignment of their profile of intelligences or the characteristics unique to students with ADHD (inattention, impulsivity, and hyperactivity), or a combination of both? Further, educators need to remind students to honor their own intelligences and to use their talents for lifelong learning.

Fourth, MIndful curriculum leaders train teachers to make connections between predominant intelligences and the curriculum to improve learning outcomes. They aid teachers in taking into account students' interests and intelligences. For example, a student with the bodily-kinesthetic intelligence who is having difficulty reading may find success with reading from a domain that is related to his intelligence, such as readings about great athletes or dancers.

Fifth, curriculum connections can be made between what needs to be learned to live responsibly and what will allow students with ADHD to make choices when possible. This is the responsibility of MIndful curriculum leaders. A curricular accent on real-life application is of utmost importance to lifelong learning.

Sixth, MIndful curriculum leaders develop and provide a curriculum that uses a multimodal approach to teaching. Students with ADHD do better in environments where they can pick and choose activities and then explore content using their senses.

Seventh, utilize the assistance of parents and students in assessing intelligences and strengths. Admittedly, students with ADHD can be challenging to reach and teach. School leaders and educators must speak with parents and students, noting abilities and talents, as opposed to opting for remediation.

These seven paths hold fundamental promise for increasing learning. MIndful curriculum leadership practice shouldn't focus on the disability, nor should it serve to remediate and pathologize students with ADHD. Rather, MIndful curriculum leadership focuses on ability, or the student's predominant intelligences, thus illustrating to the school community the promise and contributions that students with ADHD bring with them.

## School Improvement

The identification of at-risk students is easier than determining those students who should be considered at-promise students. Admittedly, underachieving students with ADHD, which is often commingled with LD, are demanding students to teach; therefore, educators must speak with parents and students, noting abilities and areas of difficulty. The placement team (PPT) or parent teacher conferences should focus on ability, or the student's predominant intelligences. Levine believes that students with learning disabilities are not really disabled; their brains are merely wired differently, and it is not helpful to reduce students to a label such as ADHD or LD (Gorrell, 2002).

Gail, an elementary school student, was diagnosed with LD and ADHD. Gail was a challenge to teach. Even her peers found her behavior difficult in the classroom. Her teacher explained that Gail caused Richard, her classmate, to become frustrated because he couldn't grasp that what was easy for him was difficult for her.

> During a logical-mathematical clue finding activity, Richard, a classmate, became frustrated with Gail. Gail was having a difficult time with the activity and he was explaining it over and over: "Can't you see this? Can't you do it? Just mark this one!" Richard got so frustrated with her. I [his teacher] was forced to say, "Some people are stronger in some areas than others. You're going to have to slow down and be more patient." I knew he was strong in logical-mathematical intelligence and that Gail was weak in this area. (Shearer, 1999, pp. 46–47)

Pairing students who have learning strengths with those who have weaknesses may create frustration in the classroom, and obviously needs to be monitored carefully. However, the right pairing can aid in the learning of both students. In one of our samples, approximately half the teachers reported that, although their students with ADHD in MI schools received good grades, they exhibited difficulty with reading and math. This may confirm that an MI curriculum may be more successful in assisting with achievement for students with ADHD. Duane (1988) states that ADHD is not synonymous with LD (p. 6). In fact, in light of MI theory, Dr. Corley, a principal of an MI school, predicts, "[I] will have fewer kids in special ed as time goes on because of our use of multiple intelligences" (Bete, 1997, p. 11).

Jim Fox, a teacher of seventh- and eighth-grade students, explained that all of his students had received "some sort of diagnosis such as LD or ADHD." He shared the description of his classroom.

My students are those who have been beaten up academically. Many are failing nearly every class. Their lowest areas are generally linguistic and logical-mathematical. Their esteem is really low. The number-one objective of the program is to increase the self-esteem of the student, and the MIDAS™ project has been a perfect fit and really helped these kids. The fruit of the MIDAS™ project has been that some of the bewilderment, intimidation, or confusion with who they are has cleared away somewhat. They now have more self-worth than they have been given credit for by the system as well as by themselves. That has been absolutely great for the students in this program.

Building on students' strengths when planning curriculum projects is rewarding for Jim. He states that this works not only for the students with ADHD but "for all of these students, I can see it in their eyes."

I can sense the joy, dignity, and self-respect that emerged as a result of this project. I found it interesting that every student in this class said, "Mr. Fox should do this project again next year" without hesitation. They weren't telling us that to make us happy or win points because they don't care if we're happy or not. . . . You can hear it in their voices that it's made a difference.

An advocate for students and teachers to take time and reflect on their own MIDAS™ profile, Jim contends that "the MIDAS™ profile sensitizes teachers to their own weaknesses and helps them to empathize with their students who are struggling."

It enhances the teacher–student relationship so that each can see the other as "real people." Students don't see the teacher as "unapproachable" or the only "intelligent" person in the classroom. Much of my work with these "at-risk" kids is like re-parenting.

## PROFESSIONAL DEVELOPMENT: WORKSHOPS

Administrative support is crucial for helping teachers overcome different kinds of resistance that may keep them from implementing accommodations that have been demonstrated effective for students with AD/HD. (Beyda & Zentall, 1998, p. 31)

Beyda and Zentall report resistance among teachers to accommodate students with ADHD when accommodations were felt to be beyond their control or when accommodations were thrust upon a teacher. Lack of training and negative reactions to noncompliant behavior were cited factors in the resistance to accommodate students with ADHD.

## Training in ADHD

Our research found that a majority of teachers never received any training in teaching students with ADHD. "Lack of training is the barrier most frequently indicated by elementary school teachers in the process of working with ADHD students" (as cited by Reid et al. in Miranda, Presentacion, & Soriano, 2002, p. 3). Teachers also come with negative preconceived notions regarding students with ADHD and, unfortunately, many students with ADHD have earned their negative reputations. Since many students in class fall somewhere on the inattentive and or hyperactive spectrum, training for teachers would benefit not only students with ADHD, but also those students on the fringe. Knowledge is power. And training in ADHD for teachers should include the *definition of ADHD* (e.g., DSM-IV, primary, secondary, and associated symptoms). Refer to Chapter 1 and Appendix A.

Second, *myths and facts about ADHD* need to be discussed. Because ADHD has been bandied about in both the private and public spheres for such a long time and has been part of our vernacular, myths abound about it. The foremost myth is that medication can cure a student with ADHD. Other myths include that all students with ADHD come from homes where there is no discipline, have behavior problems, are hyperactive, have low IQ scores, will outgrow their disorder, and so on.

Third, *current approaches for ADHD* (e.g., medication, school-based, behavioral, and so forth) should be included. Refer to Chapter 1 for an explanation of approaches.

Finally, a *multimodal approach to working with students with ADHD* seems to be the best tactic. Refer to Chapter 3 for details.

Students with ADHD in our study were asked "How hard is it for you to understand what a teacher expects of you?" Collectively, they responded that "sometimes it's hard." Sometimes, they just don't get it.

To see any progress, teachers need to recognize that ADHD is a legitimate disorder and that students with ADHD perform best in a nonthreatening, safe environment. Students with ADHD often have outgoing personalities. They have high intelligence and are original thinkers. Despite their high activity levels, they are curious and have the ability to be still and hyperfocus. Such traits can be harnessed with the right strategies and utilized to aid these students in their own learning.

## Constructive Discipline for ADHD Students

Many behavior problems can be directly linked to poor self-image. Teachers can be of vital importance in maximizing not only academic learning, but also self-esteem in students with ADHD (Murphy & Johnson, as cited in Purvis, Jones, & Authement, 1992, p. 113). The students with ADHD in our study lacked self-esteem and self-reported that they had low personal intelligences. They exhibited limited self-understanding and were not able to relate to others. Students with ADHD have difficulty with peer relations. Hence, early interventions such as social skills classes may deter poor peer relations. An intervention of this nature has the potential to improve the school experience for both students with ADHD *and* their peers.

Sydney, a middle school student with ADHD, is a tall boy. He was held back in the second grade and appears older than many of his peers. In fact, he is the same height as many of his teachers. Sydney described to us how he typically would disrupt his and his peers' learning in the classroom.

> So the teacher comes up to me . . . and asks a question, like "What's 9 × 9?" And I say, "What's 9 × 9? You don't know? Why you asking me? You're the teacher . . . we're paying you to know answers to questions. . . . You don't know answers to questions. You're coming to the kids, what are you out of your mind?" Like a rabid dog. It was just best to leave me alone . . . but now how does that teacher see me? The teacher sees me as a troublemaker. . . . So how do I see myself? As a trouble maker. . . . I'm a walking attitude that's not really a good thing.

A key to resolving behavior problems is to understand and describe possible underlying motivations for the rule-breaking behaviors. Behavior problems are often the result of a student "acting out" emotional conflicts, social difficulties, learning impairments, or family troubles. Additionally, anxiety and boredom in school are causes for misbehavior that can be addressed by better matching curricular tasks to students' abilities.

Class rules and logical consistent consequences are the foundations of good classroom management. When teachers accentuate the importance of personal intelligences, the rationale behind the rules becomes visible, with the consequences becoming naturally motivating. Sandra is an elementary teacher who accentuates the importance of personal intelligences in her classroom through this instructional strategy. She employs a responsive classroom game called "Pretzels." Its creator, Ruth Sidney Charney, describes the strategy as "a weekly activity that allows the exchange of compliments and criticism among the students in your class [which] can help resolve conflicts and teach children how to properly handle conflict" (1997, paragraph one). Sandra advises,

> Give positive and negative feedback in a quiet, respectful way. Receiving messages from their classmates in this way, helps these boys [with ADHD] to re-focus and receive some negative messages about how they are affecting others. It also gives them positive feedback in the same way. It gives them a way to share their feelings about how others are treating them—both with positive words and negatives.

Reflecting on the MI profile of an entire class allows a teacher to be alerted to a special need that the group as a whole has for instruction in the interpersonal (empathy, respect, conflict management) or intrapersonal (self-control, personal discipline, goal setting, and emotional regulation) intelligences. For specific individuals, the MI profile can be reviewed with the student in an effort to identify strengths that can be valued and directed in a constructive way. For many students, problematic behaviors may only be evidenced in certain situations and settings. The reason for behavioral difficulty in different contexts may be revealed in stories that students tell regarding their profile. The teacher's verbal acknowledgment of the student's strengths may serve to minimize unacceptable behavior. Once again, a "strengths versus deficits" approach should be employed rather than a direct attack on "the problem" without regard for student strengths.

An approach adopted by Tom, an assistant principal at a middle school, involved previewing a student's MI profile. Prior to talking with the student, teacher, or parent following a behavior problem referral, Tom would read the reflections on the student's profile. He would begin the meeting with an initial discussion of the child's interests and activities related to his MI strengths. This approach accomplished two goals. Rapport was established, and the creative use of the child's strengths was undertaken in partnership to help alleviate the "problem" behavior. This approach provides for a balanced intervention by bringing in and capitalizing on positive behaviors. This is important for ADHD students (and their parents), who receive a higher share of negative attention and limited positive support from teachers and administrators.

Elliot, a school administrator, employs a long-range approach when discussing behavioral issues with a teacher who may get frustrated with a particular student. Elliot explained that he tells the teacher, "Let's *not* focus on the moment. Let's look back 3 months, 6 months, last year. Now tell me, has that student made improvements in his/her behavior? *Yes*, we still have work to do, and *yes*, we'll continue to do that work as a team together. . . . We strive to create a culture in our school that we are not here to blame the kids."

A strong relationship exists between grades and behavior. Steve, an adult with ADHD to whom we spoke, looked back on his school experience: "I tried to fit in and compete academically for 8 years. All I could get was a D average. By the time I got to high school, I couldn't take it anymore."

> My self-esteem couldn't take it anymore. I tried to study, but I just didn't get it. My ego was taking a beating every time they would pass the test back down the line with my grade stamped in a big red letter "D" and everyone got to see it. So I decided to compete in something else. Class clown and troublemaker. If the teacher called on me, I made jokes or would argue. This way, my self-esteem was intact because my identity wasn't student, it was school hood. In high school, I rode my motorcycle right through the front door of the school and right down the main hall and right into jail, all on the idea that finals were coming next week. You see, if I could have competed academically, I would have. I just didn't have any idea how.

Steve, an inspirational speaker on ADD/ADHD and founder of the Results Project, has come full circle. By invitation, he freely walks the halls of high schools, including the one from which he was once expelled—inspiring all students who have felt stigmatized by labels.

When the intelligence profile of a student with ADHD is assessed, then strategies such as those offered in this book can help address strengths and weaknesses in an effort to curb student frustration. This aids in circumventing the student's acting out or behavior problems. As Levine maintains, "While learning represents a major challenge for all kids, it does not compare to the social aspects of school in terms of its potential to create unhappiness and maladjustment among students" (Levine, 2003, paragraph one).

Discipline problems can stem from the characteristics of ADHD and the student's learning and working styles and MI cognitive profile. For example, students with ADHD may be aural learners and may appear to be inattentive. Although their eyes may not be on the teacher while directions are imparted, the students may, in fact, be listening. Similarly, the student with ADHD who cannot sit still is informing you about the need to move while learning. An environment that is established to circumvent potential discipline problems can be created to meet the needs of students with ADHD. The danger with traditional classroom management techniques is that, for ADHD students, it can create a cycle of negativity that spirals downward. When working with ADHD students, teachers and administrators may simply "react" to the problems with criticism and slip relentlessly into "fix-it" mode, hammering away at the students' self-esteem. These negative interactions, although well intentioned, can exacerbate the problems.

George Ann, a teacher who demonstrates respect, care, and a sense of commitment, relayed her predicament with an ADHD student: "He said he was aware that he was breaking rules in class, but simply could not control himself." Medication was the tactic this boy's parents chose.

Becky's advice as a newcomer to the field of education shows how a teacher can discipline in a way that matches the MI strengths of ADHD students. A multiple intelligences–inspired perspective can help, and some MI activities can be used as incentives. She uses her student, Ron, as an example.

> He gets "happy," "OK," and "sad" faces for the following actions: I did my work, I was quiet, I stayed in my seat, and I did not distract my friends. Since he has the interpersonal and spatial intelligences, I try and match his interests with his strengths. And it seems to work. He chooses from the following rewards if he achieves three out of four happy faces: computer (spatial activity—he loves the computer and wants to be on it all the time), lunch with me (interpersonal), visit with a teacher (interpersonal).

A way to improve school climate is to manage behavior problems in students with ADHD via MI. Armstrong (1994) suggests to "select behavioral strategies that match the most-developed intelligences" (p. 106). To avoid difficult behavior, it may help to ask the student with ADHD who, for example, is strong in the logical-mathematical intelligence to sequence or outline expected behaviors prior to a proposed assignment. This tactic helps refocus the ADHD student and aids in circumventing off-task behavior.

The following activities are suggested for teachers to use with students with ADHD following a behavior problem. They provide alternatives to having the student sit quietly for time out or wait outside the principal's office. Removing recess and heatedly debating with the ADHD student are not recommended.

### Constructive Discipline for the Student with Strength in Logical-Mathematical Intelligence

- Graph (e.g., pie charts, bar graphs) the number of "time outs" over the past week or month.
- Chart the types of behavior that the teacher has had to redirect or reprimand. For example, were you distracted (e.g., "Johnny, you can draw whatever you choose after you have completed the drawing of a cat for the assignment), inattentive (e.g., Suzie, eyes on the board), or hyperactive (e.g., T. J., return to your seat)?

- Sequence or outline what behavior should have been exhibited at the time of the reprimand or off-task behavior.
- Compare and contrast behavior over time.
- The student asks and answers Socratic questions. For example, "What if" I had followed directions? "What if" I had completed the project on time?
- Identify and explain why classroom rules exist.
- Tell a story about what would happen if there were no rules.

Students with ADHD were surveyed regarding the question "Is it difficult for you to solve a problem with a friend, brother, or sister without having a big argument?" They were also asked "Is it difficult to keep your feelings and temper under control?" Collectively, they responded that it was difficult, indicating that they were self-aware regarding their impulsivity and interpersonal challenges. Lizzy, an administrator in an MI school, views discipline as a means of *honing problem-solving skills* to address larger issues: "It's not just about discipline; it's about creating strong relationships with students and assisting them to solve the problems."

### Constructive Discipline for the Student with ADHD and Strength in Musical Intelligence

- Compose music that will help change the behavior (e.g., calm down, refocus, energize you to do your work). Then listen to this tape the next time you are reprimanded or redirected.
- Recite a chant or mantra for a few minutes to help you get back on track.
- Create a rap, rhythm, or song about the appropriate, on-task behavior that should have been displayed.

### Constructive Discipline for the Student with ADHD and Strength in Bodily-Kinesthetic Intelligence

- Role-play what would be expected in class, as opposed to what transpired in class.
- Determine ways to release physical energy within the classroom as a preventative measure next time (e.g., playing with koosh ball, having two desks to move back and forth between, running an errand for the teacher, sharpening a pencil).

A simple solution suggested by Glen, an administrator we interviewed regarding discipline, was the "walk around."

We do not have a room for discipline referrals. We have found that walking and talking with a student who has been referred to us for a discipline problem helps to calm him or her down. Sometimes we just walk and walk until that barrier is broken. Some kids just need a break, and the physical activity helps.

### Constructive Discipline for the Student with Strength in Spatial Intelligence

- Conjure up mental images of the appropriate behavior that should have transpired.

- Use visualization to calm yourself in situations that you know may cause off-task behavior.
- Take pictures of classmates who exhibit the appropriate behavior that was expected of you.
- Draw a picture of yourself exhibiting the on-task behavior.
- Create a visual display of classroom rules.
- Rearrange the room or your seat to increase the likelihood of on-task behavior.
- Make a video of classroom expectations. Enlist classmates for assistance.
- Sculpt a figure to be placed in the room (e.g., desk) as a reminder to stay on-task or of what the teacher expects of you.

### Constructive Discipline for the Student with Strength in Naturalist Intelligence

- Observe someone whom you or your teacher deems a "role model" in class and note his or her behaviors.
- Identify or recognize patterns in your behavior.
- Research inappropriate behavior patterns in animals and how the animal's group responds (e.g., rejects animal from group, aggression, establishing hierarchy).
- Identify what makes plants survive and thrive, and make analogies to what behaviors are needed to be successful in class.
- Go outside the classroom with a timer, take a breath, and examine your surroundings. Recompose yourself by the time the alarm goes off and return to the classroom.

### Constructive Discipline for the Student with Strength in Interpersonal Intelligence

- Request to be a peer mediator during conflicts and find resolutions to classmates' and your own off-task behavior.
- Be a discussant leader and lead a group discussion about expected classroom behavior and the reasons behind classroom rules.
- Brainstorm solutions to your problem that arose in class, and present hypothetical solutions to problems that may arise in class.
- Interview classmates for feedback and advice on your off-task behavior.
- Empathize with the teacher and imagine what you would do to reprimand a student for this particular behavior.

For the student with ADHD and the interpersonal intelligence or the linguistic intelligence, the following technique supplied by Alfonse may prove helpful. Alfonse is a political science major who hopes to become a lawyer. He believes that the school conflicts he resolves will better prepare him for his profession. He clarifies that "As a discipline coach, I cannot emphasize enough the importance of listening to a student when a discipline problem arises." He advises teachers to "Listen, listen, listen. Listen to what they have to say. Listen to the lies, if that's the case. Listen to the tales. Listen until the child is done talking."

After listening to the student and reflecting, Alfonse redirects the conversation back to the student by saying, "We are talking about you; let's get back to talking about you. We talk about choices and consequences. I never talk down to any student. I never yell at any student. I truly believe this builds our relationship and establishes trust."

Being a discipline coach to younger students, Alfonse makes it clear that misbehavior becomes more troublesome as students proceed through the grade levels. He says, "When the younger students have discipline problems, we discuss that 'Everybody makes mistakes and how we resolve them.' Some of these students I've known for many years. And I tell the ones in fifth grade that are headed to middle school, that if they act this way in middle school, the person in charge of discipline is not going to be someone who knows you like I do. They are going to look at the behavior and not you, the student. And they will assume you are this and this [bad]."

### Constructive Discipline for the Student with Strength in Linguistic Intelligence

- Use language and words in an essay, poem, or short story to reflect on the situation and suggest a solution.
- Take dictation of classmates' stories as to how his or her behavior impacted them.
- Write an alternative ending to how the conflict might have been resolved.

Providing students with the power to make their own choices when faced with a disciplinary consequence is something that Joey, a principal, suggested: "I remember one [ADHD] student was referred to me because he would not do his reading test. He was mad."

He came to my office and asked, "How long am I going to have to sit here?" I told him, "You decide. You can sit here for a few minutes or the rest of your life." I told him, "You are going to sit here until it is finished." I don't talk down to them. I give them the straight talk. I give them choices and I am consistent. I always lay out their choices and it takes as long as it takes.

### Constructive Discipline for the Student with Strength in Intrapersonal Intelligence

- Think about how the problem could have been solved before it led to the consequence (e.g., time out).
- Journal or write about the expected behavior and the impact it had on you personally, on the teacher, and on classmates.
- Reflect on classroom expectations and how you can prepare yourself to meet them.
- Set a personal goal to improve off-task behavior.

Students with ADHD can frustrate teachers, causing them to confront the situation with anger. The vital advice above suggests that teachers "use classroom management techniques before you become irritated, impatient or upset. We are much more powerful when we are centered, when we like our students, and when we view our students with fondness rather than impatience" (California Nurses Association, 1988). You might find it hard to "like" your ADHD student, but if you keep in mind their MI strengths, then it may be easier to "like" this particular aspect. This appreciation will make it easier to maintain your composure and respond constructively to any misbehaviors.

## Raising Test Scores via MI

The demands placed on teachers for student improvement on standardized tests cannot be ignored. This has been emphasized in part due to the impact of No Child Left Behind (NCLB) legislation. Mack, a school administrator who stands 6 feet, 4 inches tall, made his convictions regarding MI clear.

> We are an MI school. When they passed the NCLB, we were forced to look at achievement. We are still accountable. We have found that our students do as well or better than their home districts, whether they are from an urban or suburban setting. We do feel MI integration is the right way to go.

From his experience, Mack suggests that MI serves as an avenue to raise test scores, parent participation, and hope for students with ADHD. According to more than 35 schools using MI (Project SUMIT), principals and administrators indicated that MI "is regarded as the prominent influence in improved test scores, improved discipline, improved parent participation, and improvements with learning disabilities" (1999, Project ZERO Outcomes, paragraph 1).

ADHD students have unique problems attaining good grades and bridging weaknesses to strengths. There are three general ways in which students can improve test scores as a result of using the multiple intelligences. First, developing intrapersonal intelligence can aid student pacing and monitoring responses to test questions. Students who are adept at intrapersonal intelligence tend to be self-directed and goal-oriented learners who can use MI strengths as study strategies to prepare for tests. Second, students should be taught test-taking skills, ranging from test-taking logic to pre- and posttest considerations to item choice. Third, general strategies can help the student, such as getting a good night's sleep and eating a good breakfast on the day of the test.

Gardner's goal is for assessment to be conducted in an "intelligence fair" (e.g., to match strengths) or authentic manner. Tests and other methods of evaluation should be conducted in situations that are identical to, or closely aligned with, the evaluated activity, whenever possible. A written multiple-choice test would not be a fair method of assessing interpersonal skill. A similar goal is to provide options other than short answers to short questions to demonstrate learning. Two students may possess an equal understanding of the information, but slower readers may not be able to perform well, despite the accumulated knowledge, perhaps because of a lack of processing time. The spatially strong student may demonstrate understanding by drawing, charting, or creating photo collages. Allow students to demonstrate knowledge via their strengths. For example, the student with ADHD and strength in spatial intelligence can show his or her understanding of a story by representing the main idea through drawing. Student knowledge can be assessed in other ways besides pen-and-paper measures (e.g., multiple-choice, short-answer).

According to Hebert (1992), "the main thrust of Gardner's theory as applied to schools is that children may demonstrate different kinds of intelligences in ways not necessarily associated with traditional school subjects and certainly not associated with traditional modes of assessment" (p. 59). To maximize achievement, teachers need to instruct students with ADHD on how to employ other intelligences for enhancing memorization, verbal responses, and logical reasoning.

MI-inspired strategies for *managing test anxiety* can be an important component of an intrapersonal curriculum. Implementing specific strategies tailored to the MI strengths of students with ADHD can alleviate test anxiety or be used as a preventative measure.

### Managing Test Anxiety via MI
- *Musical intelligence*: Help students recall songs that are calming, enhance focusing, and are energizing.
- *Bodily-kinesthetic intelligence*: Have students relax by squeezing a koosh ball. Teach them deep breathing exercises. Choose a chair and desk or table that fits their body type and size. Prior to the test, discuss ways to release excess energy (e.g., Move N Sit Wedge® seat cushions, use of two desks to move back and forth between, walk to get a drink of water).
- *Linguistic intelligence*: Encourage students to memorize positive, self-confidence-enhancing affirmations. Request that they read directions carefully.
- *Spatial intelligence*: Help students employ visualization exercises for successful test taking. Choose a location for students with minimal distractions and good lighting.
- *Naturalist intelligence*: Have students situate themselves near a window so that they can momentarily collect their thoughts by gazing outside. Help them organize materials and observe patterns in the test items (format, sequence, style).
- *Intrapersonal intelligence*: Tell students to expect anxiety, but to approach testing with self-assurance. Teach them to talk themselves through the test.
- *Interpersonal intelligence*: Warn students that they shouldn't discuss test anxiety with other anxious students. Have students discuss positive aspects of pretesting techniques (e.g., developed study guides, test preparation strategies, MI strategies).
- *Logical-mathematical intelligence*: Have students glance at the test prior to starting so that strategies can be allocated for particular questions, such as the sequence of problems to be tackled first and time allocation. Have students answer the questions they understand first.

Refer to Chapter 3 for general and specific strategies on how to overcome learning obstacles.

## Strengthening Schools by Strengthening Personal Intelligences

A lack of self-awareness combined with interpersonal difficulties can cause students with ADHD to be rejected by teachers and peers. MIndful teachers work to ensure proper social skills among all of their students. Savannah, a passionate fourth-grade teacher, taught social skills to her class, but was especially pleased with Dotty, a girl with ADHD who, unlike most of her counterparts with ADHD, had strengths in the interpersonal and intrapersonal intelligences. Savannah described Dotty as being "great at conflict resolution, a skill she learned last year."

> She asked to be the mediator to resolve issues between classmates. For example, she will sit between two students who are not getting along. She will listen to one person's story. Then she will paraphrase that person's issue and say something like, "So what you mean is. . . ." She will continue in this manner until she brings forth a resolution between the two students who are not getting along. She is a great problem solver!

Using the talents of the student with ADHD can help not only the teacher, but also the class as a whole. Abigail, a resourceful second-grade teacher who manages to successfully connect learning to students strengths, spoke to this tenet when she described Jeremy, a student with ADHD:

> Math is not Jeremy's strong suit. So I use his bodily-kinesthetic strength to help him. For example, he likes to "act out" math concepts. So I would put a multiplication table with a square on the floor. He would have to walk around once to demonstrate 4 × 1, walk around twice to show 4 × 2, etc. Jeremy struggled in math. He was a smart boy and liked to work problems out on his own. But because his strength was the interpersonal (and intrapersonal) intelligence, even though he wanted to do it on his own, he had the foresight to know that he needed help. He was very insightful like that.

Victor, a seventh-grade student with ADHD, lacked Jeremy's insight. Penelope, the assistant principal, went to great length to see that Victor's learning needs were understood and met instructionally.

> Victor's strengths were in the linguistic and bodily-kinesthetic intelligences. His weaknesses were the interpersonal and intrapersonal intelligences. One day he was out at recess playing basketball with his classmates. He had the ball and, as it happens in basketball, other kids attempted to get the ball and they grabbed for it. One kid grabbed his shirt and Victor lunged for the next person that passed by, which happened to be an innocent bystander!

Penelope tried employing a behavior modification plan that involved issuing tickets for good behavior to earn prizes. This failed to work for Victor. "Finally," Penelope continued, "we were able to get him a paraprofessional to assist him throughout the day." This paraprofessional was used to prevent Victor's frequent suspensions from school. Penelope justified this through his individualized education plan (IEP). As she explained, she used the metaphor, "Jiminy Cricket":

> The para was Victor's "Jiminy Cricket" and would figuratively sit on his shoulder, helping him to make the right choices. He hasn't been in the office, except once this year, and he was horrified when he did have to come. His behavior plan includes having one of the teachers at recess duty observe him, especially in situations that we know that are tough for him—like basketball games.

In one of our studies on MI and ADHD, we found that only two of the 76 participants had strength in the intrapersonal intelligence (reflects deeply). Lack of interpersonal intelligence (thinks by discussion and interaction with others) closely followed. Therefore, teaching a student with ADHD social skills is vitally important to his or her future, both inside and outside the classroom.

Students with ADHD need to be taught how to "read" another person, to grasp social cues that most classmates take for granted. They need direct instruction on how to make a friend and be a friend, how to resolve problems amiably, and when to stop talking. They also need to learn self-awareness and how to identify their strengths and weakness in order to circumvent problems. For many students with ADHD, their social development may lag behind their chronological age. They miss cues and can misinterpret situations. Such students will truly be handicapped unless MIndful teachers address social, nonacademic problems. The development of intrapersonal and interpersonal skills should be an explicit component of the ADHD student's education. This was the situation for Maurice, whose teacher described her school and classroom philosophy:

> Our school goal is to create a culture of respect. We have a discipline policy in place that uses choices . . . along with other approaches when an incident with behavior occurs. We lay out the scenarios regarding the choices of the student.

She adds, "Of course, there are consequences for poor choices."

Cyndi explained that Maurice, a boy with ADHD, had an "impetuous nature. He would hit others at what appeared to be the slightest provocation—if someone took his pencil, if he wanted what someone else had at [learning] centers. He had poor interpersonal and intrapersonal skills."

> One day, he was at recess and he hit someone. The reason he gave was "but I wanted to play with him." So, at our school, we lay out their choices. Do you want, for example, friendship, which we (teachers) can help you with if you approach us for assistance? Or do you want to get suspended and removed from class? The student makes the decision regarding which personal action will create his or her desired result.

The student with ADHD, who lacks a natural proclivity with interpersonal intelligence needs direct instruction regarding how to understand classmates and make distinctions between different personality types. Teachable moments can be used to instill empathy in ADHD students. Jeremiah had difficulty appreciating classmates' perspectives and displaying sensitivity to the motives, moods, and intentions of others.

Jeremiah was a fifth grader with ADHD who had difficulty relating to peers. His director Marsha, a coworker of Penelope's, explained, "If a classmate stares at Jeremiah too long [misinterpretation of classmates' intention], it sets him off. This is what happened one day during math class. Since I'm the first person called for a discipline problem, the teacher asked that I intervene."

> Jeremiah began to make a scene, started kicking and yelling. At this point, I remind him of his choices. "We can turn this around right now. You do

not have a suspension yet—but I see that this is turning ugly. It's your decision. I can restrain you and take you away or we can walk away together and talk about it."

Jeremiah made the choice to calm himself and walk with me. We—the teachers, myself, administrators—act as a team and try and stay ahead of the game with our goal being that Jeremiah tells us he needs a break before one is forced upon him.

Some students with ADHD need guidance in order to help them interact effectively with classmates. The following are ways to help students with ADHD build interpersonal intelligence.

### Strengthening the Interpersonal Intelligences
- Provide "role-taking" opportunities.
- Teach conflict resolution strategies.
- Rotate classroom leadership duties.
- Have students identify the feelings and opinions of others.
- Practice "listening for understanding" without giving opinion.
- Arrange community service activities.
- Investigate "leaders."
- Connect students to role models in the community.
- Explain the ways etiquette and manners facilitate community.

If the student with ADHD lacks self-awareness, a plan may be needed to aid him or her in identifying strengths and weaknesses. A student with ADHD who is weak in intrapersonal intelligence may have difficulty making decisions, initiating, and self-pacing during class projects. Direct instruction regarding reflection, monitoring of thoughts and feelings, and self-regulation may be a prerequisite to their attaining personal and class goals. The following are ways to help students with ADHD build intrapersonal intelligence.

### Strengthening the Intrapersonal Intelligences
- Provide self-assessment opportunities.
- Provide accurate feedback on skills and behavior.
- Schedule reflection "think time" . . . pre-, parallel, and post-reflective thought.
- Provide affirmation for feelings and opinions.
- Recognize past and current knowledge, abilities, and experiences.
- Facilitate realistic peer feedback.
- Promote a dialogue of discovery to be enacted between the teacher and student.
- Connect the student to appropriate role models in the community.
- Promote specific "goal-setting" and monitoring skills.

## Staff Development Toward an MI-Inspired School

Three basic steps may foster a professional staff development program in the creation of an MI-inspired school. Too often, schools attempt to move directly from initial MI awareness to classroom integration. The rush to implementation can result in short-lived changes and a residual cynicism regarding educational innovations. To make a genuine and successful transition to an MI-inspired curriculum, the faculty must not only comprehend but also accept the validity of MI theory and understand its practical utility.

Schools must move through several stages in the transition from an IQ-based philosophy to the adoption of an MI-inspired perspective. The first stage is awareness of MI and its implications for everyday problem solving and life in general. The second stage is acceptance. This occurs when the staff comprehends and believes MI to be a worthwhile and valuable contribution to education. The third stage is the progressive, yet active integration of MI-inspired activities in the classroom and throughout the school structure. This can be an ongoing and evolving endeavor where the school makes efforts to connect the curriculum directly to important community roles.

Among a diverse faculty there will be teachers who are operating at all levels of MI implementation and successful ADHD management. However, there is also a general level of MI readiness for a school as a whole.

**Raising Awareness of MI and ADHD.** A majority of teachers has at least heard the term *multiple intelligences*, but their understanding may be vague, misconstrued, or simplistic. The same is true for ADHD. Many teachers still assume that all children must be hyperactive in order to be identified as ADHD.

The first goal in raising awareness of MI and ADHD is to provide teachers with recent research that accurately describes the eight multiple intelligences and the cognitive and behavioral manifestations of ADHD in the classroom. There are any number of strategies for doing this that are interesting and interactive, such as role-playing, self-assessments, debates, panel discussions, videos, and so forth. Refer to Chapters 1 and 3.

If the MI transition is to move beyond the "talking stage," teacher issues regarding MI acceptance will need to be addressed.

**Acceptance of MI and ADHD.** It is one thing to know about the eight intelligences, but it is a completely different matter to accept these intelligences as legitimate and valuable. The same is true for ADHD. A (sometimes) silent, yet powerful, lack of acceptance can undermine changes to the curriculum and instructional practice. A small number of schools is fortunate enough to have teachers who have self-selected to teach in an MI-inspired school. For most schools, however, patience and persistent efforts to nurture teachers who are slow to change must be undertaken.

Generating an in-depth understanding of MI theory by teachers as well as students is the first step in the MI evolution. Teachers not only need to recognize that MI exists and that many other teachers enthusiastically embrace it, but they also need to have personal experience with its benefits. One of the most powerful experiences available is to ascertain how the use of MI influences students with ADHD. Additionally, when teachers review their own MI profile in light of personal life experiences as well as their teaching propensities, it can have a profound effect on their acceptance of the validity of MI. As one teacher explained, sharing his MI profile with his students was worthwhile: "It was good for them to see that there were many areas where I didn't do well. I think they see me more as a real person now. I see my students differently, more as real people, too . . ." (Shearer, 2004, p. 156).

**Integration of MI School and Community.** This step involves the implementation of a wide range of possible activities and approaches to curriculum, instruction, and school design. The goal of MI integration is to create a niche in the school's curriculum where MI-inspired activities can be integrated into the intellectual life of the total school. Schools are complex entities that exist in constant flux, so how a school decides to integrate MI into the fabric of each day is dependent upon decisions, and resource allocations will be unique.

It is important to provide teachers with time to discuss and reflect on an MI-inspired curriculum. Some teachers with whom the authors worked at the initial stages of implementing an MI curriculum said, "I think using MI will be a better technique of teaching reading. I want students to know themselves better so they can help themselves to deal with their reading/math problems." Another supportive teacher shared, "I used it as a complement to the existing curriculum to design new methodology and activities." One teacher remarked, "The MI approach gives the kids the chance to tap into their souls. It gives them a way to connect to their shining human potential, their strength that will unlock their potential development" (Shearer, 2004, p. 157).

MI-inspired lesson planning and a project-based curriculum represent popular approaches to implementing MI in the classroom. However, they pose particular problems for ADHD students because they require high-level self-monitoring, complex task management, and persistence and task completion. MI projects also provide opportunities for ADHD students to mobilize particular strengths through the in-depth investigation of a topic. Teachers need to be MIndful that ADHD students' deficiencies in self-regulation and task management skills may limit success on long-term, complex projects, particularly if such projects are not well structured.

The objective of an MI-inspired education is for classroom-learning activities to be closely linked to authentic, community-based adult roles. When an ADHD student's MI strengths are linked explicitly with a valued adult role or career, students who struggle with academic tasks will gain self-worth. Service learning projects provide a powerful bridge from the classroom to the community while also helping students build a sense of personal worth. ADHD students gain self-awareness and self-esteem when they are "helping," as opposed to always being "helped" on the receiving line because of academic and disciplinary problems.

## SCHOOLS IMPLEMENTING MI

Mindy Kornhaber, an MI expert states, "a school using MI may be one influenced by the theory, drawing also, and perhaps equally on many other ideas, e.g., constructivist learning, arts-integrated curriculum, which are complementary to the theory, but not necessarily driven by it" (personal communication, February 13, 1999). There is no right way to implement MI theory into a school building. However, as Linda Pfiffner (1995) states, "A first step in helping an ADHD child achieve educational success is to choose the right school" (p. 207). She goes on to say, "as with all children, academic tasks should be well matched to the child's abilities" (p. 216). The following examples of schools and projects that foster MI learning may offer insights.

### Schools in the United States

Project Spectrum, Arts PROPEL, Practical Intelligence for Schools (PIFS), Project ATLAS (Authentic Teaching, Learning, and Assessment for all Students), and Project SUMIT (Schools Using Multiple Intelligence Theory) are some of the successful research projects at Project Zero that were studied and that offer a historical or contextual frame of reference since Howard Gardner developed MI theory in 1983.

Project Spectrum "offers an alternative approach to assessment and curriculum development for the preschool and early primary years" (Project Spectrum, 1998, paragraph one). From 1984 to 1988, Project Spectrum investigated the possibility of ascertaining children's predominant intelligence at a young age. From 1988 to 1993, Spectrum researchers worked with children in grades K–2 in Somerville and Roxbury, Massachusetts. One goal of Project Spectrum was to "blur the traditional line between curriculum and assessment thus enabling students to be assessed in a natural, familiar, and nonthreatening contexts" (Blythe & Gardner, 1990, p. 34).

Arts PROPEL was a research project between Project Zero and the Educational Testing Service and the Pittsburgh Public School System. During this project, "middle school arts teachers organized their [curricula] around major student projects that emphasize both process and product" (Campbell & Campbell, 1997, p. 14). For example, "Students may work on portraiture for several weeks, learn how to work with different media, study portraits of recognized artists, and, ultimately, create, display, and reflect upon a final work, using all the principles and skills they have acquired" (Campbell & Campbell, 1997, p. 14).

PIFS was developed with the assistance of Robert Sternberg at Yale University. It consisted of "metacurricular units that can be infused into the curriculum typically taught in middle school classes" (Blythe & Gardner, 1990, p. 34). From an MI standpoint, students were instructed to draw upon their strengths as they probed for answers.

Howard Gardner, Theodore Sizer, James Comer, and the Educational Development Center in Project ATLAS joined forces and ideas and developed a model of the ideal school. Eight hundred schools under the Project ATLAS title (*Authentic Teaching, Learning, and Assessment for all Students*) served to "meld the ideas and structures of four organizations—Coalition of Essential Schools, Comer's School Development Program, the Development Group at Project Zero, and the Education Development Center . . . a huge curricular and instructional development place near Boston" (Lockwood, 1993, p. 100).

A research project at Harvard's Project Zero, Project SUMIT (*Schools Using Multiple Intelligences Theory*) investigated "ideal" schools using MI theory. Its purpose was to "identify, document, and promote effective implementations of MI. These were applications of the theory that teachers and principals associated with increases in student achievement, test scores, quality of student work, attendance, behavior, and/or parent participation" (1999, Project Zero, paragraph 3). Project SUMIT identified 40 schools using MI theory through a set of practices referred to as "Compass Points." These are routes that educators using the theory have taken and that appear to benefit students. The six Compass Points that were generated were:

- *Culture: Support for diverse learners and hard work.* Acting on a value system, which maintains that diverse students can learn and succeed, that learning is exciting, and that hard work by teachers is necessary.
- *Readiness: Awareness building for using MI.* Building staff awareness of MI and of the different ways that students learn.
- *Tool: MI is a means to foster high-quality work.* Using MI as a tool to promote high-quality student work rather than using the theory as an end in and of itself.
- *Collaboration: Informal and formal exchanges.* Sharing ideas and constructive suggestions by the staff in formal and informal exchanges.
- *Choice: Meaningful curriculum and assessment options.* Embedding curriculum and assessment in activities that are valued both by students and the wider culture.
- *Arts:* Employing the arts to develop children's skills and understanding within and across disciplines. (1999, Project SUMIT)

Harvard's Project Zero embarked upon a number of movements in educational reform that were rooted in cognitive understanding, and yet, as Smagorinsky (1996) suggests, students are concerned with grades and being prepared for the next class or for college. Hence, student performance hinges upon traditional methods of assessment unless the general rubric as we now know it changes.

## School Abroad

Gordon Dryden, coauthor of *The Learning Revolution*, suggested that the characteristics of the best schools for students with ADHD might be found in "a large K–12 international one, in Singapore: the Overseas Family School. It has more than 3,000 students from over 60 nationalities. To the best of my knowledge, not one case of what many Americans call 'attention deficit syndrome' has been presented. The reason's not hard to find: the students seem never to be bored."

> At the elementary school, the IB PYM [International Baccalaureate Primary Years Program] revolves around 6- or 7-week global themes a year: planets of the universe, endangered species, minerals of the world, and all the other building blocks of global knowledge. All other "subjects," such as math, language, and art, are woven into each global theme.
>
> Teachers are all thoroughly trained in concepts such as Howard Gardner's theory of multiple intelligences, Bloom's Taxonomy, and many others. The school is also a world model for how to use interactive and co-creative digital technology as part of the exploration process. Instead of their traditional role as students, classmates are more like multimedia journalists, using the world's best new digital technology both to use the world as their classroom and to report back their findings. This often means working together in multitalented teams, where each member not only contributes his or her own specialty but also learns from the talents of others. Children use their own natural talents to script, shoot, and edit video, and to add graphics, animations, and music that they have often composed themselves. And they easily absorb the talents of others.
>
> Strangely enough, in producing 22 television programs on the world's best learning and teaching methods, and the world's best schools, I can't recall ever running across any student with attention deficit syndrome.

Perhaps it's a label teachers (and doctors) place on kids whose learning style differs from their teachers' teaching styles.

Change is rarely easy, and institutional change is especially difficult for tradition-rich organizations such as schools. Nonetheless, instead of requiring students to conform to the demands of individual schools, a promising educational reform begins with teachers who are willing to respond to the strengths of individual students. Schools are "responsible for helping all students discover and develop their talents or strengths. In doing this, the school not only awakens children's joy in learning but also fuels the persistence and effort necessary for mastering skills and information" (Campbell & Campbell, 1997, p. 14). Schools have a tenuous grip on how students with ADHD learn best. Perhaps MI theory and curricular adaptations could aid such students in living a richer intellectual life by promoting academic self-esteem and laying the groundwork for lifelong learning.

# School–Home Partnerships

> "He's *not* dumb!" (emphatically said to a teacher by
> the mother of Aaron, a fourth-grade boy with ADHD).

CHAPTER 5 EXAMINES THE PARTNERING of schools and parents. Philosophical, theoretical, and practical suggestions for what teachers, students, and parents can do to increase learning outcomes of students with ADHD are discussed. A multimodal team approach to working with students with ADHD is described.

Parents are a child's first teachers; schoolteachers provide backup and concrete skills. Both parties struggle with the high demands of educating the ADHD student while contending with the primary (inattention, impulsivity, and/or hyperactivity) and secondary (low self-esteem, poor grades) characteristics of students with ADHD. Their partnership is essential to ensure a successful outcome.

## TEACHERS, PARENTS, AND ADHD STUDENTS WORKING TOGETHER

The 1990s ushered in a wealth of information on how educators should work with families. Such reform stressed collaboration between administrators, teachers, and parents. State departments of education weighed in by highlighting the schools' responsibility as a partner.

> The word "school" [in school–home partnerships] is placed first for a reason. It is the responsibility of the school to take the first step to building a partnership. This does not mean that the school owns the partnership, but the school does own many of the resources that will support a partnership with families. (Connecticut State Department of Education, 1998, p. 9)

### Benefits to Teachers

A school–home partnership has many benefits for the teacher, student, and parent. "Improved academic achievement, increased language achievement, improved overall school behavior, sustained achievement gains, improved parent–child relationships, increased gains in intelligence for low achievers, [and] improved home–school relationships" are among the many advantages gained by creating a cooperative relationship with parents (Connecticut State Department of Education, 1998, p. 3). Often, however, the first and only contact between administrators, teachers, and parents concerns a discipline-related incident. Although this is unfortunate, it *does* offer an opportunity for teachers to take the first step toward building a partnership.

Donna, an assistant principal in an MI school, maintains that her approach to discipline can bring about a successful school–home partnership. "I call in the social worker for many of our discipline problems. I call the families and they meet with us to solve the problem. Often, they provide consequences at home." Donna states that, in this way, "We have reduced our discipline problems *significantly*." Consequently, she continued, "We have detailed plans in place for 22 students in our school who are *not* on any mandatory individualized education plans (IEPs)."

Donna employs individualized behavioral plans and tries to give students whatever they need to prevent disruptive behaviors. She suggests that, particularly for students with ADHD, items such as handheld "focus tools" (e.g., koosh balls and stress balls) may be incorporated into classroom routines or even into behavioral plans (when necessary) "to assist students in keeping their hands occupied rather than touching classroom materials or touching others when they are supposed to be listening."

Other strategies Donna suggested for students who need to release energy include the scheduling of motor breaks (e.g., walk to sharpen a pencil or run an errand for the teacher) throughout the day. She included the caveat that "As long as the student does not abuse the privilege or use a device as a toy, we support its use."

> Whether it is jumping on the trampoline for a few minutes, a need for pressure via handstands, a walk down the hall, a Move N Sit Wedge® seat cushion, adjusting the light in the room, weighted vests, or weighted blankets, we attempt to provide students who have attention issues methods to adjust their sensory input.

Parents should be very much a part of planning for disciplinary consequences. Alfred, a discipline coach at an interdistrict magnet school, helped students make positive choices by conforming to the disciplinary techniques he learned from the child's parents and referring the child back to the parent.

> When it comes to discipline, the success stories are ones when I talk to parents. Once you know the parents, things change. After meeting the mom and establishing a relationship with her and the student, I've found that the student is less apt to exaggerate a story or lie. And the mom is more likely to trust that I have her child's best interest at heart. After meeting the parents, I try and pick up on how they might speak to their child, and then I speak to students as if their parents were speaking to them. I often ask the student misbehaving, "What would your mom think? Would your mom accept that?" This is an attempt to get them to reflect on their behavior.

Once a relationship is established with the parent, the parent may be more apt to work with teachers and administrators to improve their child's behavior. Significant improvements have been noted in hyperactive behaviors for students with ADHD in programs that included rewards both at home and at school for positive behaviors at home and school, respectively (O'Leary et al., as cited in Fiore, Becker, & Nero, 1993).

These programs have the potential to "enhance teachers' professional standing from the parent's perspective" (Epstein, 1986, p. 11). In programs that stress clear communication between parents and teachers, the need to justify professional decisions was diminished. Trust is established and parents feel comfortable becoming school volunteers (Power, 1992). Furthermore, a collaborative relationship with parents fosters academic success (Springer, 1990). If teachers can get parents involved early in a student's education, children will learn more and schools will improve (Epstein, 1986).

Start early. "If education is about initiating the young into an already existing world" (Silin, 1987, p. 3), why not start in kindergarten and work with parents as we induct children into an organization that they will be part of for the next 13 years?

Administrators, teachers, and program directors need to assume the role of "change agent." Allowing for teacher autonomy is crucial. Teachers will be most likely to enact change if they are given a "blueprint" such as MI and if they feel in control of their own professional development. Teachers should be given the freedom in how they initiate and foster parent relationships. Refer to the section on professional development in Chapter 4.

## Benefits to Parents and Students

Davies contends that "parent involvement benefits parents themselves, in terms of greater appreciation of their important roles, strengthened social networks, access to information and materials, personal efficacy and motivation to continue their own education" (Connecticut State Department of Education, 1998, p. 3).

With parent involvement, "the teachers' work can be more manageable, parents who are involved have more positive views of the teacher and the school, and parents and others who participate are likely to be more supportive of the schools" (Connecticut State Department of Education, 1998, p. 3). The hidden benefits to students when teachers and parents work together include improved self-esteem and academics, a heightened sense of security, and the provision of hope.

# WHAT SCHOOLS AND TEACHERS OF ADHD STUDENTS CAN DO

"My advice to teachers who have students that have ADHD is to have patience with them," says Connor, a middle school student with ADHD.

Patience needs to be exhibited by parent and teacher. One parent described her situation: "My son, Pablo, is 8 years old, has ADHD, and is in second grade. I have got nothing but complaints from his teachers—Pre-K, kindergarten, first grade."

His second-grade teacher was young, fresh out of college. She said he was not going to pass second grade because he is very much below grade level. The teacher shared with me that she was concerned about both his academics and behavior. I told the teacher to let me know if any situation arises. Well, she let me know, all right! I have over 300 e-mails! I counted them! I answered each and every e-mail. You know, other parents told me to "pull my child out of her class." But I stuck with her. At least she communicated with me (as opposed to his former teachers). I told her we will both learn from this. I said you'll have other kids in your class with ADHD.

### Address Learning Needs

A change in law in 1999 made it easier to address the academic needs of children with ADHD. "On March 11, 1999 . . . AD/HD was formally listed in the regulations for the first time, under the category, 'Other Health Impairment'. . . . [S]chools will . . . be required to address AD/HD systemically and systematically" (Cohen, 1999, p. 40)

### Address Social Needs

The above law has improved the academic lives of students with ADHD. Academics are first and foremost, but a student's emotional needs must also be met. Often, social needs have been given feigned regard, because of the prevalent belief that the emotional growth of students is not as important as academic development. Regarding his need to understand and be accepted, Herman, a student, confides, "I don't think all teachers understand what ADHD is and what I go through everyday."

"When children's emotional needs are met and the children feel stable and secure, only then are the children ready to accept learning experiences and changes within their lives" (McCarthy & May, 1974, p. 22). For students with ADHD, social needs may trump the need for academic skills. At times, it is their behavior that gets in the way of their learning. Indeed, many times, they've learned the wrong skills. This was the case for Alexandria. Her mother, Darlene, shared this story: "Alexandria's school life changed when she was in third grade." Her teacher, Mrs. Schumacher, met Alexandria's emotional needs.

> Her third-grade teacher could read Allie "like a book." She was a seasoned teacher and strict. And that was good for my daughter with ADHD. She can be really manipulative and I truly believe she had manipulated her prior teachers. Prior to this, I dreaded all of my parent–teacher conferences. I would hear about her bad behavior or bad grades. But Mrs. Schumacher was different. She had all positive things to say about Allie. When I questioned her about my concerns about her academics, she said, "Your daughter doesn't have a learning problem." This was confirmed by the scores she received when I had her professionally tested. Her teacher gave me tips on how to redirect Allie and to get her to focus.

Research indicates that "if emotional concerns aren't met, any attempt at cognitive learning is of no use" (McCarthy & May, 1974, p. 22). MIndful teachers address students' basic needs before addressing academic needs. A basic need for everyone, including students with ADHD, is to be in the company of people who like them. However, education may serve as a hindrance for students with ADHD. Maslow's hierarchic theory (physiological, safety, love or affection or belongingness, esteem, and self-actualization) is often represented as a pyramid. The lower levels represent basic needs, and the upper levels represents more multifaceted needs, with an ultimate need for self-actualization. "Maslow believes that the only reason that people would not move well in the direction of self-actualization is because of hindrances placed in their way by society. He states that *education* is one of these hindrances" (Maslow's Hierarchy of Need, Self-Actualization, 2007).

Not caring for the social needs of students with ADHD may cause them to avoid schooling and exhibit unmanageable behavior. Anita, Michael's grandmother, works hard to raise him, but she became confused when "Michael didn't want to go [to school] at all—he asked, 'Will you be with me? Will you stay with me?' He wouldn't get out of the car . . . he ran around the car saying, 'No, I'm not going!' I was chasing him around the car . . ."

Faith, another parent, didn't have to play tag to get her son to go to school, but she did have to play hide and seek. "One day, he was very quiet and every once in a while I'd heard him say 'I'm not going to school' and then he started telling me he's going to get undressed. . . . He started wanting to take his clothes off. . . . His shoes came off . . . and then it got completely quiet. . . . I couldn't find Josh anywhere. . . . I was looking all over the house for him . . . and in my bedroom we have a very large wicker basket . . . with a lid on it and Josh can fit into it perfectly. . . . He thought he'd be quiet as a mouse and never be found. . . . I found him . . . got him in the car kicking and screaming. He was miserable . . . and I was fighting off the tears."

Giselle's daughter, Nicole, manifested physical symptoms. "It started on Sunday afternoon . . . severe symptoms . . . crying, not eating, diarrhea . . . physical symptoms. . . ." (Schirduan & Miller, 2002, p. 10).

Students with ADHD need to experience a sense of belonging. Ian, a veteran teacher, explains how crucial the teacher–student relationship is: "I think that if you can make a personal connection for students, ADHD or not, you've got them hooked—and that personal connection is stronger than any technique."

Students with ADHD need to know that their teachers enjoy them as individuals and are working to help them in academic and nonacademic ways. Unfortunately, many students with ADHD feel that teachers dislike them. Charles's mother states, "I think Charles really thought his teacher had it out for him." A school year is a long time for a child to perceive a teacher's dislike. In one of our studies, we asked students with ADHD "Is it easy for you to sense when someone is in a bad mood?" Based on a five-point Lickert scale where one was "sometimes" and five was "all the time," their responses revealed a mean score of 3.17—meaning "most of the time/almost all the time."

It is crucial to remember that students with ADHD are perceptive and can read environmental cues. Therefore, teachers must work to create a climate that is inclusive of all students, while at the same time addressing the social needs of students with ADHD. An MI-inspired perspective can help an ADHD student feel liked by a teacher despite problematic behaviors. A teacher can say to the student, "I don't like your behavior, but I do like you. I like your understanding of animals and I share your love of dogs. I really like how you make a special effort to control your temper on bad days." Using the MI language to carefully describe what is likable about the student's thinking imparts emotional honesty beyond the unconvincing platitude "I like you."

## WHAT ADHD STUDENTS CAN DO: STUDY THE MI WAY

Students with ADHD can be taught to use their intelligences to achieve learning goals. The following are strategies that teachers can use to help students with ADHD to achieve various instructional objectives by using their strongest intelligences.

### Bodily-Kinesthetic Intelligence

Students with ADHD and bodily-kinesthetic intelligence can affirm: I can use my body to learn anything! I can try moving around while I study. I can take movement breaks or walk while I study my notes. I can manually write out the information over and over. I can "do it," not just talk about it. I can get a feel for it and follow hunches. I can physically sort out my notes and rearrange the information using notecards. I will practice, practice, and practice. I will try to imitate exactly how someone else does it. I can find ways to act out or dramatize the information. I can play make-believe and pantomime the information. I can invent gestures to describe what I'm learning. I can tinker with it and build a model.

### Spatial Intelligence

Students with ADHD and spatial intelligence can affirm: I can use my spatial imagination and artistic abilities to learn anything! I can organize my notes on the page in a clear design. I can use "mapping" to arrange new information visually. I can use different-colored pens, markers, paper, or notebooks. I will visualize "real-life" situations involving the information. I can do some drawing or building before reading to warm up my brain. I can picture myself knowing how to use the new information very well on a test or project. I will look to see how the whole problem works from beginning to end, and then break it down into chunks and pieces. I can use doodles, drawings, or other symbols to help me memorize things. I can make cartoons or a DVD to explain complicated material and practice skills. I can ask someone to show me how it works while I watch carefully.

### Musical Intelligence

Students with ADHD and musical intelligence can affirm: I can use my musical skills to learn anything! I can play familiar or relaxing music before or during my study time. I can make up fun rhymes or lyrics using new information that I must memorize. I will listen for rhythms and sound patterns in explanations. I energize my brain to study when I'm tired with strong music. I can hum to myself as I do my work. I can take musical breaks. I can make a DJ tape using the new information with appropriate music. I can create a rap song on the material to be covered. I can look for music that pertains to what I must study.

### Logical-Mathematical Intelligence

Students with ADHD and logical-mathematical intelligence can affirm: I can use my logical skills to learn anything! I can use logic to find explanations for how things work. I can create detailed plans about connections and relationships between things. I can seek out solutions like a detective. I can make a game and challenge myself to find a more efficient and better way to study. I can test myself and analyze my mistakes. I can count my errors and chart my progress. I can tackle a problem in an orderly way: first things first. I can ask why and how. I can outline the logical pattern of the information and determine what's most important and least important. I will wonder about the possibilities and test out answers.

### Interpersonal Intelligence

Students with ADHD and the interpersonal intelligence can affirm: I can use my interpersonal skills to learn anything! I can understand what the teacher wants me to be able to do and what I need to know. I will "read my teacher's mind" and then check with my teacher to see if I'm right. I will ask two or three people in the class or a friend what I'm supposed to know. I will ask the student who is a whiz to explain it to me. I will have fun "playing the role" or pretending to be the person who is an expert. I will lead a "study group." I will talk to a friend on the phone and we'll study together. I will do my best to teach the new information to someone else and then have that person teach it back to me. I will be my own best cheerleader while I'm learning something very hard. I will remind myself that someone important, a classmate, is counting on me to do my best. I will try to sell a product or persuade someone that I'm an expert. I will dramatize the information.

### Intrapersonal Intelligence

Students with ADHD and intrapersonal intelligence can affirm: I can use my intrapersonal skills to learn anything! I can first ask myself, "What do I already know about this?" and "Why is this information important to me? How does it fit in my life and my future? Will I ever need to know or use this?" I can slow down my practice or study process to find and correct my mistakes or misunderstandings. I will review my work often and ask myself, "What did I just learn? Is it important to know and remember?" As I study a new subject, I will remind myself of my learning strengths and try to use them to learn. If I become discouraged, frustrated, or sidetracked, I will think of ways to focus my thoughts and think positively. I will learn to test myself to discover whether I'm learning. I will not put myself down because of my weaknesses. I will find ways to boost my self-confidence and not give up. I will use positive self-talk when solving problems. I will remind myself that I'm my own best teacher. I will check out my new learning with teachers or parents to be sure that I've studied correctly.

### Naturalist Intelligence

The student with ADHD with a naturalist intelligence can affirm: I can use my naturalist skills to learn anything! I can first observe carefully by using my senses to watch, listen, touch, smell, and maybe even taste the new information. I can record and then organize all this data into a system that makes sense to me. I might make separate lists or use a graph, collage, mobile, or "mind-map" to show relationships and connections between the different parts. I can follow a hunch and then test it. I can build or imagine a living model. I can think of animal metaphors and symbols for the new information to help me relate to it. I can discover how this information fits into the natural scheme of plants, animals, and human life. I can see how things have developed over time and look for growth, change, and the evolution of ideas and products. I can imagine that I am a hunter tracking down the answers by following signs and footprints. I can imagine that I am gathering food for my mind so my brain won't starve. I can imagine that I am cultivating a garden or raising the next generation of good ideas.

### Linguistic Intelligence

Students with ADHD and linguistic intelligence can affirm: I can use linguistic activities to learn anything! I will read everything in the textbook carefully. I will listen to explanations and write detailed notes, which I can then rewrite and translate into my own words. I will pick out key words to memorize. I will build my vocabulary. I will learn the meaning of words that confuse me. I can use a tape recorder to help me study by talking out loud and then listening to the recording. I can make up a story. I can create a rhyme to help me remember. I can talk to someone about what I'm trying to learn and try to teach, convince, or sell them this new information. I can write a checklist of everything I need to know. I can make an outline of the information. I can make a poem out the information.

Affirmations, along with learning how and when to study, represent positive techniques that can be used with students who have ADHD. Levine (2002) advises to improve memory "long-term filing works best if you go right to sleep. The minutes before bedtime are crucial. A student shouldn't study and then place a phone call to her best friend. Call your friend, then study, then go to sleep—in that sequence—to foster optimal consolidation in memory" (p. 118). Levine's advice, coupled with positive approaches that build on intellectual strengths, can provide much-needed encouragement for students with ADHD.

## WHAT PARENTS OF ADHD STUDENTS CAN DO

Parents struggle with the demands of raising a child with ADHD. Students with ADHD have been reported to take toll on marriages and parental self-esteem. "The most important predictor of children's success is related to positive parental self-esteem" (Gestwicki, 2000, p. 133). Parents need to take care of themselves first, and then attend to their child with ADHD.

While raising a child with ADHD, parents ask themselves poignant questions such as: Why doesn't my child listen to me? How can I get her to do her homework? How can I help him get better grades? Why don't her friends from school visit? Am I a bad mother or bad father?

Matt, an adult with ADHD, put such questions to rest after an initial self-identification and subsequent medical diagnosis as an adult with ADHD. He explains how he was able to put his mother's fear regarding her child-rearing skills to rest.

> I didn't know I had ADD until I was 39 years old [when I took a checklist test in a magazine]. . . . My mom was so happy to find out I had ADHD. . . . I called her and said, "Mom there's this book you need to read" she went out and read it. "It's called *Cosmopolitan*. . . . that's me." . . . She was thrilled to death. . . . "Oh, thank God," she said. . . . "All these years I just thought I was a bad mother."

We met Matt at a conference on ADHD. Like many people with ADHD, Matt struggled with the primary and secondary characteristics associated with the disorder. He had difficulty in school. He was angry, yet his anger dissipated somewhat and he experienced a sense of relief, as did his mom, upon hearing his diagnosis. With an explanation for what he had felt for most of his life, Matt now views himself as an individual with promise. This is the goal of all parents: to be able to provide their children with explanations and coping strategies that will aid them in navigating the world successfully.

## Honor ADHD Child's MI Strengths

Typically, solutions to ADHD behaviors are focused on "fixing the child" (using admonitions such as "Pay attention!", "Stop fidgeting!", "Behave!", "Get organized!", "Find your pencil!", and "Focus!"). Such admonishments reinforce the child's behavior or, worse, serve to identify the child as being "at-risk" for failure. Repeated reprimands on behaviors that fall outside the child's abilities also fail to note the child's intellectual strengths and serve to identify the child as a "problem child." To maximize motivation and achievement, parents should keep in mind the acronym RAVE, which stands for *R*ecognize, *A*ppreciate, *V*alue, and *E*ngage or *E*ncourage.

Discovering where a student is "at-promise" for achievement begins with recognizing that we simply *recognize* the child's unique skills and behaviors. Describe what the child does well often or with enthusiasm. Many times, a child's MI strengths will be overlooked, ignored, or denigrated. It is easy for a child to take for granted and minimize the value of his/her thinking strengths when these skills may come so easily as a part of everyday life. Experts are always at a loss to describe their own talents, because these are not discrete, but rather enacted as a whole. This is also true of the skills of the ADHD child. Sometimes, it is only when others recognize what is unique about a child that strengths can be acknowledged.

The second key to fulfilling a student's potential is to *appreciate* his or her thinking skill or intelligence as an important component of an intellectual repertoire. For example, children who habitually collect and categorize things such as rocks, feathers, and sports cards can be appreciated for exercising a skill associated with the naturalist intelligence. An MI perspective can be employed to bolster children's self-confidence and self-worth when they appreciate that a normal aspect of their everyday life is truly an "intelligent" activity, worthy of investing time and energy to improve.

When a child comes to realize that his or her unique ability has *value* to other people, that student can begin to maximize learning potential. Students who are "at-risk" for failure usually do not feel that they are valued at home, in the classroom, or in the school community. When a student's intellectual strengths lie outside of what is normally acknowledged, praised, and rewarded, his or her motivation may be impaired and his or her feelings of self-worth undermined.

A student's chances for success will be increased if his or her intellectual strength is *engaged* or *encouraged*. A child's strongest intelligence may not develop fully if the child is not provided with the proper intellectual environment and encouragement. Athletes need to be challenged to build specific bodily-kinesthetic abilities. Art students need guidance to enhance their sense of color and design. Interpersonally astute children may need to learn to use win–win negotiation strategies.

Achievement is possible if the child's unique skills can be encouraged and related to necessary classroom performance and the pursuit of academic studies. "The family is the greatest influence on a child and it is the family that can make the greatest change in a child's education" (Natwick, 1991, p. 12). Teachers and parents should RAVE, understand, and "honor" each child's unique strengths.

### Recognize the Impact of Parent and Child MI Profiles

Our work with families of students with ADHD involves helping not only the student with ADHD, but also his or her parents. ADHD may be inherited and, thus, at times the entire family suffers. Pam, an 11-year-old with ADHD, lives a meager life in the South with her mother, two idolized brothers, and a father who also has ADHD. Pam illustrates ADHD characteristics as she sees them in herself and in her brothers as well. She describes her dad as having two speeds: stop and go. "He goes 100 miles per hour . . . very high strung . . . always having to do something. . . ." Many experts attest there is a genetic component to the disorder. In fact, studies indicate that close relatives in the families of ADHD children also have ADHD. "Forty to fifty percent of all children with attention deficits have at least one parent and thirty percent have a sibling with the condition" (Zeigler Dendy, 1999, Section 1, The Basics).

For example, Jeff's MI profile showed the linguistic and interpersonal strengths. His ADHD son, Gregory, displayed other strengths. Both had different interests and goals. Jeff had Gregory take trumpet lessons for 5 years and Gregory's enthusiasm waned to the point where his performance was forced and merely perfunctory.

> As a parent I am always learning about who this child is becoming in spite of *my* preferences, hopes and expectations. Meanwhile his task commitment to using the computer for making web pages and starting a tutoring business has skyrocketed. If I force my son to master the trumpet and under value his computer passion (strength in spatial intelligence), I risk endangering our relationship.

We have hypothesized that parental recognition of MI profiles within families has the potential to improve how a child with ADHD learns. It is a promising approach to improve family ties. In our study, parent interviews and anecdotes corroborated with student ratings for predominant intelligences. In other words, all parents chose at least one of the two predominant intelligences in their child, as reported in the student's MIDAS™.

"Parents who have a kid who's struggling in school need to become very knowledgeable about how learning works. Where it's breaking down in their child and what the words to describe it are" (Levine, as cited in Gorrell, 2002). Levine (2002) divides learning into six areas of weakness: "trouble mastering skills, trouble acquiring facts or knowledge, trouble accomplishing output, trouble understanding, trouble approaching tasks systematically, [and] trouble with the rate and amount of demands" (p. 248). Identify the trouble area, and following the identification of the weakness, strengthen it by bridging the child's intelligence to the area of weakness.

The knowledge regarding differing strengths highlights potentially contentious areas between parents and their child with ADHD. Thus, parents are encouraged to compare intellectual strengths and MI profiles. Problems may arise during homework sessions when parents assume that their child shares their intellectual strengths, ways of learning, or approaches to tasks. The MI profiles of parent and child may be so different that a common ground fails to be identified. If that is the case, parents may need to seek out tutors. Gardner (1999b) notes, "as my work on multiple intelligences has taught me, individuals have distinctly different kinds of minds—even and sometimes especially when they are members of the same family" (p. 3).

> Often no one is at fault when the styles of parents or teachers are counter to the learning patterns of a kid. Both sides need to put some work into the relationship and try a healthy dose of compromising and mutual acceptance. (Levine, 2002, p. 261)

## Apply MI Theory with Homework

Tamara, the mother of a 14-year-old with ADHD, does not share her son's MI strengths or his ADHD characteristics. With utter exasperation in her voice, Tamara stated, "My son, Bradley, tends to think he doesn't have a problem."

> Though he's 14, it's very difficult to instill a sense of responsibility in him. When I left it up to him to complete his homework, he started failing school. I think that's the hard part, trying to instill maturity in him. He is immature, and it can be aggravating.

Bradley, like so many students with ADHD, procrastinates. Chapman-Booth (1998) refers to procrastination as a temporal disability among students with ADHD. Parents need to provide regular guidance and supervision on planning assignments, especially large projects that are not due for weeks. Helen, Casey's mother, said that Casey received "his best grade yet" because his teacher "broke down the large science project into smaller assignments over the course of weeks." The teacher assumed the role of project manager and incorporated a timeline that Casey and his mother found to be manageable. Parents can take an active role in seeking out ways to ensure their child's success with long-term assignments such as projects or short-term assignments such as daily homework.

Parents need to feel free to approach teachers, and teachers, in turn, need to be approachable. Incorporate conventional accommodations, such as a reduction in the number of math problems assigned, if the child with ADHD takes an extraordinarily long time to complete homework compared to classmates. Allow typed versus written responses to questions if the child has poor fine-motor skills or messy handwriting. If the child is having difficulty grasping homework, parents should work jointly with the teacher to tailor homework assignments to the child's MI profile. For example, if the assignment is to read and then summarize a story by writing a one-page paper, with the lesson objective being to identify the beginning, middle, and end story parts, then an accommodation can be made for the student with ADHD and strength in bodily-kinesthetic intelligence. This accommodation can take the form of having the student act out or pantomime the main events (beginning, middle, end) in the story, as opposed to writing them down on paper.

Classmates may consider accommodations unfair. If this is the case, a "payback" for the accommodation can be made. "I often think it's a good idea to ask a child for a payback for accommodation . . . to compensate for a reduction of demands in an area of difficulty" (Levine, 2002, p. 281). A payback can entail drawing a picture for someone with strength in the spatial intelligence. A pay-back for the student with ADHD and naturalist intelligence for writing a one-page versus two-page assignment about a recent field trip to the zoo could be to use the student's keen observation skills to relay an event from the field trip to his or her parent. The parent then transcribes it on paper. The student hands in the accom-modated one-page paper along with the "payback," a one-page parent-transcribed paper.

Once a child's MI cognitive profile is related to homework assignments, the child's organizational strategies can be tackled. Organizational skills can also be linked to the child's MI profile. A student with ADHD and strength in intrapersonal intelligence may want a say in choosing and personalizing a place to study. A stu-dent with ADHD and strength in logical-mathematical intelligence may seek to create a space that has an organizational system where everything from pencils to paperclips is methodically placed. A student with interpersonal intelligence may want to have a homework buddy. A child with naturalist intelligence may seek to have a cat on the desk, or to lie with a head rested against the family dog.

Getting the child with ADHD organized invariably involves the backpack. If the backpack symbolizes the proverbial apron string between school and home life, here's what a parent can do to cut the apron strings and have the child be-come more self-regulated and self-reliant. To begin, match the child's MI profile and preferences to the contents of the backpack. For example, if the child with ADHD has strength in spatial intelligence, assign a color to a corresponding folder for each subject in a binder. Next, assign the same color when highlighting notes in books or notes written in class. And finally, use that color again to write the assigned homework in a daily planner or homework log.

To alleviate the tension that often arises between parents and students when it comes to homework, consider the above alternatives and/or the following tra-ditional approaches to homework. First, complete homework at the same time and in the same place each day. Second, choose a quiet, distraction-free environment. Third, give breaks every 15 to 20 minutes for a student with ADHD. Fourth, pro-vide a nutritious snack before or during homework. Fifth, give positive feedback even on small accomplishments. And finally, purchase a set of books for home use so your child does not have to carry books back and forth to school.

Freed and Parsons (1997) note that the ADHD child "can accomplish a tre-mendous amount [of homework] in forty-five minutes. If he works much longer, the learning curve drops and his ability to retain material will be dramatically re-duced." Freed suggests that parents "Set a timer . . . to keep him from constantly looking at the clock. If he fails to finish all his work, he can return to studying later when he's had a mental break" (p. 147). Finally, have the child assess work by asking questions that are often associated with the behavior of ADHD, such as "Have I placed my name and identifying material on my homework?", "Did I com-plete the assignment as required?", "Did I rush through my homework?", "Did I miss any questions?", "Is my work legible?", "Did I place the homework in the corresponding folder in my binder?", and "Am I ready and prepared for the next school day?".

You can personalize a checklist to include potential pitfalls, the mistakes that the child often makes following the cry "I'm done with my homework!" A list can be made of potential pitfalls with check-off marks. A list may work particularly well for those students with ADHD and strength in linguistic intelligence, but you should tailor the list to their particular MI strengths. For example, after noticing an oversight, ask the ADHD student with strength in naturalist intelligence to review homework to *observe* a pitfall. For the student with ADHD with strength in spatial intelligence, take pictures of task completion (e.g., a picture of the student placing the homework in a folder) and post the pictures to remind them what to look for upon completion of homework. Such techniques will curb potential pitfalls that many, like Jerry, a sixth-grade student with ADHD, experience: "My parents and I would get into fights because I was late all the time. . . . It is hard to get ready and organized for school."

Students with ADHD need assistance with approaches to schoolwork and homework. It is vital to address the primary (e.g., inattention or impulsiveness) *and* secondary characteristics (e.g., procrastination and organization) of ADHD when embarking upon homework strategies. While medication for students with ADHD will improve concentration in the short run, "there is not solid evidence that their schoolwork improves in the long run" (Attention-Deficit Hyperactivity Disorder, 1995, paragraph 6).

In our interviews, we saw that students with ADHD develop their own strategies for focusing and homework completion. There is much that parents of students with ADHD can do. Preparation with schoolwork and homework begins with a sense of having the parent and child recognize, understand, and honor one another's strengths and finding ways to succeed as a team.

## THE SCHOOL–HOME PARTNERSHIP PROMISE

Parents make a difference, and family relationships rank first. School relationships are a close second for making a difference in the lives of students with ADHD. When the talents of parent, child, and teacher come together, much can be accomplished.

George, a third grader with ADHD, struggled with reading and writing. His mother, Ruby, wanted to help, so she visited his classroom and talked about her job as a researcher. Wendy, George's teacher, tells the story.

> George's mother was a researcher for science. She became interested in the intelligences and offered to come to school to share her responsibilities and show students how reading and writing were such an important part of her job. George was her assistant that day, and was able to be a big help, even though he was so very excited. The presentation impressed the entire class, but it made a lasting effect on George. He began to see the need to place more emphasis on his learning with regard to reading and writing. He did become a stronger student.

Parent involvement is viewed as a cornerstone in school reform (Espinosa, 1995). It is crucial to a student's success in school (Natwick, 1991; Power, 1992). Hence, when schools and parents become partners in an effort to help a student with ADHD, success happens. Consider a pact or contract as an avenue to school success.

A School–Home Partnership Promise involves the student, parents, and teacher in addressing the difficulty that the student with ADHD is experiencing. The contract, pledge, or what will be referred to as the partnership promise can be initiated by a student, parent, or teacher. The Partnership Promise must be clear and concise, must include a manageable number of action items, and must be tailored to meet specific needs. Teachers, for example, may initiate the list of items. Parents and or the student may add an item or two. Items on the list can be negotiated. Everyone (teacher, parent, and student) signs the Partnership Promise.

Action items for the Partnership Promise (see Figure 5.1) may include areas in which the student with ADHD may struggle, such as homework, discipline, tardiness, absenteeism, study habits, effort, and neatness.

"Schools filled with students who can't control their impulses, can't focus their attention and can't regulate their emotions will not succeed" (Brooks, 2007, Family Relationships Shape Education) unless they are given promising ways to develop talents by MIndful educators and MIndful parents.

Here's some sage advice from Lance, a middle school student with ADHD who has received a few educational bumps and bruises along on his school journey: "ADHD is a big part of my life and I realize that it will not go away. I am not going to change, so the way I learn has to change. I can do anything; it just may take me a little longer or may be a little harder than [it is for] kids who don't have ADHD."

Parents' knowledge of their child with ADHD begins at birth, it spans years, and it is comprehensive. Teachers' knowledge of their students with ADHD is finite and concentrated to a particular grade with academic and social expectations. Both parents and teachers should work to complement one another to show students with ADHD that they can do anything.

**Figure 5.1.** Partnership Promise

**Student Name:**_____          **Date:**_____

*Initial*

_____1. Student will attend school on time.

_____2. Student will be positive, knowledgeable about student's MI strengths, and participate in class.

_____3. Student will take notices home from school and return homework to school on time. To that end, student will devise a method best suited to student's strength to attain goals (e.g., list-making, picture list, etc.).

_____4. Parent will check and discuss their child's homework and use child's MI strengths, MI study strategies, etc., to help them succeed.

_____5. Parent will volunteer time each week at school or at home.

_____6. Teacher will view the student from an at-promise versus an at-risk view.

_____7. Teacher will assist the student to overcome academic or social weakness via their MI strengths.

Signatures:_____

          *Student*                  *Parent*                *Teacher*

# CHAPTER 6

# At-Promise

MOMENTS ADD UP, AND IF educators are not called to action to change perceptions and instructional strategies for students with ADHD, moments of inaction may have unwelcome consequences. Every second, a public school student is suspended; every 10 seconds, a high school student drops out; every 25 seconds, a child is arrested; every 5 minutes, a child is arrested for a drug offense; and every 9 minutes, a child is arrested for a violent crime (Moments in America for Children, 2008). ADHD students' challenges can lead to antisocial characteristics and risk-taking behavior. Immediate action is required in that ADHD is one of the most common disorders in students (Kessler, Chin, Demler, & Walters, 2005).

> Between 7 and 10 years of age, at least 30 to 50% are likely to develop symptoms of conduct disorder and antisocial behavior such as lying, petty thievery, and resistance to authority. Twenty-five percent or more may have problems with fighting with other children. Those who have not developed some other psychiatric, academic, or social disorder by this time are in the minority. . . . As many as 30% may be experimenting with or frankly abusing substances such as alcohol and marijuana. Up to 58% have failed at least one grade in school, and at least three times as many hyperactive teenagers as non-ADHD children have failed a grade, been suspended, or been expelled from school. Almost 35% of ADHD children quit school before completion. (Barkley, 1992, pp. 82–83)

These grim statistics do not speak well to the overarching purpose of education, which is to educate children to read, write, reflect, and think critically. Skipping school and exhibiting defiant behavior and apathy may be by-products of the time students spend in classrooms experiencing failure. We believe that this book offers fundamental choices for teachers to improve both the tangibles (academics) and intangibles (self-concept) in the lives of students with ADHD. Classrooms in America for students with ADHD are replete with "academic" statistics. For example, "25% higher of students with ADHD have other serious learning problems" (Barkley & Zeigler, as cited in Richter, 2006) in language and math. Other problem areas range from listening to memory to organizational and fine-motor skills. "Half of all students with AD/HD are believed to have a learning disability and inadequate written expression has been cited as the most common learning problem (65%) among students with ADHD" (Zeigler et al., as cited in Richter, October 2007). These numbers pale in comparison to how many children take medication. The number of children diagnosed with ADHD and taking medication in 1985 was listed at 500,000. That number increased to 6 million children taking medication for their ADHD (Children and Adults Against Drugging America [CHAADA], Facts & Statistics, 2008). The percentages have reached "75–90% of kids with AD/HD [who] are helped by medication" (Zeigler et al., as cited in Richter, October 2007).

Educators must realize that the definition of *education* involves more than students' academic selves. "We have to get over the definition of education as something that takes place in schools between the hours of 8 and 3, between the months of September and June, and between the ages of 5 and 18" (Brooks, 2007, [editorial]).

Our research indicates that students with ADHD can achieve academic and social success. Rethinking ADHD through the lens of MI theory enables educators to view the ADHD student through a prism of strengths.

## SUCCESS IN HIGH SCHOOL

Individuals are drawn to what they do well; yet students with ADHD struggle to find their place in the world. It is the educator's responsibility to introduce students to life choices and vocations that reflect their MI cognitive profile. This chapter recommends life choices for students with ADHD. Data on which intelligences correlate to various careers and jobs are presented.

In order to work toward success in high school, teachers, parents, and students with ADHD should focus on the "ability," as opposed to the "disability," of the student. The musician John Lennon was not known for his LD but for his music. Comedian Robin Williams, who has ADHD, may not have fared well in schools that stressed the three Rs (reading, writing, and arithmetic). Both are revered because of their ability, *not* their disability.

As students progress from elementary to middle and on to high school, MI strengths take hold and have the potential to blossom as students begin to think about their life choices. However, for many, lack of exposure to the eight intelligences combined with a lackluster curriculum can prevent growth and contribute to apathy regarding a postgraduation future.

Manny, a student with ADHD, attended private elementary, middle, and high schools that focused on language arts and math. Budget money for science, as well as other subject areas, was considered a frill. Thus, students like Manny may underperform in science classes, but have notable naturalist strengths that involve physical, earth, and life sciences. Manny chose to learn about the weather through practical experience rather than through the classroom. Manny's mother mentioned her son's affinity for science and his obsession with the weather:

> As a child, when the warning signs appeared on TV notifying us that a thunderstorm is headed our way, my son would put us in "lock down" even though the sun was shining! He would go around the house and lock all the windows.

Manny's love of weather continued, and he is an avid watcher of the Weather Channel. His mother tells us, "when a storm is coming, he gets all in a rage about it . . . he loses his mind" Manny becomes hyperfocused on the weather, following it on the computer, noting warning systems, and downloading Doppler weather onto his phone. His mother says that weather is "both interesting and fearful to him," and tells the story of every parent's nightmare:

I remember watching the news, and it was predicted that the next town over was going to get a big hail storm, thunderstorms, and high winds. It was all over the news. Manny was supposed to drive home before the weather got bad. But Manny decided to drive to the next town to see the storm. It reminded me of what a storm chaser would do. Anyway, he ended up hydroplaning and getting into an accident. No one was hurt, but the car was damaged. Manny went over a curb, knocked down a sign, and now he is learning a lesson by paying back the [insurance] deductible!

Bad choices may be a consequence of not having specific talents recognized and deficient intrapersonal awareness. These problems, combined with low academic self-esteem due to negative school experiences and limited exposure to the multiple intelligences, can propel a student onto a crash course. Given a history of struggle with classroom tasks and failures, high school students may overgeneralize their deficits, assuming that they are inept both in class and beyond school borders.

The ultimate challenge is for a student's school career to represent the springboard for quality, lifelong learning. The goal is for all students to become community leaders and valued members of a chosen profession.

## SUCCESS IN COLLEGE

Although IQ tests may predict school success, "they have been found to be much less predictive of success in post-secondary academic and occupational domains" (Ackerman, 1996, paragraph 3). Many students go to college because they want to be successful and instead find that they become unhappy and confused, and fail at subjects. The first step to discovering the subject areas in which they'll be successful is to provide them with a cognitive profile that illuminates their multiple intelligence strengths and limitations. This responsibility must be jointly shared among student, parent, teacher, and school personnel (e.g., guidance counselor). These individuals should act as boundary spanners between the student's high school and the postsecondary world (e.g., college, training programs). For a parent working alone to pave a child's way to college, the path may be frustrating.

Rachel speaks to changing notions of success when working with her son: "I realized I was getting extremely frustrated with my ADHD son, Frank." Frank was getting poor grades, and Rachel explained that she had to change her own personal view of success. She learned "that success is not measured by the grade a child receives in school." When speaking of Frank's future college career, she confirms that "of course, I expect him to go to college."

And yes, I expect him to do his best, but I accept Cs. But I no longer hold him to artificial standards. I now measure his success by how happy he is and if he is pursuing his interests. There is so much to do in this world, so many ways to be successful. . . . I want Frank to find something that he loves to do and do it well.

Of the dozens of ADHD college students and adults with ADHD we've counseled over the years, the naturalist and spatial intelligences were listed as strengths among the top four of the eight intelligences. Linguistic and logical-mathematical intelligences were ranked in the bottom half. This represents a pattern that crosses grade levels. The intrapersonal intelligence is ranked at number eight, indicating a perceived weakness among elementary and middle school, high school, and college students and adults with ADHD. However, the interpersonal intelligence was reported in the top half by college students and the lower half among high school, middle school, and elementary students. Perhaps as students become more social among peers during their final years of schooling, the development of crucial interpersonal skills improves somewhat.

Though respondents were small in our study of college students with ADHD, when asked "Do you think your ADHD interferes with your studies at college?", all but one responded "yes," indicating that once they are beyond the walls of K–12 classrooms, students with ADHD continue to need assistance in seeking a promising future.

## SUCCESS IN LIFE

"Children's minds flourish when they feel upbeat about their prospects for the future . . . there are countless individuals who find it much easier to be an adult than they found being a child" (Levine, 2002, p. 306). Barkley (1995) cites a Biederman and Faraone study that conservatively states that over 25% of ADHD children have at least one parent who has ADHD. Martin and Ben are father and son. Martin shares that both diagnosed and suspected ADHD tendencies are part of their extended family history. In this excerpt, Martin explains how he came to accept Ben's choices and how, through that acceptance, he became a role model in his son's life. His advice is that "Parents should not lose heart."

> My son Ben was diagnosed with ADHD at 7. He's 17 now. Over the years, I would question myself and ask, "Is what I am doing meaningful? Will he ever be different?" Ben was running through life and making poor choices. And I would say, "Son, you don't want to go down that road, I've been there." But he'd say, "Dad, that's just the way I want to be."

Time and time again, Martin said that Ben "would go off in a bad direction and suffer for it." Ben often asked his father, "Why don't you just give up on me?" Martin would reply, "I will never give up on you!" Martin continues to advise parents, maintaining that "even though we love our children, at times we are tempted to give up, and I am no exception. But I made a conscious decision not to give up, but I needed a strategy. So after a while, I decided to step back and accept Ben and let him be his own person." This acceptance involved accepting "that jacket day in and day out that he found at the Salvation Army [thrift store], compliment him on the berets he wore." Ben's father also asked him about his most recent interests and "decided to stop swooping down to 'save Ben' and let him be the person he needed to be, to grow his way." Martin's hypothesis was that "maybe letting go some was just what might bring him [Ben] around someday." Martin happily notes that "Ben is doing much better now, still very set on trying things on his own. But a friend in a similar situation with her daughter shared with me that she bumped into my son and asked, 'Ben, can you give me any advice about my daughter?' And Ben's response was, 'Don't give up.'"

Success in life involves acceptance and a discovery of passions. Gardner (1993b) states:

> In my view, the purpose of school should be to develop intelligences and to help people reach vocational and avocational goals that are appropriate to their particular spectrum of intelligences. People who are helped to do so, I believe, feel more engaged and competent, and therefore more inclined to serve the society in a constructive way. (Gardner, 1993b, p. 9)

## Careers Associated with MI

When MIDAS™ strengths are matched to career skills, then the chances for students' success become greater. Interest and motivation are key ingredients, but the right intellectual dispositions to develop the necessary work skills are essential. Careers reflect a combination of intelligences, with two or three predominant intelligences. Thus, career categories may overlap.

*Careers and MI*
- *Musical*: music teacher, instrumentalist, singer, disk jockey, song writer, music critic, choir director, composer, sound engineer, recording technician, manager, promoter
- *Bodily-kinesthetic*: athlete, rodeo rider, acrobat, jockey, actor, clown, equestrian, juggler, magician, craftsperson, dancer, coach, stunt man, gymnast, aerobics teacher, drama coach, sports trainer, choreographer, surgeon, manual laborer, builder, assembler, physical therapist
- *Linguistic*: writer, poet, journalist, storyteller, teacher, manager, supervisor, lawyer, public relations, playwright, editor, salesperson, reporter, interpreter, translator, librarian, proofreader
- *Logical-mathematical*: bookkeeper, records clerk, accountant, financial services, lawyer, paralegal, inventory control, electrical engineer, systems analyst, statistician, biologist, researcher, computer programmer, chemist, investment broker, pharmacist, mechanical engineer
- *Spatial*: landscape designer, interior designer, architect, advertising executive, navigator, artist, craftsperson, seamstress, tailor, draftsperson, mechanic, builder, engineer, graphic design, photographer, fashion designer, surveyor, set designer, urban planner, cartographer, carpenter, builder, film editor, makeup artist, hairdresser, commercial artist, sign painter, furniture restorer, geographer, pilot
- *Interpersonal/intrapersonal*: teacher, counselor, public relations/promoter, child-care provider, salesperson, politician, secretary, nurse, coach, social worker, bartender, homemaker, probation officer, recreation aide, manager, receptionist, clergy, psychologist, waiter/waitress
- *Naturalist*: animal trainer, farmer, fisherman, hunter, astronomer, chef, forester, doctor, scientist, biologist, veterinarian, meteorologist, naturalist, guide/tracker, physicist, horticulturist

Justin, an adult with ADHD, wasn't identified until later in his life. He comments that he learned that "the way his brain works holds specific, potentially life-saving talents and also may imply a tendency for certain careers for individuals with ADHD."

I discovered [certain things about ADHD that might actually be helpful in particular jobs] when I was riding. . . . I used to ride Harleys . . . I'm flying down the road. I'm doing about 90 miles per hour . . . and somebody's trailer just disconnects from the car and goes sideways and hits the rail and flips over, and cars are screeching like this (arms crisscrossing) and I'm doing 90 like an idiot, and I'm flying down the road and smoke and cars are spinning, and I went right through the middle of it and my bike is following the spin, and I went right though it, pulled over to the side of the road, pulled off my glove, and my hand was calm. . . . I couldn't figure that out. . . . It wasn't because I was [macho] 'cuz I just wet myself . . . but my hand was calm. . . . I couldn't figure that out, 'cuz adrenaline calms me down . . . so there's gotta be jobs for people who have ADD. . . . That's what it's like. . . . Cops, or working in an ER (emergency room), or as an air traffic controller.

At times, testing requirements may actually conflict with recruiting the best candidate for a job. Ironically, this may occur in educational testing, which has extensive practice with measuring performance. Years ago, during the piloting of a statewide 6½-hour assessment for administrators, Harry, a former school superintendent, was overheard to comment sarcastically, "That's all we need, principals who can sit for 6 hours."

I want the ones who'd be bouncing off the walls after only an hour. Those with ADHD, who cruise the halls with eyes in the back of their heads and leave their offices to connect with students and see what's going on.

### Life Trajectories

Gardner (1993b) maintains that education needs to "transcend common knowledge" (p. 205). Although it is important to know about history and literature, "it is at least as important for students to identify their strengths, to pursue areas where they are comfortable and in which they can achieve a great deal" (p. 205). He wrote of "life trajectories" that reflect an individual's developed abilities and skills that, in turn, "are determined in significant measure by the profile of intelligences with which they have been endowed and/or nurtured in early life" (p. 205). The life trajectories of Thomas Edison, Winston Churchill, and Pablo Picasso were not defined by their learning problems (Edison and Picasso were dyslexic and Churchill stuttered) but were determined by their learning strengths.

Shawn, a pragmatist and adult with ADHD, put it this way: "[I read a book titled] *Soar With Your Strengths*. . . . In Chapter 3, it says find out what you do well and do more of just that. Chapter 4 says find out what you don't do well, and stop doing that." For Shawn and for others, that's the secret to living with ADHD.

### AT-PROMISE

We conclude the book as we began, by examining students as "at-promise." Students with ADHD have been excised from the mainstream. Teachers seek answers to dealing with ADHD in a host of traditional ways that may have little to do with how ADHD students function best. To overcome academic and social failure, teachers must come to know and reflect on their own intelligences and the intelligences of their students. We have found that the pattern of intelligences of students with ADHD is not the same as the intelligences that are emphasized in the traditional school setting. In fact, our studies cite the pattern of intelligences of students with ADHD as fitting the naturalist and spatial profile, not the language-logic profile that is so highly prized in schools and society. The students in our studies at schools using MI felt competent and self-assured across a wide range of cognitive and interpersonal situations. They felt positive with regard to academic tasks. And despite self-reports of difficulty in reading and math, students with ADHD in this study collectively achieved average success according to report card grades.

The underestimation of a student's intelligence has a profound impact on a child's success at home, school, and in life. Further research is needed as we rethink ADHD through the lens of MI theory and examine the connection between the onset of problems (both academic and social) and school entry. Further investigation into students' profile of intelligences and the use of labels (ADHD, LD) is also critical to the understanding of how such labels correspond to teacher perceptions of student efficacy. Although we are not advocating pigeonholing students with ADHD or the "tracking" of children in general, for that matter, schools need to identify the predominant intelligences of students with ADHD. Proper identification would allow teachers to select appropriate pedagogical practices. In short, teachers could implement instructional interventions and differentiate the curriculum to have the match be the most appropriate one for the student with ADHD.

Students with ADHD feel a keen sense of failure as early as elementary school, and as a result, may begin to withdraw intellectually, emotionally, or physically from formal school experiences. It is not that the disciplines of language or logic have failed, or even that the intentions of teachers have gone unnoticed. On the contrary, research has indicated that teachers, school staff, and parents respond helpfully when students with ADHD are entrenched in school failure. However, focusing on student weakness through remediation instead of strengths dooms the student to prolonged failure.

For students with ADHD to overcome academic failure, schools must act in concert with their students' intelligences. Today, the growing interest in MI theory offers educators new hope and real tools to support the academic achievement and positive self-concept of ADHD students. MI theory offers promise for students with ADHD. Gardner (1993b) states, "In my own view nothing is more important in a student's educational career than the encountering of a discipline or craft that fits a particular blend of intelligences—a pursuit worthy of a student's efforts for years or even a lifetime. Individuals of accomplishment often attribute enormous importance to crystallizing experiences where they first confronted a pursuit that fit their learning strengths and styles. All too often, these matches occurred completely by chance" (p. 73). Gardner affirms the power of acknowledging and utilizing all the intelligences—including those typically emphasized in schools (linguistic and logical-mathematical) and those that have traditionally received less attention, such as spatial, bodily-kinesthetic, musical, interpersonal, intrapersonal, and naturalist.

He suggests that the "challenge confronting educators is to figure out how to help individuals employ their distinctive intellectual profiles to help master the tasks and disciplines needed to thrive in the society" (p. 4). For kids like Manny, we cannot afford to delay their promise any longer.

Wayne, an entrepreneur and adult with ADHD, explains how ADHD is a crucial part of an individual's character. He answers the question "Would I push a button to become normal?":

> I mean, I think 1,000 miles an hour (I don't want to get rid of that), I've got energy to burn (I don't want to get rid of that), I'm real creative (I don't want to get rid of that). I don't want to get rid of the things that ADD gives me that I like . . . so *no*, I don't want to push that button to get rid of my ADD. . . . Why? Because I like my ADD. . . . See, I had a problem that I was trying to solve because I was told it was a problem. . . . Then I'm thinking there are other things I like . . . sure, there are things that cause problems . . . but I also have some things that solve problems . . . that make things unique for me. . . . So no, I don't want to get rid of my ADD. . . . [He sighs.] As a matter of fact, I *like* my ADD.

# Diagnostic Criteria for ADHD

**A.** Either (1) or (2):

1. Six (or more) of the following symptoms of *inattention* have persisted for at least 6 months to a degree that is maladaptive and inconsistent with developmental level:

   **Inattention**

   a. Often fails to give close attention to details or makes careless mistakes in schoolwork, work, or other activities

   b. Often has difficulty sustaining attention in tasks or play activities

   c. Often does not seem to listen when spoken to directly

   d. Often does not follow through on instructions and fails to finish schoolwork, chores, or duties in the workplace (not due to oppositional behavior or failure to understand instructions)

   e. Often has difficulty organizing tasks and activities

   f. Often avoids, dislikes, or is reluctant to engage in tasks that require sustained mental effort (such as schoolwork or homework)

   g. Often loses things necessary for tasks or activities (e.g., toys, school assignments, pencils, books, or tools)

   h. Is often easily distracted by extraneous stimuli

   i. Is often forgetful in daily activities

2. Six (or more) of the following symptoms of *hyperactivity-impulsivity* have persisted for at least 6 months to a degree that is maladaptive and inconsistent with developmental level:

   **Hyperactivity**

   a. Often fidgets with hands or feet or squirms in seat

   b. Often leaves seat in classroom or in other situations in which remaining seated is expected

   c. Often runs about or climbs excessively in situations in which it is inappropriate (in adolescents or adults, may be limited to subjective feelings of restlessness)

   d. Often has difficulty playing or engaging in leisure activities quietly

   e. Is often "on the go" or often acts as if "driven by a motor"

   f. Often talks excessively

   **Impulsivity**

   g. Often blurts out answers before questions have been completed

   h. Often has difficulty awaiting turn

   i. Often interrupts or intrudes on others (e.g., butts into conversations or games)

**B.** Some hyperactive-impulsive or inattentive symptoms that caused impairment were present before age 7.

   **C.** Some impairment from the symptoms is present in two or more settings (e.g., at school [or work] and at home).

   **D.** There must be clear evidence of clinically significant impairment in social, academic, or occupational functioning.

   **E.** The symptoms do not occur exclusively during the course of a pervasive developmental disorder, schizophrenia, or other psychotic disorder and are not better accounted for by another mental disorder (e.g., mood disorder, anxiety disorder, disssociative disorder, or a personality disorder).

## Code based on type:

*314.01 Attention-Deficit/Hyperactivity Disorder, Combined Type*: If both Criteria A1 and A2 are for the past 6 months

*314.00 Attention-Deficit/Hyperactivity Disorder, Predominantly Inattentive Type*: If Criterion A1 is met, but Criterion A2 is not met for the past 6 months

*314.01 Attention-Deficit/Hyperactivity Disorder, Predominantly Hyperactive-Impulsive Type*: If Criterion A2 is met, but Criterion A1 is not met for the past 6 months

*Coding note*: For individuals (especially adolescents and adults) who currently have symptoms that no longer meet full criteria, "In Partial Remission" should be specified.

*Source*: American Psychiatric Association (2000), pp. 83–85.

# Online Multiple Intelligences Developmental Assessment Scale (MIDAS™) Directions

C. Branton Shearer

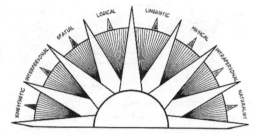

**Multiple Intelligences Research and Consulting, Inc.**

**www.MIResearch.org**

### ONLINE MIDAS SYSTEM INSTRUCTIONS

1. Make sure you are connected to the Internet. Open a browser such as Internet Explorer, Netscape, Safari, or Firefox. The OMS system may not function properly on computers with strong security systems such as public Internet cafes or in some schools.

2. **DISABLE YOUR SPAM/JUNK** e-mail filter if you have one. (**This is important to do!**)

3. Go to the following link: *http://www.MIResearch.org/assessments*

4. Click on the button: "**Login to take M.I.D.A.S. Assessment.**"

5. Enter **Login, Password,** and **Org Code** exactly as provided (case sensitive!): "**Submit**":
   Login = _____Refer to inside back cover_____
   Password = _____Refer to inside back cover_____
   Org Code = _____Refer to inside back cover_____

   *Note*: There are *two* login numbers. Use one per profile. The password and org code remain the same for both profiles.

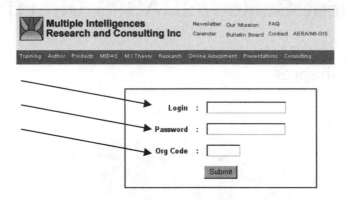

6. It will first ask for information about you (name, education, e-mail). Be sure to **carefully** enter an accurate e-mail address where the profile will be sent **(very important!).** Respond to each question thoughtfully. You cannot skip questions, but you may answer: "I don't know."

7. The questionnaire will take about 20 minutes to complete. It will stop at the end of each section so you may correct any of your responses.
   If you must stop before completing, you may login again later. You will have to start from the beginning, using the same login codes. Once you have responded to all questions, you can no longer login using those codes.
   *The Web is inherently unstable, so you may need to be patient and persistent.*

8. When finished, the program will automatically e-mail the profile to the e-mail address that you provided (usually within a few minutes).

9. The **MIDAS profile** is e-mailed as a .PDF document with a **Brief Interpretative Packet**.
   Follow those instructions to maximize the benefit that you will receive from a MIDAS profile. It is important to verify your profile for yourself!
   If you do not have **Acrobat** to open these documents, you can download it for free at: *www.adobe.com/products/acrobat/readstep2.html*
   For more information about **multiple intelligences** and your MIDAS profile, visit: *www.MIResearch.org*

If you experience any problems send an e-mail to *sales@miresearch.org*

Best of Luck!

**Branton Shearer, Ph.D.**
M.I. Research and Consulting, Inc.

# MIDAS™
# Interpretative Packet

## C. Branton Shearer

**Multiple Intelligences Research and Consulting, Inc.**

**www.MIResearch.org**

**Hello—**

   **This profile** was compiled from The MIDAS–KIDS questionnaire. The scales are based on the theory of multiple intelligences as described by Howard Gardner, who defines intelligence as: " . . . *an ability to solve a problem or create a product that is valued in your community."*

   The MIDAS profile can be used to gain a deeper understanding of a child's skills/abilities and preferred learning style. **This is not a test**. These scores are not absolute. It is up to you to determine if these scores are a good description of your child's intellectual and creative life.

   **If this profile appears** to be lower than what you know to be true, then you probably underreported your child's abilities. Factors that can lower scores are modesty, excessive criticalness, or lack of knowledge. To verify this profile, first review pages 1 and 2 by asking these questions, and then create a Brief Learning Summary.

   **Page 1**: Does this profile accurately picture your child's general overall level of abilities?
   **Page 2**: Are the subscales listed in an order that matches strengths and weaknesses?
   **Page 3**: Create a *personalized* brief learning summary

### Brief Learning Summary

   **1. Main Areas**: List the 8 main scores from high to low in the approximate categories.
   
   High =    2 highest scales
   Middle = 3 middle scales
   Low =    2 lowest scales

   **2. Specific Areas**: From page 2, write in the five highest and lowest subscales in categories.

   **3. Preferred Activities**: Describe actual activities that your child does the most or the best. For example, *"played the trumpet for 5 years."* Also, from the bottom of page 1, write in the highest of the intellectual style scales (technical, innovation). These indicate if your child tends to have more inventive or practical problem-solving skills.

**Validate** this summary by discussing it with your child or other people who know him or her well, and also compare it to other test results, such as school grades or feedback from teachers.

**Now** you may review the MIDAS–KIDS scale descriptions and study strategies to learn how the different intelligences are used to enhance life and learning. Additional information is available from the author, which you may obtain from the website: *www.MIResearch.org*

**Branton Shearer, Ph.D.**

## THE MIDAS

### Brief Learning Summary

Name: _____ Date: _____ # _____

The following profile was compiled from data provided by you. It represents areas of strength and limitation as described by you. This is preliminary information to be confirmed by way of discussion and further exploration.

**MAIN AREAS**                                      **SPECIFIC SKILLS**

**HIGH**

**MIDDLE**

**LOW**

*Preferred Activities:*

## MIDAS–KIDS SCALES

**Musical:** *To think in sounds, rhythms, melodies, and rhymes. To be sensitive to pitch, rhythm, timbre, and tone. To recognize, create, and reproduce music by using an instrument or voice. Active listening and a strong connection between music and emotions.*

> **Musicality:** awareness of and sensitivity to music, rhythms, tunes, and melody

> **Instrument:** skill and experience in playing a musical instrument

> **Vocal:** a good voice for singing in tune and along with other people

> **Appreciation:** actively enjoys listening to music

**Kinesthetic:** *To think in movements and to use the body in skilled and complicated ways for expressive as well as goal-directed activities. It involves a sense of timing and coordination for whole body movement and the use of hands for manipulating objects.*

> **Physical Ability:** ability to move the whole body for physical activities such as balancing, coordination, and sports

> **Dance, Acting:** to use the body in expressive, rhythmic and imitative ways

> **Working with Hands:** to use the hands with dexterity and skill for detailed activities and small work

**Logical-Mathematical:** *To think of cause-and-effect connections and to understand relationships among actions, objects, or ideas. To be able to calculate, quantify, consider propositions, and perform complex mathematical or logical operations. It involves inductive and deductive reasoning skills as well as critical and creative problem solving.*

> **Problem Solving:** skill in organization, problem solving, and logical reasoning; curiosity and investigation

> **Calculations:** ability to work with numbers for mathematical operations such as addition and division

**Spatial:** *To think in pictures and to perceive the visual world accurately. To be able to think in three dimensions and to transform one's perceptions and re-create aspects of one's visual experience via the imagination. To work with objects effectively.*

> **Imagery:** use of mental imagery for observation, artistic, creative, and other visual activities

> **Artistic Design**: to create artistic designs, drawings, paintings, or other crafts

> **Constructions:** to be able to make, build, or assemble things

**Linguistic:** *To think in words and to use language* to express and understand complex meanings. *Sensitivity to the meaning of words as well as the order among words, their sounds, rhythms, and inflections. To reflect on the use of language in everyday life.*

> **Linguistic Sensitivity:** skill in the use of words for expressive and practical purposes

> **Reading:** skill in reading

> **Writing:** ability and interest in writing projects such as poems, stories, books, or letters

**Interpersonal:** *To think about and understand another person.* *To have empathy and recognize distinctions among people and to appreciate their perspectives with sensitivity to their motives, moods, and intentions.*

> **Understanding People:** sensitivity to and understanding of other people's moods, feelings, and point of view

> **Getting along with Others:** able to maintain good relationships with other people, especially friends and siblings

> **Leadership:** to take a leadership role among people through problem solving and influence

**Intrapersonal:** *To think about and understand one's self.* *To be aware of one's strengths and weaknesses and to plan effectively to achieve personal goals. It involves reflecting on and monitoring one's thoughts and feelings and regulating them effectively. The ability to monitor one's self in interpersonal relationships and to act with personal efficacy.*

> **Self-Knowledge:** awareness of one's own ideas, abilities; personal decision-making skill

> **Goal Achievement:** awareness of goals and self-correction and monitoring in light of a goal

> **Managing Feelings:** ability to regulate one's feelings, moods, and emotional responses

> **Effective Relationships:** ability to regulate one's mental activities and behavior with other people

**Naturalist:** *To understand the natural world, including plants, animals, and scientific studies.* *To be able to recognize and classify individuals, species, and ecological relationships. To interact effectively with living creatures and discern patterns of life and natural forces.*

> **Animal Care:** skill for understanding animal behavior, needs, characteristics

> **Earth Science:** ability to work with plants, i.e., gardening, etc., and knowledge of natural science

### Intellectual Styles

**Innovative:** To work in artistic, divergent, and imaginative ways. To improvise and create unique answers, arguments, or solutions.

**Technical:** To work accurately, carefully. To strive for just the right answer and perform activities in the exact way they are shown.

# Multiple Intelligences Research and Consulting, Inc.

**Hello!**

The **MIDAS** assessment provides information to help students and parents understand themselves better so they may be successful in life as well as in school. After the **Brief Learning Summary** has been created, you should review it carefully to determine if it is accurate. Students and parents often have differing views and so it is important that you use the MIDAS Profile as a means of having an understanding and respectful discussion. It is O.K. to agree to disagree about the results.

This **MIDAS Profile** indicates areas of skill, knowledge, and disposition as reported by the individual or parent. These scores represent the approximate level of development in each area *at the present time*. **All of these abilities may be improved over time and with effort and guidance.** To determine the accuracy of the MIDAS Profile, use the form on the next page and follow these steps:

**First**, look over the MIDAS Profile and make note of high and low areas. You will want to become familiar with each area by reading the information in this packet.

**Second,** ask yourself, a family member, or a close friend if they agree with these areas of strength and weakness.

**Third**, compare this profile to other sources of information, such as:

- feedback from teachers and other knowledgeable adults

- other test results

- grades in school subjects and projects

- after-school and weekend activities

**Fourth**, discuss all this information with the student and if necessary revise the **Brief Learning Summary** to create a Verified Profile that better represents what the student is really capable of doing.

**You are now ready** to use the verified MIDAS Profile to make plans to increase intellectual development, achieve better performance in school and to promote personal satisfaction and greater fulfillment. Completion of the activities in this workbook will result in a greater appreciation for the student's strengths and how these can be activated and used to create workable plans for enhanced development.

## Multiple Intelligences in Daily Life

### C. Branton Shearer, Ph.D.

| | Activities | Study Skills | Just for Fun | School Major | Careers |
|---|---|---|---|---|---|
| Musical | Singing, listening, playing instruments | Rhyme, rhythm, song, lyrics, repetition, sing it with gusto! | Hum, sing, drum, rhyme, compose, strum, whistle | Band, vocal, composing, choral, orchestra | Choral director, musician, sound engineer, DJ, critic |
| Kinesthetic | Sports, dance, handicrafts, jogging, acting, mime, dexterity | Gestures, write large 3x, act it out, dramatize it, make models | Wrestle, touch football, soccer, magic tricks, juggle, dance | Recreation, dance, leisure, fitness, physical education | Actor, coach, assembler, laborer, dentist, choreographer |
| Linguistic | Speaking, reading, writing, storytelling, poetry | Note taking, checklist, outline, tape record, teach | Word play, poetry, story telling, lyrics, read aloud | Journalism, education, sociology, literature | Writer, editor, librarian, teacher, translator, sales |
| Logical/Math | Calculating, investigation, problem solving, strategy, logic | Question, categorize, explain, analyze, compare | Chess, mysteries, challenges, puzzles, computers | Engineering, accounting, medicine, computers, science | Lawyer, chemist, analyst, bookkeeper, engineer |
| Spatial | Map reading, artistic design, crafts, mechanical | Watch, mind-map it, visualize, colorize notes, cartooning. | Doodling, photography, modeling, clothing design | Architecture, engineering, aviation, graphic design | Landscape design, artist, interior design, pilot |
| Interpersonal | Empathy, leadership, manage relationships | Study groups, teach it to someone, role-playing discuss | Team games, sports, chatting, helping, volunteering | Ministry, public relations, management, nursing | Teaching, nurse, counselor, sales, politician |
| Intrapersonal | Personal knowledge, opinions, judgment, self-direction, goal | Test yourself, ask why it's important to me, ask what do I know now | Reflection time, surveys, planning life goals, journals | Creative writing, philosophy, psychology, leadership | Minister, psychologist, writer, artist, pilot, engineer |
| Naturalist | Understanding animals, working with plants, science | Use your senses, observations, metaphors | Train a pet, fish tanks, nature hikes, plant flowers | Biology, ecology, horticulture, zoology | Naturalist, forester, farmer, botanist, greenhouse worker |

### Profile Reflections
### on *Brief Learning Summary*

The areas on the summary that I think are too high or low are:

| | High | OK | Low | | High | OK | Low |
|---|---|---|---|---|---|---|---|
| **Linguistic** | ___ | ___ | ___ | **Musical** | ___ | ___ | ___ |
| **Spatial** | ___ | ___ | ___ | **Kinesthetic** | ___ | ___ | ___ |
| **Logical-Mathematical** | ___ | ___ | ___ | **Intrapersonal** | ___ | ___ | ___ |
| **Naturalist** | ___ | ___ | ___ | **Interpersonal** | ___ | ___ | ___ |

Overall, I think the profile is:  **OK**____  **Too high**____  **Too low**____  **Mixed up** ____

My _____ scale **surprises** me because . . .

_____

_____

My _____ scale **puzzles** me because . . .

_____

_____

What I **learned** about myself from this assessment is . . .

_____

_____

**Other Comments:**

# MIDAS™
# Profile Report

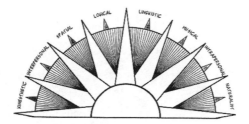

# M.I.D.A.S

## Multiple Intelligences Developmental Assessment Scales
*"Discover Your Royal Road to Learning, Achievement, and Personal Development."*

Name: A. Student          ID Number: 610          Code:
Birth Date: 31 May 1998   Education: Primary       Sex: Male

These main scales represent your multiple intelligences profile as reported by you. You should review and verify this profile via reflection, discussion, and in comparison with other information.

## Main Scales
| | |
|---|---|
| Linguistic | *********** |
| Interpersonal | ******** |
| Intrapersonal | ********* |
| Logical-Mathematical | **************** |
| Spatial | ********************* |
| Musical | ******************* |
| Kinesthetic | *************** |
| Naturalist | *********************** |

The following profile represents your intellectual style. These scales indicate if you tend to be more social, practical, or inventive in your problem-solving abilities.

## Style Sales
| | |
|---|---|
| Technical | ******** |
| Innovative | ************************* |

Processed 4-05-2008    Percent answered items = 90%

The MIDAS subscales are ranked below in the left column from the highest at the top to the lowest at the bottom. The shaded top group represents skills that you identified as strengths. Areas that are least well developed are in the shaded area at the bottom.

| Rank | Specific Skill | Main Scale |
|------|----------------|------------|
| High | | |
| | Vocal | Musical |
| | Self-knowledge | Intrapersonal |
| | Imagery | Spatial |
| | Earth science | Naturalist |
| | Artistic | Spatial |
| | | |
| | Dance | Kinesthetic |
| | Problem solving | Logical-mathematical |
| | Appreciation | Musical |
| | Constructions | Spatial |
| | Writing | Linguistic |
| | | |
| | Animal care | Naturalist |
| | Musicality | Musical |
| | Leadership | Interpersonal |
| | Physical ability | Kinesthetic |
| | Effective relationships | Intrapersonal |
| | | |
| | Reading | Linguistic |
| | Managing feelings | Intrapersonal |
| | Hands | Kinesthetic |
| | Calculations | Logical-mathematical |
| | Goal achievement | Intrapersonal |
| | | |
| | Getting along with others | Interpersonal |
| | Linguistic sensitivity | Linguistic |
| | Understanding people | Interpersonal |
| Low | Instrument | Musical |

The following are percentage scores based on the total number of completed items for the main scales and subscales. This profile should be carefully verified before assuming the validity of these scores.

| All Scales | Score | Category |
|---|---|---|
| *Linguistic* | 31 (Low) | |
| Linguistic sensitivity | | 13 (Very Low) |
| Writing | | 50 (Moderate) |
| Reading | | 25 (Low) |
| *Interpersonal* | 19 (Very Low) | |
| Leadership | | 42 (Moderate) |
| Understanding people | | 13 (Very Low) |
| Getting along with others | | 13 (Very Low) |
| *Intrapersonal* | 25 (Low) | |
| Self-knowledge | | 75 (High) |
| Managing feelings | | 25 (Low) |
| Effective relationships | | 25 (Low) |
| Goal achievement | | 20 (Low) |
| *Logical-mathematical* | 40 (Moderate) | |
| Problem solving | | 60 (High) |
| Calculations | | 20 (Low) |
| *Spatial* | 55 (Moderate) | |
| Artistic | | 67 (High) |
| Constructions | | 50 (Moderate) |
| Imagery | | 70 (High) |
| *Musical* | 50 (Moderate) | |
| Musicality | | 44 (Moderate) |
| Vocal | | 100 (Very High) |
| Appreciation | | 58 (Moderate) |
| Instrument | | 0 (Very Low) |
| *Kinesthetic* | 41 (Moderate) | |
| Physical ability | | 35 (Low) |
| Dance | | 63 (High) |
| Hands | | 25 (Low) |
| *Naturalist* | 61 (High) | |
| Animal care | | 45 (Moderate) |
| Earth science | | 69 (High) |
| *Technical* | 21 (Low) | |
| Innovative | 68 (High) | |

# References

About QuickReads. (2006). QuickReads: A research-based fluency program. Retrieved May 27, 2008, from http://www.quickreads.org

Ackerman, P. (1996, September). *Adult intelligence*. Department of Education. Office of Educational Research and Improvement. The Catholic University of America. (ERIC/ AE Digest Series EDO-TM-96-03)

American Psychiatric Association. (2000). *Diagnostic and Statistical Manual of Mental Disorders* (4th ed.). Washington, DC: Author.

Armstrong, T. (1987). Describing strengths in children identified as "learning disabled" using Howard Gardner's theory of multiple intelligences as an organizing framework. *Dissertation Abstract International*. (UMI No. 872584A)

Armstrong, T. (1994). *Multiple intelligences in the classroom*. Alexandria, VA: Association for Supervision & Curriculum Development (ASCD).

Armstrong, T. (2003). *The multiple intelligences of reading and writing*. Alexandria, VA: ASCD.

Attention-Deficit Hyperactivity Disorder. (1995). Treatment. *Harvard Mental Health Letter*. Retrieved February 28, 1998, from http://www.concentric.net/~skiplac/sx1.html

Bailey, S. (2003). Rxboard. Message posted to Strattera-Info From About.com Forum. Retrieved July 19, 2008, from http://mb.rxlist.com/rxboard/general.pl?noframes; read=1709

Barkley, R. (1992). ADHD: *What do we know? Program manual*. New York: Guilford.

Barkley, R. (1995). *Taking charge of ADHD: The complete authoritative guide for parents*. New York: Guilford.

Baum, S., Viens, J., & Slatin, B. (2005). *Multiple intelligences in the elementary classroom: A Teacher's toolkit*. New York: Teachers College Press.

Bete, T. (1997, August). Renovating to support the seven ways students are smart. *Planning and Management, 36*, 8:14–19.

Beyda, S., & Zentall, S. (1998, Winter). Administrative responses to AD/HD. *Reaching Today's Youth, 31*–36.

Bishop, P., & Beyer, R. (1995, Summer). Attention Deficit Hyperactivity Disorder (ADHD): Implications for physical educators. *PALESTRA*, 39–46.

Black, S. (1994, January). Different kinds of smart. *The Executive Editor, 16*(1), 24–27.

Blythe, T., & Gardner, H. (1990). A school for all intelligences. *Educational Leadership, 47*(7), 33–37.

Braswell, L., Bloomquist, M., & Pederson, S. (1991). *ADHD: A guide to understanding and helping children with attention deficit hyperactivity disorder in school settings*. Minneapolis: University of Minnesota.

Brooks, D. (2007). *Family relationships shape education. The Day* (New London, CT), editorial.

Brown, A. (1998). Research Newsletter. *NARSAD, 10*, 34–38.

Butler, R. (1994). Geography and vision-impaired and blind populations. *Transactions of the Institute of British Geographers, New Series, 19*(3), 366–368.

California Nurses Association. (1988). Difficult behaviors in the classrooms: Keys for managing challenging student behaviors. Retrieved November 15, 2007, from http:// honolulu.hawaii.edu/intranet/committees/FacDevCom/guidebk/teachingtip/behavior .html

Campbell, B. (1992, Summer). Multiple intelligences in action. *Childhood Education,* 197–202.

Campbell, B., & Campbell, L. (1997). How teachers interpret MI theory. *Educational Leadership, 55,* 14–20.

Chapman-Booth, R. (1998). List of appropriate school-based accommodations and interventions: For a 504 adaptations and modifications section of an IEP. Retrieved May 27, 2008, from http://www.insource.org/pdf/504acom.pdf

Checkley, K. (1997). The first seven . . . and the eight: A conversation with Howard Gardner. *Educational Leadership, 55,* 8–14.

Children and Adults Against Drugging America (CHAADA). (2008). Facts and statistics. Retrieved April 4, 2008, from http://www.chaada.org/Page3.html

Cohen, M. (1999). The quest for recognition of AD/HD within the IDEA: A case study in public policy advocacy, perseverance, and grassroots effort. *Attention!®,* 38–40.

Connecticut State Department of Education Association of Boards of Education Parent-Teacher Association of Connecticut Special Education Resource Center. (1998, June). Policy action packet for school-family-community partnerships: A guide to developing partnership programs for student success.

Dalke, J. (2006). Venn Diagrams©. Retrieved May 16, 2006, from http://www.lessonplanspage.com/lAMathVennDiagAPromise/Apromise24.htm

D'Alonzo, B. (1996). Identification and education of students with attention deficit and attention deficit hyperactivity disorders. *Preventing School Failure, 40,* 88–94.

Damico, S., & Armstrong, M. (1996). Intervention strategies for students with ADHD: Creating a holistic approach. *Seminars in Speech and Language, 17,* 21–35.

DeNoon, D. (2001). New ADHD drugs—new problems. *Medical News Archives.* Retrieved January 18, 2002, from http://www.future-horizons.org

Duane, D. (1988). The classroom clinician's role in finding the cause of ADD/LD. *Learning Disabilities Focus, 4,* 6–8.

DuCharme, C. (1995). Valuing differences: The children we don't understand. *Journal of Learning Disabilities, 28*(9), 582–585.

Dunlea, H. (2006). Box and Deliver©. Retrieved May 16, 2006, from http://www.lessonplanspage.com/MathSSLatLongPlotting-BoxAndDeliver56.htm

Dyson, L. (2000, April). *From the classroom to the community: Evaluation of attention deficit hyperactivity disorder (ADHD) by teachers and mental health professionals.* Paper presented at the Annual Meeting of the American Educational Research Association. New Orleans, LA.

Emig, V. (1997). A multiple intelligences inventory. *Educational Leadership, 55,* 47–50.

Epstein, J. (1986). Parents' reactions to teacher practices of parental involvement. *The Elementary School Journal, 86*(3), 277–294.

Espinosa, L. (1995). Hispanic parent involvement in early childhood programs. ERIC ED 382412. ERIC Clearinghouse on Elementary and Early Childhood Education, Urbana, IL.

Fagella, K., & Horowitz, J. (1990, September). Different child, different style. *Instructor,* 49–52.

Feinberg, B. (2007). The Lucy Calkins project. *Education Next®, 7*(3). Retrieved June 13, 2007, from http://www.hoover.org/publications/ednext/75558137.html

Fine, L. (2001, May). Paying attention. *Education Week,* 26–29.

Fiore, T., Becker, E., & Nero, R. (1993). Educational interventions for students with attention deficit disorder. *Exceptional Children, 60*(2), 163–174.

Freed, J., & Parsons, L. (1997). *Right-brained children: Unlocking the potential of your ADD child in a left-brained world.* New York: Simon & Schuster.

French, T. M. (1939). Primary mental abilities by L. L. Thurstone. [Review.] *Psychoanalytic Quarterly, 8,* 534–535.

Gardill, C., & DuPaul, G. (1996). Classroom strategies for managing students with attention-deficit/hyperactivity disorder. *Intervention in School & Clinic, 32*(2), 89–94.

Gardner, H. (1989). Balancing specialized & comprehensive knowledge: The growing educational challenge. In T. J. Sergiovanni & J. H. Moore (Eds.), *Schooling for tomorrow: Directing reforms to issues that count*, 148–164. Needham Height, MA: Simon & Schuster.

Gardner, H. (1992, July/August). Multiple intelligences: Putting research to work. *Instructor*, 48–49.

Gardner, H. (1993a). *Frames of mind: The theory of multiple intelligences* (10th anniversary ed.). New York: Basic Books.

Gardner, H. (1993b). *Multiple intelligences: The theory in practice.* New York: Basic Books.

Gardner, H. (1995). Reflections on multiple intelligences: Myths and messages. *Phi Delta Kappan*, 77(3), 200–209.

Gardner, H. (1997, February). Letters to the editor. *NASSP Bulletin*, 81(586), 121–22.

Gardner, H. (1999a). *Intelligence reframed: Multiple intelligences for the 21st century.* New York: Basic Books.

Gardner, H. (1999b). A Prescription for peace. *Time.* [Electronic Copy] Retrieved February 17, 2008, from http://www.time.com

Garrett, A. (1994, November). *What is curriculum history and why is it important?* Paper presented at the Annual Meeting of the American Educational Studies Association, Chapel Hill, NC.

Gestwicki, C. (2000). *Home, school, and community relations: A guide to working with families* (4th ed.). Albany, NY: Delmar-Thompson Learning.

Gorrell, C. (2002). The classroom revisited. *Psychology Today*, 35(4), 54–56.

Hamilton, R., & Ghatala, E. (1994). *Learning and instruction.* New York: McGraw-Hill.

Hatch, T. (1997, March). Getting specific about multiple intelligences. *Educational Leadership*, 26–29.

Hawkins, J., Blanchard, K., & Brady, M. P. (1991). Teacher perceptions, beliefs, and interventions regarding children with attention deficit disorders. *Action in Teacher Education*, 8, 52–59.

Hazelwood, E., Bovingdon, T., & Tiemens, K. (2002). The meaning of a multimodal approach for children with ADHD: Experiences of service professionals. *Child: Care, Health and Development*, 28(4), 301–308.

Hearne, D., & Stone, S. (1995). Multiple intelligences and underachievement: Lessons from individuals with learning disabilities. *Journal of Learning Disabilities*, 28, 439–448.

Hebert, E. (1992). Portfolios invite reflection from students and staff. *Educational Leadership*, 58–61.

Henderson, J., & Hawthorne, R. (1995). *Transformative curriculum leadership.* Englewood Cliffs, NJ: Prentice Hall.

Hoagwood, K., Kelleher, K., Feil, M., & Comer, D. (2000). Treatment services for children with ADHD: A national perspective. *American Academy of Child and Adolescent Psychiatry*, 39(2), 198–206.

Hoerr, T. (1996a, November). Focusing on the personal intelligence as a basis for success. *NASSP Bulletin*, 36–42.

Hoerr, T. (1996b, November). Introducing the theory of multiple intelligences. *NASSP Bulletin*, 80(583), 8–10.

Hoerr, T. (2000). *Becoming a multiple intelligences school.* Alexandria, VA: ASCD.

Howard, J. (1990). *Getting smart: The social construction of intelligence.* Lexington, MA: The Efficacy Institute.

Jensen, E. (1998). *Teaching with the brain in mind.* Alexandria, VA: ASCD.

Jordan, S. (1996, November). Multiple intelligences: Seven keys to opening closed minds. *NASSP Bulletin*, 80(583), 29–35.

Kaplan, S. (1995). The restorative benefits of nature: Toward an integrative framework. *Journal of Environmental Psychology*, 15, 169–182.

Kessler, R., Chiu, W., Demler, O., & Walters, E. (2005). Prevalence, severity, and comorbidity of twelve-month DSM-IV disorders in the National Comorbidity Survey Replication (NCS-R). *Archives of General Psychiatry*, 62(6), 617–627.

Keys for managing challenging student behaviors. (1988). Retrieved November 15, 2007, from http://honolulu.hawaii.edu/intranet/committees/FacDevCom/guidebk/teachtip/behavior.html

Krechevsky, M. (1994). *Project Spectrum: Preschool assessment handbook.* Cambridge: Harvard College.

Kugelmass, J. W. (1996). *Foxfire classrooms in alternative views of learning disabilities: Issues for the 21st century,* pp. 257–261.

Kuo, F., & Faber Taylor, A. (2004, August 30). Children with ADHD benefit from time outdoors enjoying nature. *Science Daily,* Champaign, IL: University of Illinois at Urbana-Champaign news release. Retrieved September 3, 2004, from http://www.sciencedaily.com

Levine, M. (2002). *A mind at a time.* New York: Simon & Schuster.

Levine, M. (2003). What's seen on the social scene. *Schwab Learning, August Newsletter.* Retrieved July 19, 2008, from http://www.nldline.com/information_page.htm

Levine, M. (2007, July 30). Retrieved July 19, 2008, from http://www.malaya.com.ph/jul30/livi2.htm

Levine, M. (n.d.). All kinds of minds: A message from Dr. Mel Levine, founder and Co-Chairman of All Kinds of Minds. Retrieved October 20, 2002, from http://www.allkindsofminds.org/perspective.

Linksman, R. (2007). Reading and ADD or ADHD. Retrieved December 22, 2007, from http://www.readinginstruction.com/abriclin.html

Lockwood, A. (1993, Fall). Multiple intelligences theory in action. *Research and the Classroom, 4,* Madison, WI: Board of Regents, University.

Louv, R. (2005). Last child in the woods: Saving our children from nature-deficit disorder. Chapel Hill, NC: Algonquin Books.

Mash, E. J., & Barkley, R. A. (2006). *Treatment of childhood disorders.* (3rd ed.). London: Guilford Press.

Maslow's Hierarchy of Needs. Retrieved November 15, 2007, from http://honolulu.hawaii.edu/intranet/committees/FacDevCom/guidebk/teachtip/m-files/m-maslow.htm

McCarthy, J., & May, C. (1974). Providing the best for children. *National Association for the Education of Young Children, 222.*

McCormick, K. (1994). *The culture of reading and the teaching of English.* Manchester, UK: Manchester University Press.

Miller, M. (2006). Using word syllables to create rhythmic sentences. Retrieved May 16, 2006, from www.lessonplanspage.com/musicLAmathcreateRythmicsentenceswithsyllables38.htm

Miranda, A., Presentacion, M., & Soriano, M. (2002). Effectiveness of a school-based multicomponent program for the treatment of children with ADHD. *Journal of Learning Disabilities, 35*(6), 546–562.

Moments in America for Children, American Defense Fund. (2008, March). Retrieved May 29, 2008, from http://www.childrensdefense.org/site/PageServer?JServSessionIdr007=vd4taneyn3.app13a&pagename=research_national_data_moments

Moore, D. (2000). *Barkley: ADHD theory, diagnosis, treatment-lecture summary.* Schwab Learning. June 17, 2000. Retrieved October 27, 2003, from http://www.future-horizons.org

Mosey, C. (2002). *Buzz words in education: A joy for ADHD.* Retrieved July 28, 2002, from http://www.future-horizons.org

National Institute of Mental Health (2003). *Attention deficit hyperactivity disorder.* Bethesda, MD: U.S. Department of Health and Human Services.

National Institute of Mental Health. (2006). Attention deficit hyperactivity disorder. Retrieved November 11, 2006, from http://www.nimh.nih.gov/health/publications/adhd/complete-publication.shtml

National Institute of Mental Health (2007). Attention deficit hyperactivity disorder. Retrieved November 12, 2007, from http://www.nimh.nih.gov/health/publications/adhd/complete-publication.shtml

National Institutes of Health. (1998). Diagnosis and treatment of attention deficit hyperactivity disorder (ADHD). [Electronic version]. *NIH Consensus Statement, 16*(2), 1–37.

National Institutes of Health (2000). National Institutes of Health consensus development conference statement: Diagnosis and treatment of attention-deficit/hyperactivity disorder (ADHD). *Child & Adolescent Psychiatry, 39*(2), 182–193.

Natwick, K. (1991). *Preparing the Head Start children for kindergarten through parent and teacher education.* Unpublished master's thesis, Nova University, Florida.

Neisser, U., Boodoo, G., Bouchard, T. J., Boykin, W. A., Brody, N., Ceci, S. J., et al. (1996, February). Intelligence: Known and unknowns. *American Psychology, 77*–101.

Parmet, S., Cassio, L., & Glass, R. (2002, October). Attention-deficit/hyperactivity disorder. *Journal of the American Medical Association, 288*(14), 1,804.

Perie, M., Baker, D., & Bobbitt, S. (1997). Time spent teaching core academic subjects in elementary schools: Comparisons across community, school, teacher, and student characteristics. *National Center for Educational Statistics: Statistical Analysis Report.* U.S. Department of Education. Office of Educational Research and Improvement, Washington, D.C.

Pfiffner, L. (1995). Enhancing education at school and at home: Methods for success from kindergarten through grade 12. In R. A. Barkley (Ed.), *Taking charge of ADHD: The complete authoritative guide for parents* (pp. 206–221). New York: The Guilford Press.

Piers, E. (1984). *Piers-Harris children's self-concept scale.* Los Angeles, CA: Western Psychological Services and Distributors.

Poplin, M., & Cousin, P. T. (1996). *Alternative views of learning disabilities: Issues for the 21st century.* Austin, TX: PRO-ED.

Power, J. (1992). Parent/teacher partnerships in early literacy learning: The benefits for teachers. Paper presented at the AARE Conference, Victoria, Australia.

Project Spectrum. (1998). *Project Spectrum.* Retrieved March 23, 1998, from http://pzweb.harvard.edu/Left/PZInfo/Research/Restxt/Spectrum.html

Project Zero (1999). *Project SUMIT.* Retrieved January 15, 1999, from http://pzweb.harvard.edu/SUMIT.html

Purvis, J. R., Jones, C. H., & Authement, C. (1992). Attention deficit hyperactivity disorder: Strategies for the classroom. *Journal of Special Education, 16,* 112–119.

Richter, M. (2006, October 8). Quick stats of ADHD. Retrieved July 20, 2008, from http://www.adhdnews.com/blog/archives/2006/10/index.html.

Robelia, B. (1997). Tips for working with ADHD students of all ages. *The Journal of Experiential Education, 20*(1), 51–53.

Rosselli, H. (1998). From Passow to Gardner: curriculum for talent development. *Gifted Child Quarterly 42*(3), 245–252.

Schirduan, V. (2000). *Elementary students with attention deficit hyperactivity disorder (ADHD) in schools using multiple intelligences theory: Intelligences, self-concept, and achievement.* Ann Arbor, MI: UMI™ Dissertation.

Schirduan, V., & Case, K. (2004, January). Mindful curriculum leadership for students with attention deficit hyperactivity disorder: Leading in elementary schools by using multiple intelligences theory (SUMIT). *Teachers College Record, 1*(106), 87–95.

Schirduan, V., Case, K., & Faryniarz, J. (2002, Summer). How ADHD students are smart. *The Educational Forum, 66,* 324–328.

Schirduan, V., & Miller, R. (2002). Why must a child's first encounter with school be filled with worries, misgivings, and fears, and not wonder, magic, and fun? *Journal of Early Education and Family Review, 9*(5), 6–17.

Schlozman, S., & Schlozman, V. (2000, November). Chaos in the classroom: Looking at ADHD. *Educational Leadership, 58*(3), 28–33.

Shearer, B. (1999). *The MIDAS handbook: Multiple intelligences in the classroom*. Kent, OH: MI Research and Consulting.

Shearer, B. (2004). Using a multiple intelligences assessment to promote teacher development and student achievement. *Teachers College Press, 106*, 147–162.

Sidney Charney, R. (1997). Pretzels. *Education World®*. Retrieved February 11, 2008, from http://www.educationworld.com/a_lesson/lesson/lesson009.shtml

Silin, J. G. (1987). The early childhood educator's knowledge base: A reconsideration. In L. G. Katz and K. Steiner (Eds.), *Current topics in early childhood education* (vol. 7). Norwood, NJ: Albex Publishing Corporation.

Silverman, L. K. (2002). *Upside-down brilliance: The visual-spatial learner*. Denver, CO: DeLeon Publishing.

Silverman, L. (2008). Visual spatial resource. Retrieved May 29, 2008, from http://www.visualspatial.org/Product_Marketing/UDB/udb.htm

Smagorinsky, P. (1996, November). Multiple intelligences, multiple means of composing: An alternative way of thinking about learning. *NASSP Bulletin, 80*(583), 11–17.

Smerechansky-Metzger, J. (1995, May/June). The quest for multiple intelligences. *Gifted Child Today, 18*(3), 12–14.

Springer, R. (1990). The pre-kindergarten educational program: An overview. *Kamehameha Journal of Education, 1*, 1–3.

Stagg-Elliot, V. (2000). Doctors caught in the middle of ADHD treatment controversy. *American Medical News*, 22.

Stanberry, K. (2003). AD/HD with other disorders. *A parent's guide to helping kids with learning difficulties*. For Schwab Learning.org. Retrieved July 21, 2003, from www.future-horizons.org

Sternberg, R. (1996, November). IQ counts, but what really is successful intelligence. *NASSP Bulletin, 80*(583), 18–23.

Swadener, B., & Lubeck, S. (1995). *Children and families "at promise": Deconstructing the discourse*. Albany, NY: State University of New York Press.

Sylva, K. (1992). Conversations in the nursery: How they contribute to aspirations and plans. *Language and Education, 6*(2–4), 141–148.

Tanksley, M. D. (1994). *Building good self-esteem for certain fifth grade children through cooperative learning, individualized learning techniques, parental involvement, and student counseling*. Practicum paper. (ERIC Document Reproduction No. ED 367 095).

Taylor, A., Kuo, F., & Sullivan, W. (2001). Coping with ADD: The surprising connection to green play settings. *Environment and Behavior, 33*(1), 54–77.

Thompson, S. (2007, April 26). Encouraging residents to visit the state's parks and forests. *The Thames River Times, 3*(17), 8.

U.S. Department of Education. (1994). *Attention deficit disorder: Beyond the myths*. Washington, DC: Division of Innovation and Development Office of Special Education and Rehabilitative Services. Retrieved March 7, 2002, from http://www.future-horizons.org

Viadero, D. (2005, January). Mixed methods' research. *Education Week*. Retrieved May 20, 2008, from http://www.edweek.org

Viens, J. (1999). Understanding multiple intelligences: The theory behind the practice. *NCSALL*, 6–9.

Watkins, C. (2002). Attention deficit disorder and co-morbidity: What's beneath the tip of the iceberg? For Northern County Psychiatric Associates. Retrieved September 29, 2002, from http://www.future-horizons.org

Wilhelm, J. (2004). *Reading is seeing: Learning to visualize scenes, characters, ideas, and text worlds to improve comprehension and reflective reading*. New York: Scholastic.

Zeigler Dendy, C. (1999). *Teaching teens with ADD and ADHD: A quick reference guide for teachers and parents*. (1st ed.). Bethesda, MD: Woodbine House.

Zentall, S. (1993). Research on the educational implications of attention deficit hyperactivity disorder. *Exceptional Children, 60*, 143–153.

# Index

# About the Authors

**VICTORIA PROULX-SCHIRDUAN**, Ed.D., an educational consultant, has taught for the past 18 years at the elementary, middle school, high school, and college level, and has counseled individuals with ADHD in private practice. Her research, state and national presentations, and related articles are in the area of attention deficit hyperactivity disorder and multiple intelligences theory.

**C. BRANTON SHEARER**, Ph.D., completed his undergraduate degree at the age of 28 after many years as a carpenter, teacher's aide, roustabout, poet, and traveler. He then received his master's in counseling and consulting psychology at Harvard University and completed his doctoral studies in neuropsychological rehabilitation at the Union Institute in Cincinnati, Ohio. He is a teacher, writer, researcher, and licensed clinical neuropsychologist.

Dr. Shearer created the Multiple Intelligences Developmental Assessment Scales (MIDAS™) in 1987 to assist in the rehabilitation of persons recovering from traumatic brain injury. Since then, the MIDAS™ has been translated into 12 different languages and used in more than 23 countries as a research-based tool to further the educational and career development of students and adults.

He works with teachers, schools, and businesses around the world to assist their efforts to inspire the multiple intelligences for everyone. He has written eight books, including his latest with Mike Fleetham, *Creating ExtraOrdinary Teachers: Multiple Intelligences in the Classroom and Beyond!*, published by Continuum Network Education International Publishing Group, London, UK. Learn more about his work at www.MIResearch.org.

**KAREN I. CASE**, Ph.D., is an associate professor at the University of Hartford in the Department of Educational Leadership. Previously a language arts middle school teacher, she completed her doctoral work at the University of Connecticut. She has taught at the University of Iowa and the University of Connecticut. With over 25 years of teaching experience in higher education, Dr. Case has published numerous articles on curriculum and leadership theory, and has presented at national and international conferences. Her research is concerned with employing curriculum modifications to ensure equity for disenfranchised student populations. More specifically, she is interested in the value and importance of nontraditional educational curricula for those students who have been marginalized within the current educational system.